Constantin Bergander
With photography by Peter Besser

Audi RS

History · Models · Technology

DALTON WATSON FINE BOOKS

GERMAN EDITION:
AUDI RS – Geschichte, Modelle, Technik

HEEL Verlag GmbH
Gut Pottscheidt
53639 Königswinter
Telefon 0 22 23/92 30-0
Telefax 0 22 23/92 30 26
Mail: info@heel-verlag.de
Internet: www.heel-verlag.de

RESPONSIBLE FOR CONTENT:
Constantin Bergander
With photography by Peter Besser

EDITING:
Sven Wedemeyer, www.wheelsofstil.de

DESIGN:
Astrid Kalandrik, Bonn
www.akalandrik-design.com

PHOTO CREDITS:
Audi AG, Porsche AG, Constantin Bergander, Peter Besser, Jan Nischan, Jonas Seidel, Gunter Stachon

ENGLISH EDITION:
Dalton Watson Fine Books
Glyn and Jean Morris
Deerfield, IL 60015 USA
www.daltonwatson.com

TRANSLATION:
Peter Albrecht

DESIGN:
Jodi Ellis Graphics

PRINTER:
Interpress Ltd, Hungary

ISBN: 978-1-85443-321-3
Published: December 2021

Constantin Bergander
With photography by Peter Besser

Audi RS

History · Models · Technology

DALTON WATSON FINE BOOKS

IN GT 118 E

CONTENTS

"Anything other than all-wheel drive is a compromise."

Walter Röhrl

Dear Audi enthusiasts and RS community:

Cars are my career, but above all my passion. Although (or perhaps because?) I deal with them daily, I never grow tired of them. I recall many quite fondly – the red Audi Sport quattro with which I conquered the Grossglockner Pass. Or my old Audi 80 Competition; in the hands of its new owner, it now boasts well over 700 horsepower as an homage to the German STW (Super Touring Car Cup) Series, and is well known throughout the scene. And most especially the Audi S1, with which Stig Blomqvist and I drifted through a Swedish forest.

In this age of downsizing and "green" awareness, I am all the more fascinated by raw, powerful cars. That is why I compiled the history of all Audi RS vehicles to create this book. Before you dive into the reading matter, I beg you for a moment of indulgence. None of this would have been possible if so many great people had not helped me. Because not all of them will fit on the covers of this book, I would specifically like to thank the following:

First, I am indebted to Peter Besser, whose fabulous talents have captured many beautiful themes for this book. My girlfriend, Sarah Schröder, who often goaded me to get to work (and helped me). Timo Friedmann, who once upon a time taught me the art of journalistic writing (and continues in this task to this day). My fantastic colleagues Björn Tolksdorf, Heiko Dilk and Sven Förster, for their selfless efforts and endless patience. Fabian Hoberg and Joachim Walter, as well as my father Michael Bergander, for proofreading and corrections. Jan Nischan and Jonas Seidel, who also enriched the illustrative material, and Henry Reimer of the Audi RS Club Deutschland, who provided significant advice.

My thanks also go to Stephan Reil, Udo Rügheimer, Michael Hölscher, Roland Heiler and Walter Röhrl, who gave me fascinating insights into the RS world. Dr. Tobias Beck and Ralf Friese of Audi Tradition, as well as Frank Jung and Jens Torner of Porsche Tradition, who richly provided me with numbers, photographs and facts, and Eva Stania, Susanne Mellinghoff, and Tanja Lehner of the Audi press department for their support. Furthermore, I am excited that this book is now reaching a much wider audience with an English translation by the talented Peter Albrecht from the USA. I want to thank him for his vivid and thorough work.

In case you, the reader, have not jumped past this section yet, I would like to thank you as well. Because this increases the odds that, along with the striking photographs, you will also honor the text with your attention. This describes the story of an automobile manufacturer that pulled itself together in the rough years, and evolved from bland fare to filet mignon. It is hard to believe that prior to this book, none had ventured to tell the tale. Now it is here – and I wish you great joy in the reading.

Sincerely,
Constantin Bergander
Berlin, Winter 2021

For Opa.

26
25
IN NW 30
Audi Tradition

PROLOGUE

Sometimes it takes two tries; the first one went like this…

As early as 1971, Audi used the slogan "VORSPRUNG DURCH TECHNIK" (advancement through technology), but was unable to deliver on the promise. It was not the fault of the technology, because Audi NSU Auto Union AG, as it was then known, built innovative, economical, and lightweight cars with front-wheel drive – quite advanced for the time. Only, Audi was unable to engineer an advancement on that existing technology. Although successful in the marketplace, the Audi 100 barely kept the brand alive; what was lacking was money and resources. Insiders reported the offices and test cells looked like something from the middle ages.

First the technology, then the advancement

Engineer, visionary, manager. Ferdinand Karl Piëch aggressively spearheaded the Audi brand's sporting direction. Austrian by birth, he hired on to Audi in 1972.

Immortalized in the cylinder head, the firing order 1 – 2 – 4 – 5 – 3 gave the Audi five-cylinder engine a distinctive sound.

The five-cylinder engine out of Ingolstadt debuted in 1976 in the Audi 100 C2 model line. In the 5E version, it delivered 136 hp from a displacement of 2.1 liters.

With the 200 model line, Audi made its first foray into the premium class.
Beginning in 1980, Audi installed a five-cylinder turbo developing 170 horsepower (the 5T) in the four-door sedan.

A MANAGER SEEKS TO RESTRUCTURE THE COMPANY

In 1972, after stints at Porsche and Mercedes, a young Ferdinand Piëch joined Audi, at the age of 35. From 1974, he was head of engineering development; a year later, Audi moved him onto the board of directors. He set a goal for himself – to turn the burned-out manufacturer into a premium brand. Instead of competing with Opel and Ford, his cars would battle with Mercedes and BMW for market share. He personally contributed to the marque's sporting image: Piëch would drive his company car at particularly high speeds to Ingolstadt or Neckarsulm. As related by his co-drivers, Piëch felt that any BMW or Mercedes driver that he passed could be a future Audi customer. Still, Audi did not have at its disposal any powerful engines. Inline six-cylinders, as commonly found in other south German manufacturers or Opel, would not fit in the Audi chassis. Longitudinally mounted engines with front-wheel drive would have such a detrimental effect on the center of mass that no engineer could achieve a balanced suspension; the car would be too nose-heavy, and undrivable. Audi lacked the money to design a shorter V6 engine.

THE AUDI FIVE-CYLINDER LAUNCHED IN 1976

Piëch initiated a compromise solution. In his time as an independent designer at Daimler (1972) he had conceived a five-cylinder engine. Now at Audi, he built another, based on the existing four-cylinder. This would be something special, as it would be capable of high engine speeds. Working with his engine developer, Franz Hauk, Piëch extended the EA 827 engine by one cylinder, to create the EA 828. Crankcase reinforcement would minimize vibration. With its 136 horsepower, the Audi 100 5E could compete with the Mercedes-Benz 250 or BMW 520i.

In order to move forward, Piëch hired engine wizard Friedrich Indra away from independent BMW tuning company Alpina. Indra was considered an expert in turbocharging and assisted in boosting power output by means of an exhaust turbocharger. Working with the first prototypes, Indra optimized the cooling system and service intervals in order to achieve acceptable durability. With 170 horsepower, Audi no longer had to trail behind the competition; the powerful Audi 200 5T could go head to head with other premium sedans – at least in terms of engineering. Still, the stigma of boring conventionality clung to Audi like an oil film to a cylinder wall.

SPORTING AMBITION

The Audi 200 was not the sort of car to inspire children to display its posters on their bedroom walls, or scale models on their shelves; rather, it was the sort of car that came with velour-covered pillows to match the interior trim.

Piëch wanted to escape from the buttoned-down image of the Audi-driving schoolteacher or retiree. His cars were to be desirable, covetable. He

Audi delivered the 200 with soft pillows, matching the interior upholstery.

knew that the road to such desirability could only run through motorsports and luxury. With its turbo engine, the manufacturer was certainly headed in that direction. However, the once so highly regarded front-wheel drive layout was now up against its physical limitations.

QUATTRO DELIVERS SUCCESS

While conducting road tests of the VW Iltis, suspension engineer Jörg Bensinger hit upon the idea that all-wheel drive would be a good fit for the Audi brand. The concept was revolutionary; today, one might call it disruptive. To date, no manufacturer had successfully offered full-time all-wheel drive in a passenger car. During cold-weather testing in the winter of 1976-1977, the sluggish military vehicle with its mere 75 horsepower was able to handily outrun the entire Audi test fleet, including the pre-production Audi 200.

Bensinger convinced Walter Treser that all-wheel drive and an abundance of horsepower could "blow everyone into the weeds." Along with a small group of engineers, Treser, director of advanced engineering for special vehicles at Audi, built a prototype, secretly and without official orders. Piëch supported the effort; he had already taken a liking to all-wheel drive during his time at Porsche. He screened the project from VW's directors and his co-conspirators would quietly build a car that would function in a motorsports environment.

Indeed, the first attempts were made with precisely such objectives. Equipped with a rigid all-wheel drive system, without a center differential, the test model, carrying Audi 80 bodywork, exhibited outstanding traction but could be coaxed through corners only with great difficulty. The development team accepted this handicap, because in motorsports, comfort counts for nothing.

The crew thought that four hundred production examples, needed for homologation, could somehow be sold to purists. But when Piëch invited the decision makers of the parent company to a test drive, they rejected the drivetrain concept; it would bind when steered around turns. After a test drive with his wife, Lilly, VW development chief Ernst Fiala complained that while negotiating a cramped parking garage, the car would literally hop in tight turns. Piëch, heading his project, gradually felt his way toward the executive floor.

Inspiration and realization: VW Iltis and Audi quattro during test drives in the snow on the Turracher Höhe. With its maximum 34% grade, it was for many years Europe's steepest road.

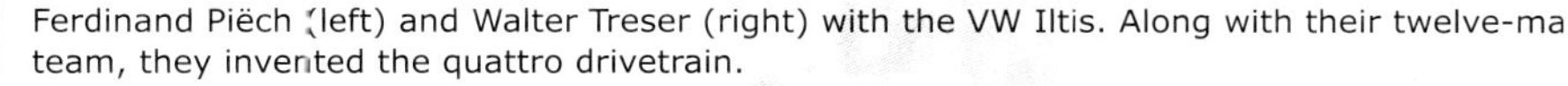

Ferdinand Piëch (left) and Walter Treser (right) with the VW Iltis. Along with their twelve-man team, they invented the quattro drivetrain.

"Qua-" up front

A hard consonant bringing up the rear

ALL-WHEEL DRIVE AS A SELLING POINT

Even the greatest of ideas may fail at the hands of the wrong decision makers. This nearly caused Audi's demise. Within the marque, the responsible parties quickly arrived at a name for the all-wheel drive coupe: it would be called the Audi quattro. However, the final decision lay with the parent company, Volkswagen, in Wolfsburg: if VW had its way, the car was to be called the CARAT, short for "Coupe mit Allradantrieb und Turbolader" – Coupe with All-Wheel Drive and Turbocharger. Project leader Walter Treser got wind of these plans and obtained a cheap perfume with the same name. When the Wolfsburgers announced their proposal during a conference, he pulled out the perfume bottle and said, "I hope you aren't suggesting we debase our fine automobile with the name of a *hausfrau* perfume." Volkswagen agreed and approved the name quattro.

This name was born of the conversation among the participating Audi protagonists. Treser had in his mind the concept "Quadra-Trac." This was Jeep's own label for its all-wheel drivetrain. He latched onto the name, noted the syllable "Qua" and derived "Quadro" for Audi. He felt that customers would make the connection between the concept of "quadratic" and four driven wheels. The team discussed the meaning, the translation from the Italian ("picture frame") and the pronunciation. Piëch did not like the soft consonant; he expanded the concept to the lower-case "quattro." He felt that sounded more masculine.

Before Audi, other manufacturers had sold a few all-wheel drive passenger cars. At Jensen, due to the high price in its V8-powered FF coupe, the concept devolved into a rear-drive variant. Subaru initially built cars with selectable all-wheel drive. It was not until Audi came on the scene that full-time all-wheel drive became successful in the marketplace. Quattro won races, quattro drove up ski jumps, quattro became a brand, a recognition feature. Long-serving VW chairman Martin Winterkorn later named quattro as a unique selling feature that resulted in marketplace success. Ultimately, it prompted corporate leadership to position Audi as the corporation's enduring premium brand.

A SALES SUCCESS

The one millionth Audi quattro, an Audi allroad model, was presented by the manufacturer at the Geneva Motor Show, 21 years after the premiere of the archetypal quattro. Audi board chairman Franz-Josef Paefgen presented the car to the SAC, the Swiss Alpine Club, for mountain rescue service. At that time, the quattro represented over 30 percent of Audi's overall production.

The five millionth quattro was built in 2013, again an allroad. In 2020, for the 40th anniversary of the concept, Audi reported that it had produced 10.5 million examples of its all-wheel drive cars. Five different quattro systems were shared among almost all Audi models; since transition to its second generation, only the subcompact A1 is available with front-wheel drive only. Meanwhile, nearly 45 percent of all Audis ever built have been driven by all four wheels.

The first all-wheel drive Audi debuted in 1980, with an open, manually lockable bevel-gear center differential. Forty years later, five different all-wheel drive technologies were available, for example the Torsen CSM in the Audi RS 5.

Strong in the snow: with its all-wheel drive, the Audi S1 shines wherever conditions get difficult.

For Audi, the quattro is synonymous with serious sporting ambitions. With 200 horsepower and all-wheel drive, the coupe could sprint to 100 km/h (62 mph) in about seven seconds, and top out at 220 km/h (137 mph).

The Audi quattro at its debut, Geneva Motor Show, 1980.

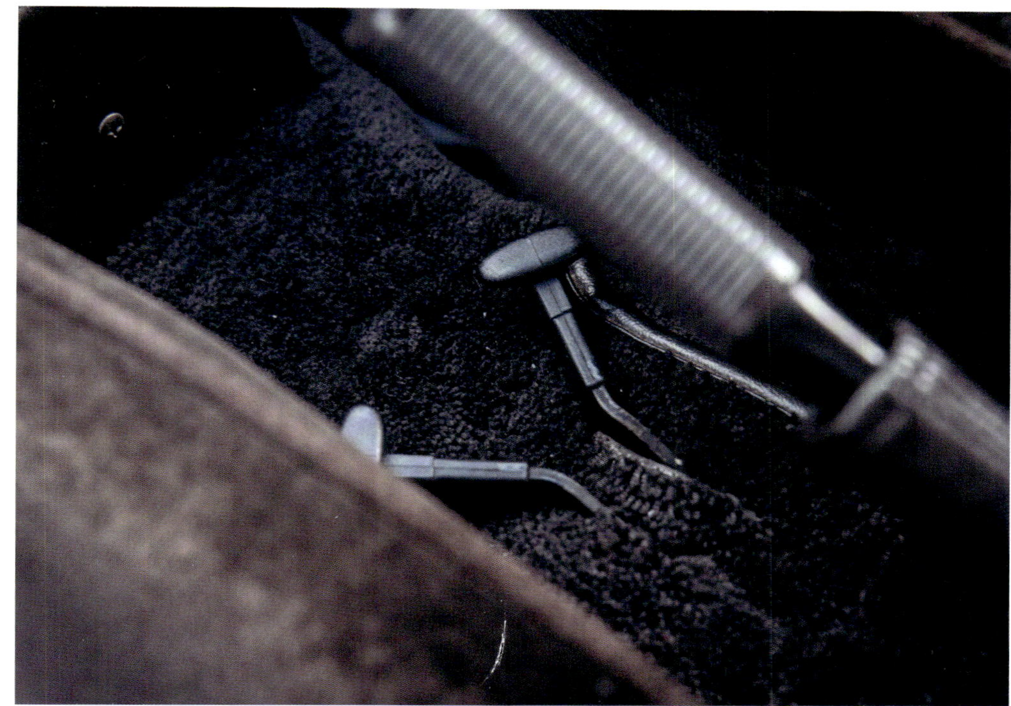

Audi's first all-wheel drive system did not lock automatically, but rather manually by means of cable pulls. The levers were located below the handbrake.

VW director of sales, Werner P. Schmidt, drove the prototype up the snow-covered Turracher Höhe in Austria faster than a front-wheel-drive car equipped with snow chains. The most important man in the company, chief executive Toni Schmücker, tried the first all-wheel drive Audi on a grassy slope in Ingolstadt, watered down by the Audi company fire department. Comparison with a rear-drive car (BMW 3-series) and front drive (Audi 80) convinced him. He approved a development budget of three million Deutschmarks. The all-wheel drive experiment officially transformed into Entwicklungsauftrag (EA, Development Order) 262. One key requirement: the car would have to stop hopping through corners.

DIFFERENTIAL INSTEAD OF RIGID ALL-WHEEL DRIVETRAIN

The problem, according to the engineers, could be solved in the same way as on an off-road vehicle, with a transfer case. However, this solution was less than optimal for a coupe with sporting ambitions. The component weighed too much. Transmission development engineer Franz Tengler was able to solve the problem with a breakthrough. During a meeting, he sketched a compact bevel-gear differential with a hollow shaft, which could be integrated in the existing transmission. Audi then combined the new all-wheel drive system with a powerful, turbocharged five-cylinder engine and widened coupe bodywork, called the resulting vehicle the Audi quattro, and presented it at the 1980 Geneva Motor Show. The motoring press cheered and wrote of a revolution in automotive construction.

A year later, the quattro made its first appearance in the World Rally Championship. In the Monte Carlo Rally, the car outclassed its competitors on the snow-covered stages. Audi's all-wheel drive, piloted by Stig Blomqvist, Walter Röhrl, Michèle Mouton and Hannu Mikkola, became an unbeatable institution in the legendary Group B. Instead of the originally planned production run of 400 cars, Audi sold 11,452 examples of the quattro.

Indicator lights in the Audi quattro's center console illuminated to show which differentials were locked.

FINALLY, THE AD SLOGAN FITS

When Audi again applied the slogan "Vorsprung durch Technik" (Advancement through Technology) a good ten years after its first appearance, the phrase was finally justified. In just a few years, the marque distanced itself from the competition. Five-cylinder turbo and all-wheel drive created a sporting, progressive image. In these forms, both applications were novel innovations in automotive construction.

Audi also invested in developing its international recognition. In 1984, ad agency BBH (Bartle Bogart Hagerty) produced advertising spots for British television. These ended with the old, rediscovered slogan, spoken by British actor Geoffrey Palmer, in German – "Vorsprung durch Technik – as they say in Germany." Few knew what that meant, but it had the ring of quality. The ads achieved cult status, especially when spoken by a Briton. Musicians including the bands U2 and Blur used it in their music. Audi would henceforth sell every innovation under this slogan: aluminum body, TDI engine, twelve-cylinder engine in W layout, direct fuel-injection and hybrids would represent "advancement through technology" in the years to come.

A DEDICATED DEPARTMENT FOR MOTORSPORTS

The Audi Motorsport department was founded in 1978. As of 1980, it was renamed Audi Sport. Success in rally competition drew the attention of the motoring world. On the basis of the Audi quattro, the Audi Sport quattro was created, "the short one," a rally car that, thanks to its short-wheelbase and powerful engine, was hard pressed to drive in a straight line. The car won the 1984 Championship, and in 1987 set a new record and won the Pikes Peak International Hill Climb. The Sport quattro S1 covered the 1,425 meter (4,675 foot) climb in 10:47.85 minutes.

In 1981, Audi proceeded to demonstrate the quattro's capabilities. In its original form, it brought home two driver and two manufacturer titles.

The production version was the most expensive series-built German car of its time; at introduction, it cost 195,000 DM, as much as two Porsche 911 Turbos – or four Audi quattros.

Expensive cars and motorsports are too abstract for many customers. For them, Audi found other means to market all-wheel drive and five-cylinder engines. In 1986, a TV ad spot showed an Audi 100 CS quattro (price: 42,440 DM) driving up a snow-covered ski jump. Racing driver Harald Demuth used the car's 136 horsepower to master the 80 percent grade. A steel cable acted as a safety measure for the effort. The climb was made under the car's own power (with spikes in the tires). Those who were not exposed to the quattro through the rally sport, learned of it during television commercials.

The five-cylinder engine accompanied Audi primarily in its more sporting models. In the search for a market niche, Porsche came to Audi's aid. The Stuttgart carmaker transformed the Audi S2 into the Audi Avant RS2. Its success further motivated Audi to build cars suitable for everyday service, on performance-oriented mechanicals. In 1996, this task was taken over by a subsidiary firm, quattro GmbH, initially with the Audi S6 plus, then four years later with the Audi RS 4. The cars' aspirations and execution were in keeping with the *zeitgeist*. The abbreviation RS established itself and attracted many fans. Organizations such as the Audi RS Club Deutschland e.V. celebrated these, the marque's most sporting models.

In 1988, Audi entered the 200 quattro in the Trans-Am series. Although rules changes in the course of the season severely curtailed the effort, Audi won both the driver and manufacturer titles.

As of the 1984 season, Audi sent the short-wheelbase Sport quattro S1 into the World Rally Championship fray. Later, the engineers would optimize its aerodynamics by means of huge wings, and even tested a dual-clutch transmission.

Advertising that sells: in 1986, racing driver Harald Demuth drove an Audi 100 CS quattro up the ski jump in Kaipola, Finland.

The Audi climbed the ski jump under its own power. Three safety measures were employed: a taut cable attached to the underside, a large fork activated by the handbrake lever, and a catch fence.

All RS vehicles (and the S6 plus) were equipped with all-wheel drive and, as of 1996, init ally with at least six-cylinder engines. The five-cylinder's run ceased in 1997, with the end of Audi S6 (C4) production. It took some time for Audi to find its way back to the inline-five. It was not until 2009 that the manufacturer brought forth a new generation of engines, which would remain in the model line. Despite the long hiatus, the asymmetrical sound of the five is firmly bound to the Audi marque, and to the quattro brand.

FAREWELL TO PIËCH

Piëch, inventor of the first Audi five-cylinder engine and proponent of the quattro, continued his climb within the Volkswagen corporate hierarchy, all the way to the head of the corporation. "The Old Man" left an enduring imprint on the Audi brand's character; many developments can be traced directly to his ideas.

Ferdinand Piëch passed away unexpectedly in 2019 at the age of 82. His former colleagues remember him as an impassioned manager, brilliant engineer and visionary entrepreneur.

Quattro GmbH & Audi Sport

FROM LICENSOR TO AUTOMAKER

After the premiere of the quattro, Audi often appeared in court to contest trademarks. To avoid such problems in the future, the manufacturer established a wholly-owned subsidiary, quattro GmbH, in 1983. At first, its sole mission was to issue licensing rights to the quattro Concept, and to prevent other firms from establishing claims. Only later was quattro GmbH given a tangible assignment: it was to reinforce the Audi brand image. Its themes were lifestyle, merchandising and brand loyalty.

1985: QUATTRO SELLS AUDI ARTICLES

Beginning in 1985, quattro GmbH marketed accessories and collectibles. The program encompassed trifles such as pens and parking discs bearing the brand logo, but also covered a number of curious, elegant, and expensive articles. The catalogs included, among other things, yo-yos and Frisbees, and umbrellas with a shift lever handle. Even hair dryers, electric razors and thermos bottles were offered, along with various watches, pins, model cars, tie tacks, wallets, clothing items, key fobs and briefcases. Human models posed with the articles in front of Audi automobile models.

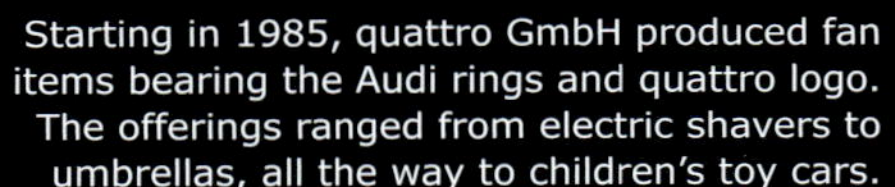

Starting in 1985, quattro GmbH produced fan items bearing the Audi rings and quattro logo. The offerings ranged from electric shavers to umbrellas, all the way to children's toy cars.

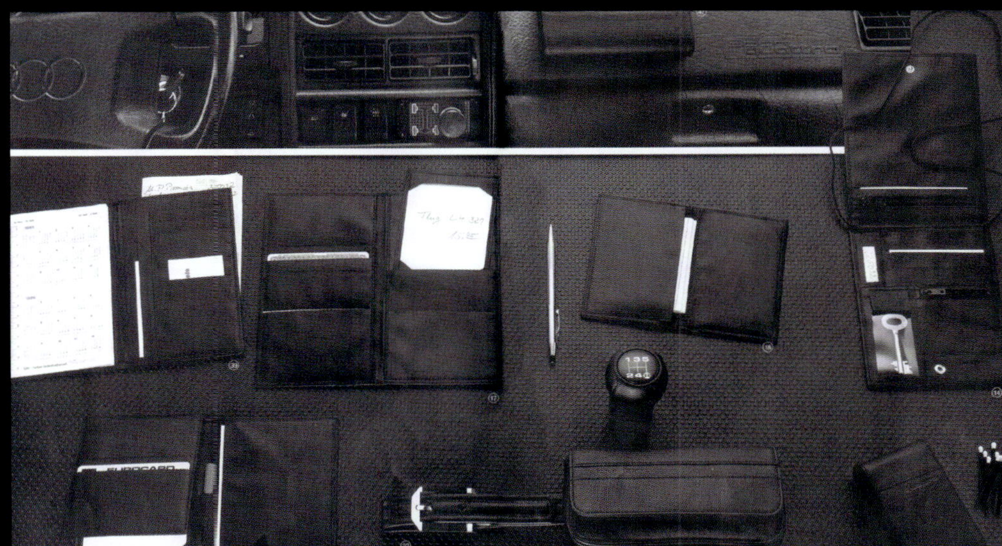

The Audi Q7 Coastline study debuted at the 2008 Geneva Motor Show. It featured white paintwork, fine leather, wool carpeting and waxed walnut veneer in the luggage compartment.

A large portion of the catalog showcased everyday items bearing the Audi rings or quattro emblem. In addition, quattro offered accessories for various sporting activities. For golfers, a variety of golf club sets, club head covers, and golf balls were available. In 1989, quattro GmbH offered one of the first mountain bikes with a titanium frame, in a limited, special edition. The quattro Pikes Peak weighed a scant 11.8 kg (26 lbs). One hundred and fifty standard examples were sold; to fulfill the wishes of an Audi supervisory board member, two more were made, in a ladies' version.

In 1990, quattro GmbH also took responsibility for advertising materials to grace the showrooms of Audi dealerships. The first drivable car entered the program in 1991: on July 1 of that year, quattro offered a miniature version of the Audi Cabriolet for children. Alpha of Krakow, Poland, built twenty examples of the two-meter-long toy per month, powered by a single-cylinder gasoline engine. Each cost 4,900 Deutschmarks.

1995: QUATTRO CUSTOMIZES CARS

Genuine points of contact with actual Audi models appeared in 1995. Finally, twelve years after the founding of the firm, the Audi subsidiary offered personalization of production cars. Anything that pleased the customer was on the program. Quattro associates assisted the prospective clients, but discouraged extremely discordant color combinations. In a press release, quattro GmbH explained that in general, only legal requirements, customs and decency set limits to the offerings; the company would gladly realize any other wishes. In the first year, quattro customized 2,000 cars. For 2012, it recorded 160,000 personalizations.

The changes cover everything not included in the option lists for production cars. Customers could order their cars painted in special colors, or order the application of soft leather or unique décor. Auxiliary heaters, flag standards, or entire mobile offices could be provided by quattro GmbH. Production logistics permitting, the company coordinated its modifications directly with the production line. If that was not possible, the conversion would be carried out with individual hand craftsmanship.

Along with individual customization, quattro GmbH offered limited runs of especially elegant trim options. These include, for example, the Audi A8 L W12 Audi exclusive concept, with its Monsoon Gray paintwork and leather interior by Poltrona Frau, or the Audi Q7 Coastline with wool floor mats and walnut veneer in the luggage compartment.

1996: QUATTRO BECOMES A VEHICLE MANUFACTURER

While the first customer cars were being personalized, the Audi subsidiary struck out in a new direction. It began development of its first (full size) car. Quattro GmbH, with a staff of only twenty-five, received an assignment from its parent company. After the success of the Porsche-Audi Avant RS2, the next task was to create a sporting Audi without the influence of an external company. The Audi S6 plus premiered in 1996; a total of 952 examples were built.

Quattro GmbH's personalization portfolio included soft leather, exotic wood and elegant colors. Specially-trained advisors assisted customers in selecting their individual options, and were aware of tasteful combinations.

Snapshot of the 2020 RS portfolio: Avant, Coupe, Sportback, SUV and SUV Coupe.

1999: THE FIRST HOMEGROWN RS AUDI

The S6 plus was followed in 1999 by the Audi RS4, the marque's first RS model to be developed in-house. In 2002, this was complemented by the RS 6, following the same principle but with new nomenclature: a space is inserted between the letters and number. Henceforth, quattro GmbH would extend the RS idea to most Audi model lines, although none dared to address the S1. The quick little subcompact already put out 231 horsepower. An RS 1 would have to be even more powerful to differentiate itself from the base model, and there simply was not a market for that performance class.

quattro also did not build an RS version of Audi's luxury class. Only a few studies hinted at what the RS concept would look like, in the subcompact or luxury classes. However, the concepts never went into production. Still, quattro GmbH got approval for the sport-oriented Audi S8 plus.

2006: A QUATTRO SUPER SPORTS CAR

Sales of the first vehicle to be developed completely in-house by quattro GmbH began in 2006. The Audi R8 super sports car was introduced on the market as a sister model of the Lamborghini Gallardo (first-generation R8) and Lamborghini Huracán (second-generation R8). In addition, quattro GmbH turned its attention to other extreme developments, for example the Audi Q7 V12 TDI.

The marketplace dictates the offerings. Quattro GmbH experimented with different body shapes and created more cars than would ultimately appear on the market. A finished design for an Audi RS Q5 exists, somewhere in a secret drawer. The success of the SQ5 put an end to that project, but not the idea behind it. RS models are in the form of the Avant, sedan, coupe, cabriolet, roadster, spyder, SUV and SUV coupe.

2011: QUATTRO TAKES RESPONSIBILITY FOR CUSTOMER SPORTS

In addition, from 2011 onward, quattro GmbH took charge of supporting customer motorsports activities. The Customer Racing department sold FIA-certified racing versions of sporting

Motorsports play a vital role at Audi. The manufacturer contests a number of GT racing classes, as well as LMP prototypes. Beginning in 2011, quattro GmbH has been responsible for customer racing, and sells race-ready versions of the TT RS, RS 3 and R8.

Audi models to private racing teams. The models offered included three variants of the Audi R8 LMS for the GT1, GT2, GT3 and GT4 racing classes, as well as the Audi RS 3 LMS for the TCR International Series touring car championship.

In 2016, quattro GmbH changed its name to Audi Sport. Shortly thereafter, the first, and so far only, quattro vehicle without all-wheel drive took to the track; the Audi R8 RWS (since 2020: R8 RWD) was powered through its rear wheels only.

Today, Audi Sport supports all RS models, the R8 sports car, the Audi S8 plus, Audi exclusive special customizations, the S line trim variant, the Audi Collection as well as customer racing activities. Audi Sport employs more than 1,300 specialists.

The brains behind quattro GmbH and Audi Sport

DIRECTORS AND DEVELOPMENT CHIEFS

Rudolf Gölz (1995 – 1998)

As quattro GmbH's first boss, Gölz shepherded the market launch of the brand's first car. On March 20, 1995, Audi promoted the industrial business manager to its board of directors, with responsibility for merchandise, accessories, vehicle development and modifications. He was highly regarded by his colleagues because he was largely a "hands off" manager, and had confidence in his specialists. After he left the company in 1998, quattro GmbH moved from Ingolstadt to Neckarsulm.

Werner Frowein (1998 – 2012)

Frowein moved from motor sports to vehicle construction. He assumed leadership of quattro GmbH between the phaseout of the Audi S6 plus and introduction of the first RS4, and significantly expanded the brand's portfolio. The firm grew from manufacturing just a single model to offering vehicles in several classes. Frowein's time as chief of quattro GmbH also covered development of the Audi R8 as well as a new edition of the five-cylinder engine for the Audi TT RS and the RS 3. He retired from the company in 2012.

Audi Sport
Vorsprung durch Technik
Audi Sport
customer racing
100
Audi Sport
BILSTEIN
Audi quattro GmbH

Francíscus van Meel (2012 – 2014)
Prior to his move to quattro GmbH, Meel led Audi's electromobility strategy. Upon assuming office, Audi announced that he would bring his experiences in electrification to the performance marque. However, after just two years at quattro GmbH, he was slated to move to China as head of research and development. Instead, Van Meel decided to switch to BMW, where he headed the M GmbH operations.

Heinz Hollerweger (2014-2016)
Audi veteran Hollerweger gave the original quattro comfortable road manners. In its experimental phase, he eliminated unpleasant front suspension vibrations. Later, he was head of vehicle development in Ingolstadt. In 2014, he assumed leadership of quattro GmbH. He retired after two years in Neckarsulm but continued to serve as an advisor. Among other projects, he assisted SEAT with its León Cupra.

Stephan Winkelmann (2016-2017)
Winkelmann switched from Lamborghini to quattro GmbH in 2016. In his last full year with the Italian carmaker, the firm sold 3,245 vehicles – a record. Winkelmann unified Audi's sporting departments to form the brand Audi Sport. In January 2018, he left his post to take over leadership of Bugatti.

Michael-Julius Renz (2018-2019)
After more than 20 years at Audi, Renz switched to Audi Sport in early 2018. Before taking on his leadership role in Neckarsulm, he was responsible for distribution and presence of the core brand in the Chinese market. He retired after a year and a half.

Julius Seebach (2019-present)
Seebach came to Audi after seven years at sister brand Porsche. Initially, he led the drivetrain and engineering development departments. From 2017, he headed the RS 4 through RS 7 platforms at Audi Sport. In May 2019, at the age of 39, Seebach became the youngest managing director of Audi's performance-oriented subsidiary.

Stephan Reil (1996-2017, and 2020-present)
Reil joined quattro GmbH in 1996 as department head for individual vehicle personalization. In 1998 he became director for development and production. From 2001, he was responsible for overall vehicle development as well as personalization. In 2017, he left his long-term employer and shifted to the core brand. Since 2020, he has been responsible for engineering development at the Neckarsulm facility.

Oliver Hoffmann (2017-2020)
After stints at Lamborghini, Hoffmann became responsible for engineering development at Audi Sport in 2017 at the Győr (Hungary) Audi plant, in Audi engine development and as director of drivetrain development. In 2018, his employer appointed Hoffmann to a seat on the management board. In 2019, he also took on the directorship of drivetrain development at Audi, and engineering development in Neckarsulm. In July 2020, Hoffmann became chief operating officer of all Audi development, and head of development in March 2021.

RS 3
D
IN RS 3002

COMPACT CLASS

It took some time for Audi's compact models to become decidedly sporty. The Ingolstadt-based brand had been selling RS models since 1994, but it was not until 2011 that a compact car was allowed to carry the initials signifying higher performance. The Audi RS 3 became the entry-level model in the quattro GmbH portfolio. In this case, entry represented five cylinders, 340 horsepower and an unmistakable sound.

Audi's reasons for building the RS 3 were explained in a rational, but rather disingenuous way. At its premiere, a press spokesman was happy that the firm was finally able to offer a more affordable RS model, within reach of younger buyers. The Audi man did not elaborate on what sort of young people could spend at least 50,000 euros for a compact car with 340 hp.

Young or old, the RS 3 attracted its own coterie of customers, who loved the unmistakable engine and practical qualities. The sales numbers justified additional generations of RS models, and continued existence of the five-cylinder engine.

2011

Audi RS 3 Sportback (8P)

RS Premiere in the compact class

For the first compact RS Audi, quattro GmbH's calculations were presumably very simple – bodywork from the Audi A3 Sportback + drivetrain of the Audi TT RS = Audi RS 3 Sportback. A 340-horsepower engine was to propel the five-door just as dramatically as it had in its drivetrain donor. Still, a car can not be conceived on the basis of such simple arithmetic, certainly not an RS model. Some adjustments would be needed before the engineering package would fit its shell.

A look back: engine boss Michael Ganz and chief engineer Stephan Reil converted the lethargic inline five-cylinder engine of the VW Jetta (U.S. model) into a potent turbo engine. With extensive changes to the crankcase, cylinder head, cooling system, fuel-injection system, and a K16 turbocharger, the engineers doubled its output – 170 hp turned into 340, and the humble engine was transformed into a superb sporting powerplant. The engine debuted in 2009, in the quickest version of the Audi TT.

Even during its conception, it had been decided that in the long term, the engine would propel a car based on the A3. It could be coerced into the tight engine bay, but caused problems of its own. Weighing 185 kilograms (408 pounds), plus heavy accessories, it put enormous pressure on the front axle – too much for the standard tires of the A3. The problem was that Audi wanted tires no wider than 225 mm in the compact body's tight wheel wells. With an intended wheel diameter of 19 inches, such tires would not have sufficient load capacity. Tires in size 225-35 R19 can carry, at most, 560 kg (1,235 lbs) each. For an axle load of 1,150 kg (2,535 lbs), tires with a load rating of 580 kg (load index 89) would be required.

A few years earlier, in the TT RS, quattro GmbH did not face any such worries. Wide wheels were factory standard on the sports car, and tires with a higher load rating were optional even on the base model. The A3, on the other hand, arose from a different world of conventions. Quattro GmbH would first have to undertake extensive modifications before wider rubber would fit under its fenders. The target: 235 mm section width. Such tires would be capable of carrying the heavy powerplant.

BROAD CHEST, SLIM WAIST

To this end, for the front of the RS 3, quattro GmbH formed new, wider fenders – in keeping with RS tradition. These were made of composite material, and widened the bodywork by about 10 centimeters (4 in.). Compared to the sheetmetal of the Audi A3, the new panels were a total of 2.1 kilograms (4.6 pounds) lighter. Most important, they provided the desired extra space for suitable wheels and tires.

The rear bodywork remained as before. Audi wanted to position the RS 3 in the market segment around 50,000 Euros, 20,000 Euros less than the previous entry-level model, the RS 4. For this part of the project, different considerations applied: new quarter panels with wider wheel wells would be too expensive. Technically, this did not pose a problem, because the rear load was not much different from that of the A3 quattro. Tires of 225 section would serve in this capacity.

What quattro GmbH ultimately designed was unconventional, but logical. The top model of the A3 line kept its narrow rear flanks, but had a wider front end. Many mid- and rear-engined sports cars carry wider tires on the axle nearest the powerplant. What works on a Porsche 911 or Lamborghini Gallardo, should work just as well on an Audi RS 3.

For the first RS 3, quattro GmbH dispensed with any sort of engine cover. The five-cylinder put its ignition coils and red valve cover on display.

Ultimately, quattro transferred the familiar concept to its front-engined compact car.

In stock form, the first RS 3 rolled on 235/35 tires at the front, and 225/35 at the rear. These were a good fit to the vehicle weight, and its bodywork, but did not quite meet the engineers' aspirations. Driven hard, the Audi understeered in corners. From August 2011, this could be addressed by an option: for an extra 950 Euros, Audi would mount wider front wheels (8.5 instead of 8.0 in.) carrying even wider 255-series rubber. The goal of this investment was to move the adhesion limit. Race drivers and engineers know this as "Kamm Circle" or the "friction circle." This physical diagram graphically shows when the combination of cornering forces and acceleration or braking forces exceed the traction limits. Wider front tires expand the circle's radius: the RS 3 could corner faster, and understeer later.

The RS 3's mixed tire sizes led to discussions among its owners. Some mounted wider tires at the rear, above all for aesthetic reasons. The independent German technical inspection agencies, TÜV and Dekra, responsible for certifying vehicle modifications as roadworthy, generally accept conversions to 235-series rear tires. Audi had imagined it differently.

A DRIVETRAIN LIKE THE TT RS

Elsewhere, things went more smoothly for the RS 3. From engine to brakes, it copied the technology of the TT RS. Both cars shared the five-cylinder engine and its cooling system, dual-clutch transmission, Haldex all-wheel drive and brake system – in other words, the entire drivetrain. However, because the A3 was a practical compact car, while the TT was a quick, agile sports car, the engineers in Neckarsulm had to fine-tune a few details.

These included, above all, the suspension tuning. Differences in wheelbase, track, weight, suspension geometry, and wheels all called for engineering changes. To this end, quattro GmbH developed a sport suspension, stiffer and lowered by 2.5 cm (one inch).

Another difference: in the little TT, Audi was installing a dual-outlet exhaust system, and the starter battery was located at the rear. In developing the A3, these packaging factors did not come into play. Quattro GmbH carried over the layout of the Audi A3 with the 3.2-liter engine, and mounted the battery at the right side of the trunk. This, however, occupied the space that would be needed for an exhaust system of suitable size.

For nearly ten years, all RS models had borne dual oval exhaust tips. To give the RS 3 something similar, quattro GmbH would have had to design a new trunk floor. For the compact class, this would be too expensive. So the RS 3 was given two round exhaust tips on the left side, and a final muffler with a controllable exhaust flap. The end result did not quite look like its bigger brothers, but sounded the same.

DUAL CITIZENSHIP

In its manufacturing process, the RS 3 again demonstrated its kinship to the TT RS. As it did for its technological sibling, Audi arranged for production in two different plants. Ingolstadt assembled and painted the bodies, while Győr assembled the complete car. The two plants are separated by 475 km (295 miles) as the crow flies. The body shells were shipped by rail from Germany to Hungary.

By the time production got under way (late 2010), the Győr plant had already gained a year and a half of experience in shoehorning the hot five-cylinder and its dual-clutch transmission into a tight engine bay. The Hungarian workers were already familiar with the compact Audi: between 2001 and 2003, they built its predecessor to relieve the load on the Ingolstadt plant. From 2007, Győr also built the A3 Cabriolet.

The widened fenders of the Audi RS 3 were made of composite material. A new front fascia with larger air inlets visually differentiated the top-of-the-line model from its less powerful siblings.

The first Audi RS 3 lacked space at the right rear for an exhaust tip. If it had wanted to retain the classic RS visual cues, quattro GmbH would have had to develop a new trunk floor. The costs for this could not be justified.

Brakes were a recurring theme on the RS 3. On the race track, they had to endure extreme loads. Audi subsequently improved the system with a brake cooling duct.

In contrast to the TT RS, the RS 3 did not offer a manual transmission. The only choice in the compact sporter was a dual-clutch (automatic) transmission.

Audi understated the performance data: according to works numbers, the RS 3 could sprint to 100 km/h (62 mph) in 4.6 seconds. In tests, it beat this official time by four-tenths of a second.

In its first generation, Audi converted only the five-door A3 Sportback into the RS 3. The shorter three-door body achieved its performance pinnacle in the form of the Audi S3, with 265 hp. The A3 Cabriolet was only available with front-wheel drive. Audi did not experiment with other body styles for the RS 3 until much later. In the beginning, it was believed, such model proliferation would only be self-defeating in the marketplace.

WINNER BY A (HEAVY) NOSE

When the RS 3 rolled out to the dealerships in the spring of 2011, there were no competing offerings in the marketplace. At the time, hot compacts usually had about 200, or at most 300 hp. The new Audi even relegated rally virtuosi Mitsubishi Lancer Evolution and Subaru WRX STI to the sidelines. The RS 3, however, was only able to claim the horsepower crown thanks to perfect timing: just before its market introduction, the limited-edition Ford Focus RS500, with its 350 horsepower, ceased production.

With a lack of competing offerings in the same production timeframe, Audi's compact sport coupe was best compared with the BMW 1-series M Coupe (with its flared front and rear fenders). Both cars offered similar power output, and were similarly priced. However, they differed significantly in character. BMW built a dynamic two-door with limited rear-seat room, limited utility, and rear-wheel drive, while Audi built a practical sport sedan with ample room for four and all-wheel drive. German trade publication *Auto Zeitung* felt the RS 3 was a better concept. The RS 3 applied its superior traction to compensate for handling and slalom deficits. It was more comfortable, more practical, more powerful in sprints, and just a shade more affordable. Audi won the comparison test.

Another German publication, *auto motor und sport*, compared the RS 3 to the same offering out of Munich, as well as a coupe out of Stuttgart. Porsche sent the mid-engined, 330 hp Cayman R into the fray. Again, the winner was the Audi RS 3: "Even if it could not deny its front-drive heritage, the all-wheel drive RS 3 beat all competitors. Powerful, with secure traction and everyday utility, ultimately the four-door finished in the lead."

These praises did not come without reservations. With an eye to the road test opponents, the enthusiast magazine opined that "For the race track and pure driving enjoyment, there are more fascinating offerings in the marketplace." These caveats were above all due to the heavy engine over the front axle. Even the fat, optional front tires could not hide this physical reality.

In its own "Supertest," *sport auto* explored the question of when front-axle loading became excessive: "At the latest, at the start of the third lap on the Hockenheim short course, front-end understeer would become counterproductive to the point that any further attempt to explore the limits of the Audi RS 3 Sportback's dynamic handling would justify a charge of malicious tire destruction." The 255-series tires got hot if the RS 3 used them too hard.

BRAKING PROBLEMS IN THE AUDI RS 3

In addition, under load the brakes would suffer, audibly and perceptibly. One problem was that Audi employed ventilated brake discs with curved cooling channels to ensure continuous cooling, but did not take into account directionality. Both sides of the front axle used identical discs; in directing the airstream through the discs, the cooling channels only worked optimally on one side of the car. Audi improved discs and brake pads in the course of a service campaign, and installed new air ducts for improved brake cooling. This however did not eliminate the problem of mediocre deceleration.

Despite its flaws and several compromises, the RS 3 is an impressively fast car. *sport auto* lapped the Nürburgring north circuit in a time of 8:20 – only eleven seconds slower than the equally powerful, but 150 kg (330 lbs) lighter Audi TT RS. In the sprint to 100 km/h (62 mph) the RS 3 bettered the official works number (4.6 seconds) by 0.4 seconds. Lateral acceleration was most impressive in the wet. Talents like these could compensate for many weaknesses – above all, the poor fuel economy criticized by ADAC, the German auto club.

The first RS 3 ended production after just two years – an exception in the current RS program. Meanwhile, quattro boss Werner Frowein moved the production start of RS models into the first half of the product cycle. He was unable to meet this timetable with the premiere of the compact RS 3. Its successor, however, followed with less delay. Initially, Audi had planned on building about 2,500 examples of the first-generation RS 3. Eventually, it made about 5,400 copies.

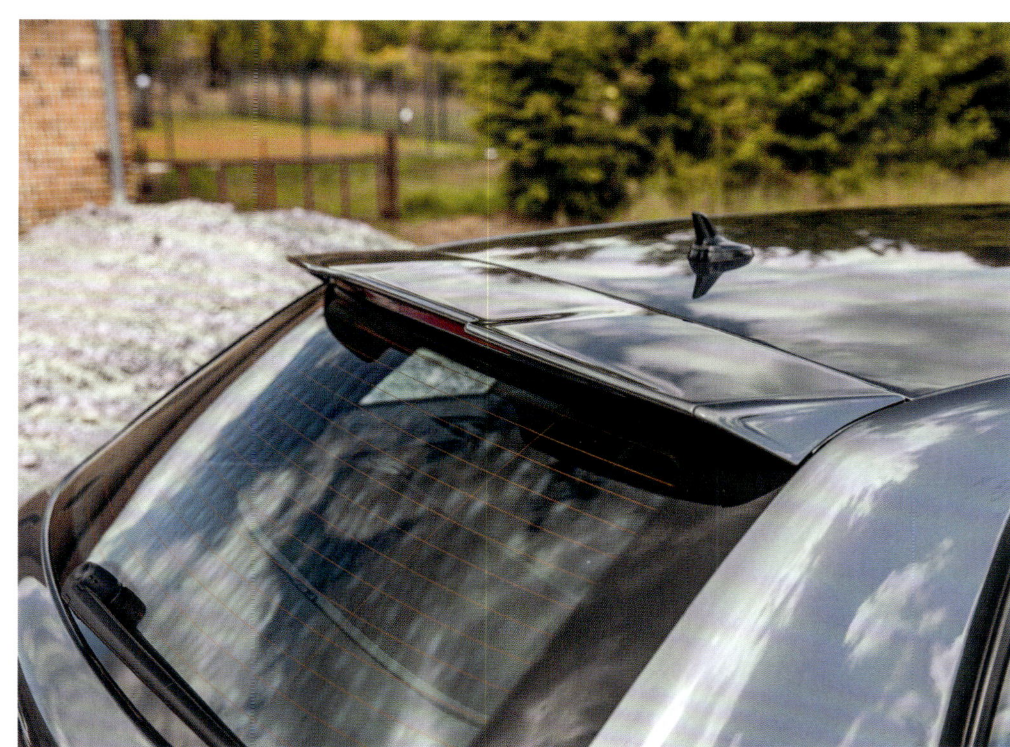

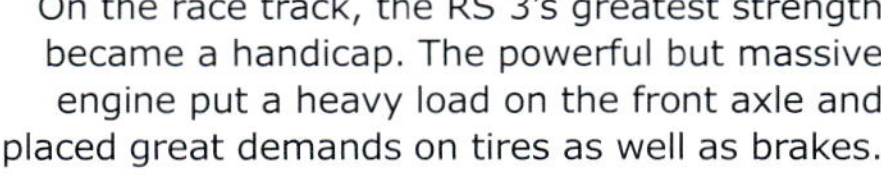

On the race track, the RS 3's greatest strength became a handicap. The powerful but massive engine put a heavy load on the front axle and placed great demands on tires as well as brakes.

PAINT CHOICES (EXCERPT)

Solid color: Ibis White
Metallic: Brilliant Black, Suzuka Gray
Pearl effect: Phantom Black, Misano Red, Daytona Gray

STANDARD EQUIPMENT (EXCERPT)

Exterior:

- 19-inch aluminum wheels with 235/35 tires (front) and 225/35 (rear)
- Xenon plus headlamps with cleaning system
- Wide fender flares, roof spoiler
- Matte aluminum-look outside mirrors

Audi sold the first RS 3 strictly as a five-door Sportback. Airdams, rocker panels and wheels significantly differentiated it from the A3 model.

Sporty, but practical: the interior of the RS 3 was not functionally different from the regular A3.

INTERIOR

- Sport seats with fine nappa leather and contrasting stitching
- Décor: piano black look
- Sport multifunction steering wheel with flattened bottom; shift knob with perforated leather cover

FUNCTION

- Automatic climate control
- "Chorus" audio system
- RS 3 sport suspension
- 18-inch brake system

2015-

Audi RS 3 Sportback & Sedan (8V)

A revival in two acts

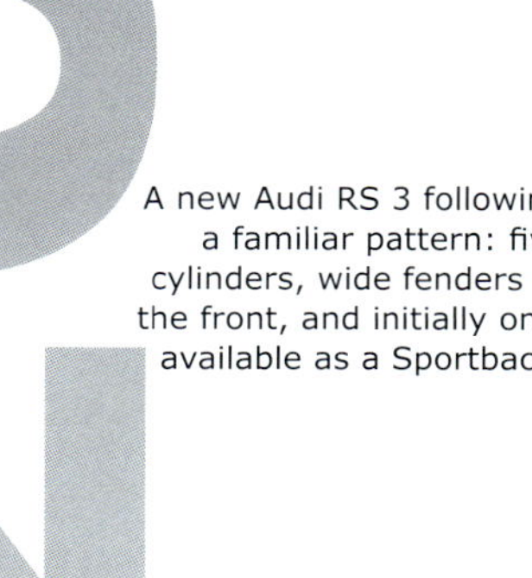

A new Audi RS 3 following a familiar pattern: five cylinders, wide fenders at the front, and initially only available as a Sportback.

Only just arrived, and gone already? The rumor mill soon questioned Audi's recently rediscovered love for the five-cylinder. After five wonderful years and three exciting cars, the iconic engine might soon be discontinued. That, at least, was the speculation in the spring of 2014. The reason was parked on the display floor of the Geneva Motor Show: a TT study with 420 horsepower from 2.0 liters suggested that in the future, a simpler four-cylinder engine might deliver RS-worthy performance. It would be more economical and lighter, and address the five-cylinder engine's weaknesses. Potential application: the Audi RS 3 of the 8V model line, anticipated for the following year.

Despite these theoretical advantages, the 2.0-liter four never got past the rumor stage. Later, insiders would reveal that a four-cylinder for the RS 3 was never under consideration. It was said, with a wink, that anyone who suggested downsizing of that model soon found themselves out of favor at Audi. In the RS models, the engine was a character-forming element. It not only had to deliver performance; it was also intended to evoke desire. This would hardly be possible with an ordinary four-cylinder, but the somewhat unrefined five-holer could do that all the better. The Geneva show study? A finger exercise. A red herring. The reality? Traditional five cylinders, and appropriately powerful.

In secret, Audi and quattro GmbH were even working on an all-new five-cylinder. The future of the powertrain was assured. To tide the model over until the powerplant was sufficiently developed, the old engine was given an update: starting in 2015, a gently reworked version of the five-cylinder, in-house designation EA 855, propelled the new Audi RS 3. Its most important new features: more power, lower emissions. With 367 hp, it was the most powerful performance-oriented compact on the market.

A NEW CONSTRUCTION SET IMPROVES THE AUDI A3

The 2.5-liter turbo engine, with firing order 1 - 2 - 4 - 5 – 3, became an enduring constant in the RS 3. Besides its powertrain, the car also highlighted several new features. These were, in part, the work of quattro GmbH in Neckarsulm. Beginning in 2012, Audi had been building a new, improved base vehicle. The newest generation of A3 was lighter, more rigid, roomier, but hardly any bigger – all establishing a good basis for the new sports model.

Many optimized features were made possible thanks to a new vehicle architecture. The Volkswagen group combined these into a "modular transverse toolkit," with the German acronym MQB (for "Modularer Querbaukasten.") This concept, intended to serve as a long-term basis for many cars, debuted in the Audi A3, the first vehicle built on this basis. The VW Golf and SEAT León followed in the same year, the Audi TT somewhat later.

In the new architecture, weight was reduced through the use of hot-formed, ultra-high and high-strength steels, while simultaneously increasing rigidity. Audi designed especially lightweight doors and rear hatch. Front and rear crossmembers, engine hood, and fenders were made of aluminum. These were expensive but costly optimizations that had a distinct effect on the resulting vehicle's technical specifications. In its concept of the new car, Audi also considered the deficits of the older sports model. Its rear-wheel wells now housed wider tires, and the floorpan provided space for an exhaust system meeting RS standards.

Other toolkit functions also benefited the top model of the platform. The new generation of Haldex all-wheel drive was more compact and 1.4 kg (3.1 lbs) lighter than the previous version and responded more quickly. Going forward, the all-wheel drivetrain would work in conjunction with the braking system. On braking of individual wheels, engine power followed the path of least resistance and was diverted to the

With increased boost pressure and larger intercooler, the familiar five-cylinder produced 367 hp in the new RS 3.

Exhaust emissions standards also apply to sporty top-of-the-line models. The engine of the RS 3 had to stretch to develop more power while also meeting more stringent emissions standards.

other, unbraked wheels. Audi called this targeted manipulation of power flow "wheel-selective torque control." This strategy increased the variability of the all-wheel drive system.

MORE POWER IN THE AUDI RS 3

Quite sporty, these new Audi developments. But first, quattro GmbH would subject the compact car to its own performance sports training program. The sister organization pumped up the five-door Sportback to create the muscular RS 3. The development targets demanded improvements wherever the predecessor had slipped up: brakes, tires, and balance all demanded an update. Special front steering knuckles, newly tuned steering, wider track and (optional) adjustable shock absorbers were intended to improve drivability. In addition, the program called for power training and a detox regime.

In the new car, the five-cylinder engine needed to meet Euro 6 exhaust emissions standards. Stephan Reil explained that this would in effect come at the cost about five percent of engine power. With that, and no other changes, the five-cylinder would be hardly any more powerful than the engine in an Audi S3. The solution: with more boost pressure (1.3 bar, or 19 psi) and a larger intercooler, the direct-injection engine developed 465 Newton-meters (343 foot-pounds) and 367 hp. In absolute terms, this was not a great leap; after all there was already one performance level with 360 hp. But this was a significant step, because more power represents more waste heat. A new cooling system was needed to regulate temperatures.

A specially-tuned transmission was mounted between the engine and the intelligent all-wheel driveline. The seven-speed dual-clutch automatic shifted more quickly than before, stayed in gear in manual mode, and automatically applied throttle during downshifts. In general, quattro GmbH had bid farewell to manually shifted transmissions just before introduction of this newest generation; it was never an option in the RS 3, even though it would have significantly reduced weight on the front axle. Audi transferred the blame to its customers, who had not lobbied for manual shift energetically enough.

New, improved brakes would provide the compact sporter with superior deceleration capability. To dispose of the topic once and for all, Audi installed eight-piston brake calipers at the front. "Wave design" discs at the front, with greater surface area, cooled more rapidly. The construction, with an aluminum rotor hat and pinned friction ring, further reduced weight. This came in handy, because above all, the RS 3 needed to lose front-end weight. Taken together, these changes on the new car accounted for a weight reduction of 55 kg (121 lbs) Weight distribution shifted rearward by one percent.

Only a handful of customers asked for a manual transmission on the RS 3. For that reason, the second generation offered the dual-clutch automatic as its only transmission choice.

BRAKES AND SEATS: PROMISES NOT KEPT

When Audi first showed the RS 3 in December 2014, the manufacturer announced that the car could be ordered with an optional ceramic brake system. At an added cost of 4,000 Euros, the manufacturer would install lighter, heavier duty discs of composite material on the front axle – a first in the compact class. However, price lists, from their first printing, deferred this to some later point in time, and customers were advised to ask their dealers regarding future availability. Upon doing so, they were given dates that, in the end, Audi was unable to meet. The optional brakes would only be available after the next major platform revision.

A similar tale was told with the optional RS bucket seats, which the RS 3 was to borrow from the R8. Sales brochures, price lists and owner's manuals featured the seats, but they were never included in the vehicle configurator. Audi delayed their introduction several times, and offered no further comment. Rare examples did appear; Audi installed the bucket seats in the press fleet, and these cars eventually found their way to the open market.

DRIFTING IN THE SNOW, HIGH SPEED ON ASPHALT

Audi wanted an impressive demonstration of how the new RS 3 differed from its predecessor. The mental image of the first-generation's understeering debut in 2011 was still a painful memory. So the successor was presented with pronounced oversteer: the first test drives with the motoring journalists were carried out in Ivalo, Finland. On packed snow, the car displayed its wild, drifting side. Audi's message: criticism acknowledged, solution provided.

Audi could hardly have chosen a better location for the RS 3 press premiere. Whirled-up snow contrasted to the striking Ara Blue of the test cars; added to the aggressive five-cylinder engine sound, it all felt like Rallying à la Röhrl. Above all, it disguised the fact that the

Chief developer Stephan Reil accompanied the first RS 3 test drives in Ivalo,Finland. He personally got behind the wheel to create spectacular photographs.

car continued to struggle against the laws of physics, especially given its portly belly. At the front, Audi offered, at additional cost, 255-series tires in order to broaden the Kamm Circle and attempt to find balanced handling.

The RS 3 showed its real talents not by sliding sideways over forest roads near the Arctic Circle, but rather in real road testing on asphalt. There, it shone. The German car magazine *auto motor und sport* summarized its testing: "The Audi RS 3 Sportback negotiates entire corners in a more neutral manner, occasionally even lifts the rear end, and in the course of the turn, develops more cornering force than its admittedly more clumsy predecessor – including, and above all, under load." The car had still not solved the front-axle load problem, but was better able to manage it: "The front-heavy weight distribution is more removed from the cornering behavior, although the actual change [in weight distribution] only appears behind the decimal point." *Auto Zeitung* confirmed that "The engineers have banished the predecessor's understeer; the front-end stays glued to the asphalt." Thanks to this reworking of several problem areas, the RS 3 drove significantly faster than its predecessor.

THE 2017 FACELIFT, AND A BACK END FOR THE ENTIRE WORLD

There were a lot of changes to the RS 3. Still, quattro GmbH (meanwhile renamed Audi Sport) held back the most important developments for the planned model maintenance. The facelift of the A3 kicked off in the spring of 2016; the reworked premium model appeared a year later. A new model was added to the line: along with the RS 3 Sportback, Audi's Hungarian plant in Győr now also built an RS 3 sedan. The North American and Asian markets preferred cars with conventional trunks. In those markets, cars with a smooth line between backlight and bumper enjoy only mediocre sales. The expansion to the model line was obvious, as both variants rolled on the same wheelbase. The two hardly differ in weight, and the added development cost was reasonable. In other areas, more effort was put into the cars. After an intermezzo with the modernized but aging five-cylinder engine, a new powerplant came on the scene. In the reworked RS 3, Audi installed its "EA 855 evo" engine, developing 400 hp. The engine first appeared in August 2016 in the new TT RS. The first RS 3 with this engine rolled off the assembly line on March 10, 2017. Audi later shipped this sedan to New Zealand.

In Oman, the reworked RS 3 variant demonstrated the qualities of the new, lighter fivecylinder engine.

For the facelift, all A3 derivatives were given a new edge in the headlamp covers. For the first time, Audi offered a sedan alongside the RS 3 Sportback.

The new engine completed the RS 3. Since the model change, the car had battled its nose-heavy handicap with considerable success. Now, the front end was perceptibly lighter. With an aluminum block and any number of engineering tricks, the weight of the five-cylinder engine was reduced by 26 kg (57 lbs). It now weighed about as much as a four-cylinder developing the same power.

In addition, Audi finally kept its promise of 2015. After long delay, the RS 3 now offered optional ceramic front brake discs. These remained steadfast even beyond the point where steel brakes would no longer be able to reject heat. The manufacturer expected that they would never again hear any complaints about "undersized brakes."

DRIFT SHOW IN OMAN

The big news about the facelifted RS 3, however, was not its optional brake package. For its first outing, the car appeared in Oman. There, it showed a hitherto unknown side – the RS could drift! And not just on snow, like two years earlier in Finland, but rather on asphalt. Testers experienced power-on oversteer in a car with which, given such a high coefficient of friction, it should not even have been physically possible – because only half of the engine output was delivered to the rear axle, along with power flow modulation by means of targeted brake application. Still, both Sportback and sedan got so spectacularly sideways that several trade publications alluded to this ability in the titles of their initial reports.

This wild side of the RS 3 ended soon enough. As Audi placed examples in its test fleet and distributed them to the various publications, the back end refused to break away. *Auto Bild sportscars* and *sport auto* revised their verdict after testing on home turf. Nothing could get the car going sideways anymore; the rear wheels politely followed the fronts. What could explain the change? Presumably, it was sand present at the first appearance in Oman. The press enthusiasm was limited to "longitudinal dynamics and very ebullient five-cylinder" *(sport auto)*. Best of all, the RS 3 continued to be the master of acceleration. Audi published a 0-100 km/h (62 mph) time of 4.1 seconds, but in multiple magazine tests, it broke the 4.0 second barrier. The car was so vocal with every movement that many owners installed (technically illegal) aftermarket exhaust flaps to at least avoid trouble with the neighbors when starting their engines. This in itself is curious, because such measures usually amplify noise levels instead of diminishing them. The issue soon resolved itself: Audi discontinued the RS 3 for one year, beginning in April 2018, in order to bring the engine up to the level of the next emissions standard. In 2019, it reappeared on the market with a particulate filter and new engine management software. Since then, it has been running cleaner, quieter, and somewhat more lethargically – the exhaust emissions standard inevitably pushed the engine power curve downward.

PAINT CHOICES (EXCERPT)

Solid colors: Nardo Gray, Kyalami Green
Metallic: Glacier White, Catalunya Red, Florett Silver, Mythos Black
Pearl effect: Daytona Gray, Sepang Blue, Ara Blue
Crystal effect: Panther Black, Ara Blue

STANDARD EQUIPMENT (EXCERPT)

Exterior:

- 19-inch aluminum wheels with 235/35 tires
- LED headlamps with cleaning system, LED taillamps
- Wide fender flares and rocker panels; roof spoiler
- Matte aluminum-look outside mirrors

With better weight distribution, the new RS 3 was more pleasant to drive than ever. The biggest changes were attributable to the intelligent all-wheel drive system.

In its second generation, the Audi RS 3 finally made room for a dual exhaust system, visually linking it to its larger siblings.

Contrasting stitching, leather, Alcantara, carbon, aluminum: Audi and Audi Sport placed a high value on a sporty interior for the RS 3.

INTERIOR

- Sport seats with fine nappa leather and contrasting stitching
- Décor: 3D optics
- Sport multifunction steering wheel with flattened bottom; shift knob with leather cover; as of facelift, shift knob with Alcantara cover
- Slotted interior door latches

FUNCTION

- Automatic climate control
- Multi Media Interface (MMI) Radio plus
- RS sport suspension
- RS brakes
- RS exhaust system

As early as 2014, the A3 Clubsport study heralded the RS 3's second generation, and an additional body style.

Under maximum-effort braking, an automatically deployable rear wing was raised into the slipstream to reduce stopping distances on the Clubsport study.

THE STUDY: AUDI A3 CLUBSPORT QUATTRO CONCEPT (2014)

From the beginning, it was an open secret that someday, the Audi A3 Clubsport quattro Concept would grow up to become the new RS 3. The powerful five-cylinder engine, all-wheel drive, oval exhaust tips, sport seats... one could hardly make it more obvious. Still, at its premiere at the Wörthersee, a lake in Austria, Audi insisted that it was an A3 study. Audi also stated that the firm was not willing to comment on speculation about future models – not even after a couple of journalists turned a few laps with the model on the Audi proving grounds in Neuburg.

The 2014 premiere of the actual RS 3 was only a year away. Audi wanted to get its fans excited, and this would only be possible with some effort. Thanks to the application of 125 new components, the concept car had wider bodywork, improved aerodynamics, and sharper optics. Some of these would later become standard equipment in the production RS 3, albeit on a less drastic scale.

The drivable version of the concept car turned out less spectacular than the car displayed at the Wörthersee in 2014. The "driver" lacked the wider track. Project director Ernst Scharl admitted that he was always a bit uncomfortable when somebody else drove "his" car; after all, the concept represented a great deal of love and labor. In less than five months, his team even implemented an air brake: in the event of brake line pressure in excess of ten bar (145 psi), a spoiler deployed into the slipstream to assist in deceleration. Theoretically, in maximum-effort braking from 250 km/h (155 mph), the spoiler would cut 12 meters (nearly 40 feet) off the braking distance.

In practice, nothing came of this idea. All production examples of the RS 3 braked in completely normal fashion. The engine, too, appeared only partly as hinted by the concept. The five-cylinder configuration remained, but developed considerably less than 525 hp and 600 Nm (442 ft-lbs) of torque. As a tradeoff, the production cars gave quicker throttle response; the study had to catch its breath before gathering up its skirts and sprinting away. Dual-clutch transmission, all-wheel drivetrain, and brake system were largely the same as the later production version. The dual exhaust, not available on the old RS 3, also made it into production.

Five cylinders and all-wheel drive were *verboten* in the international TCR Touring Car series, so the motorsports RS 3 entered the fray with four cylinders and front-wheel drive.

THE AUDI RS 3 IN MOTORSPORTS

Beginning in 2016, Audi's compact sports car competed in the TCR Touring Car racing class. Naturally, it bore the name and look of the fastest roadgoing derivative: in many aspects, the Audi RS 3 LMS resembled the RS 3 sedan, which did not even exist at the time of introduction. In terms of powertrain, the racer had no actual relationship to the road car. The racing rules limited engine displacement to two liters, and front-drive only. The unique characteristics of the RS 3 – five-cylinder engine and all-wheel drive – did not find their way to the racer.

The bodywork of the RS 3 LMS was largely derived from the production car. Its four-cylinder gasoline turbo provided 330 to 350 hp, and transmitted power to the front wheels via a sequential six-speed racing gearbox and mechanical limited slip differential. As an alternative, Audi offered a six-speed dual-clutch automatic transmission. With the near-production gearbox, curb weight increased from 1,180 to 1,215 kg (2,601 to 2,679 lbs). With racing rubber on 18-inch wheels, the car could sprint to 100 km/h (62 mph) in about 4.5 seconds, and, depending on gearing, could top out at 245 to 265 km/h (152 to 165 mph).

TECHNICAL SPECIFICATIONS

		Audi RS 3 (8PA)	Audi RS 3 (8V)	
MODEL	Body style	Sportback		Sedan
	Production timeframe	2011-2012	2015-2016	2017 -
ENGINE	Engine configuration	Transverse front-mounted inline five-cylinder Otto cycle engine		
	Engine designation	CEPA	CZGB	DAZA, as of 2019: DNWA
	Displacement, cc	2,480		
	Bore x stroke, mm	82.5x92.8		
	Power output, hp (kw) @ rpm	340 (250) @ 5,400-6,500	367 (270) @ 5,550-6,800	400 (294) @ 5,850-7,000
	Torque in Nm (ft-lbs) @ rpm	450 (332) @ 1,600-5,300	465 (343) @ 1,625-5,550	480 (354) @ 1,700-5,850; as of 2019, 480 (354) @ 1,950-5,850
	Valvetrain, valves per cylinder	Timing chain, dual overhead camshafts, active intake and exhaust valve timing control, four valves per cylinder		
	Fuel delivery	Direct gasoline injection, map ignition, exhaust gas turbocharger, Bosch MED 9.1.2 engine control system	Direct gasoline injection, map ignition, exhaust gas turbocharger, Bosch MED 17.1.1 engine control system	Direct gasoline injection, manifold injection, map ignition, exhaust gas turbocharger, Bosch MED 17.1.62 engine control system
	Compression ratio	10:1		
POWERTRAIN	Transmission	Seven-speed S-tronic dual-clutch automatic		
	Drivetrain	All-wheel drive on Haldex principle, 4th generation	All-wheel drive on Haldex principle, 5th generation; ESP with wheel-selective torque control	

		Audi RS 3 (8PA)	Audi RS 3 (8V)		
CHASSIS AND SUSPENSION	**Front suspension**	MacPherson struts with lower A-arms, tubular anti-roll bar, aluminum subframe	McPherson struts with steel lower A-arms, aluminum steering knuckles, aluminum subframe, tubular anti-roll bar		
	Rear suspension	Four-link rear axle with separate springs and shock absorbers, tubular anti-roll bar, subframe	Four-link rear axle with separate springs and shock absorbers, subframe, aluminum hubs, tubular anti-roll bar		
	Steering	Electromechanical rack-and-pinion steering		Electromechanical progressive steering	
	Turning circle, m (ft)	10.7 (35.1)	10.9 (35.8)	11.0 (36.1)	11.0 (36.1)
	Brake system	Dual-circuit brake system with ABS, ESP, four-piston calipers at front, ventilated discs front and rear	Dual-circuit brake system with ABS, ESP, eight-piston calipers at front, ventilated discs front and rear		
	Brake discs	Front: 370x32 mm Rear: 310x22 mm	Front: 370x34 mm (wave design) Rear: 310x22 mm	Front: 370x34 mm (wave design) Rear: 310x22 mm Optional: front ceramic brake discs	
	Wheel size, in.	8x19 all around Optional 8.5x19 front	8x19 all around Optional: 8.5x19 front		
	Tire size	Front: 235/35 Rear: 225/35 Optional: 255/30 front	235/35 all around Optional: 255/30 front		
DIMENSIONS AND WEIGHTS	**Length/width/Height, mm (in.)**	4,302/1,794/1,402 (169.4/70.6/55.2)	4,343/1,800/1,411 (171.0/70.9/55.6)	4,335/1,800/1,411 (170.7/70.9/55.6)	4,479/1,802/1,411 (176.3/70.9/55.6)
	Wheelbase, mm (in.)	2,578 (101.5)	2,631 (103.6)		
	Track, front/rear, mm (in.)	1,564/1,528 (61.6/60.2)	1,559/1,514 (61.4/59.6)		1,559/1,528 (61.4/60.2)
	Empty weight, kg (lbs)	1,650 (3,638)	1,595 (3,516)	1,585 (3,494) as of 2019: 1,605 (3,538)	1,590 (3,505) as of 2019: 1,610 (3,549)
	Trunk volume, liters (cu ft)	302 (10.7)	280 (9.9)	335 (11.8)	315 (11.1)
	Fuel capacity, liters (U.S. gal)	60 (15.9)	55 (14.5)		
PERFORMANCE	**Top speed, km/h (mph)**	250 (governed) (155)	250 (governed); Optional: 280 (governed) (155; Optional: 174)		
	Acceleration, 0-100 km/h, sec (62 mph)	4.6	4.3	4.1	4.1
	Fuel economy, liters/100 km (U.S. mpg)	9.1 (25.8)	8.1 (29.0)	8.5 (27.7) as of 2019: 9.4 (25.0)	
MISCELLANEOUS	**Number built, by year**	2010: 15 2011: 2,235 2012: 3,433	2014: 40; 2015: 4,865; 2016: 5,818	2016: 23; 2017: 5,535; 2018: 4,548; 2019: 6,408	2016: 83; 2017: 5,884 2018: 4,129; 2019: 4,267
	Total number built	5,683	10,723	In production	In production
	Price at market introduction	49,900 €	52,700 €	54,600 €	55,900 €

Source Audi AG

M
IN RS 4350
IN RS 1996
IN RS 4001
IN RS 4002

ID-RANGE MODELS

Audi's RS program began in its mid-range models. Beginning in 1994, the hitherto comparatively unsporty manufacturer, in cooperation with Porsche, built the Avant RS2, and from 1999, with subsidiary quattro GmbH, the first RS 4 Avant. Audi produced more RS generations and derivatives in the mid-range segment than in any other vehicle class. As Audi felt its way toward new possibilities, it also produced RS Cabriolets and RS Sedans.

Tradition has always played a major role in these cars. Whenever a new mid-range RS rolled into the spotlight, its predecessors supported it with validation from the pages of history. For Audi, this is a well-trod path; the firm repeatedly rolled out special editions that masterfully celebrated Audi's legacy as the pioneer of all-wheel drive. The firm's own history even served as justification for fashionable downsizing: as engine size diminished, a long-retired powerplant delivered new inspiration. The key features of the RS identity were always retained – all-wheel drive, abundant power, and a wagon body existed in every model generation.

1994–

Audi Avant RS2 (P1/B4)

The first RS Audi

Porsche designer Roland Heiler drew this early rendering of the Audi S2 Avant, incorporating Porsche components and a distinctive radiator grille.

Most participants agree on the origins of Audi's first RS model. In 1994, Porsche CEO Wendelin Wiedeking and Audi chairman of the board Herbert Demel announced, in the German news magazine *Der Spiegel*, that their two marques had jointly conceived a new sports wagon. In a sense, they were correct, because the Audi Avant RS2 was a project dear to the heart of automotive sage, Ferdinand Piëch. A talented developer at the time of the Avant's conception, Piëch was head of Audi and also a family shareholder in Porsche. He initiated the development of what was, at that time, the most powerful production Audi to date.

In brainstorming the idea, Audi drew on the support of a motor sports business, Konrad Schmidt Motorsport GmbH (SMS) of Cadolzburg, near Nuremberg. A look back: a long-time partner with Audi, SMS was also tasked with developing a successor to the sporty Audi quattro. The result was the Audi 20V Turbo quattro Coupe. After Audi made a few modifications to appearance and brakes, this became the S2 Coupe.

On its own initiative, SMS also modified the engine. The Cadolzburg operation created higher-output versions of the five-cylinder powerplant. Dubbed "Revo," these various performance stages put out 286 to 303 hp. It was no surprise that performance fan, Piëch, had an affinity for powerful engines, so he contracted SMS to build an even more powerful S2.

RS2 PROTOTYPE BY THE DEVELOPERS OF THE S2

SMS designed a coupe, which it delivered to Audi. On the basis of this car, the idea was born in Ingolstadt for their own car, but with bigger bodywork. Audi analyzed, speculated, fantasized... at the expense of the prototype. After several months, Audi sent this back to SMS, partially disassembled. Then the manufacturer contracted the sport wagon project with Porsche.

It was an opportune project for Porsche. Shortly after German reunification, the Zuffenhausen sports car maker found itself in crisis, with losses of 240 million Deutschmarks. Even before the project got underway, Porsche was thinking of offering Audi a cooperative project, and proactively generated proposals for sporty Audi derivatives.

Once Audi issued the contract, young Porsche designer Roland Heiler sketched several proposals for sporty wagons. The first renderings were based on the Audi S4, whose most powerful version would compete with the BMW M5 Touring. However, the decision makers felt the smaller Audi 80 Avant to be a better basis. The renderings known today show the RS2 with a distinctive radiator grille and classic Porsche elements.

Contemporary witnesses reported animated discussions regarding the scope of visual changes. Or, to put it in less politically correct terms, there were arguments. Both marques wished to have their presence known on the car. It was not until the end of May 1993 that the Porsche wheels would have center caps bearing Audi's four-ring logo. In particular, the participants were not in agreement about the design of the joint logo. Heiler was given the assignment to add a stripe to the S2 emblem and integrate Porsche script. Work stretched into the summer of 1993.

Early in the RS2 project, the car still did not have a continuous light band at the rear, but rather a valance bearing the four Audi rings.

Tuned by Porsche, the Audi Avant RS2 contained many components that were originally intended for sports cars out of Zuffenhausen. These included wheels, brakes, turn signals and skirt design.

THE AUDI/PORSCHE

Things ran more smoothly on the engineering side. In the second half of 1992, Porsche project manager Michael Hölscher took charge of Project P1 (for Porsche 1). His catalog of project specifications described a car that would have an enormous influence on Audi's future. Its brief was to develop 300 to 320 hp, differentiate itself from the normal production car through added parts and technology, yet remain close to the normal car. It was also to have a distinctive Porsche aura – this at a time when Porsche's reputation was suffering as badly as the carmaker itself. And it all had to be done quickly, because the regular Audi 80 on which it was based was scheduled to cease production in late 1995.

Hölscher and his team reworked the axles, suspension, drivetrain and visuals. The engineers adapted the brakes of the Porsche 968, initially with a detrimental effect on noise. Audi suggested using the more comfortable HP2 brakes of the Audi S4. Porsche countered by optimizing production of its own brake system, thereby validating its original choice. Many suspension components were unique to the RS2. Because the planned 215-series tires lacked the required load carrying ability beyond 250 km/h (155 mph), special hubs had to be designed to make room for 245-series Dunlop rubber. The fatter anti-roll bars, in particular, markedly improved handling in comparison to the base car.

To save time, the engineers did not design their own exhaust manifold for the five-cylinder turbo, but instead bought a ready-made commercial part. It was sourced from Lehmann Motorentechnik of Switzerland. The same component was already being used by SMS in its Revo vehicles. The team cut development time of the front valance from the usual 18 months to just nine. The quattro all-wheel drivetrain, including Torsen differential and equal power split, was taken over from the S2 without modification.

The team was unable to completely avoid all bodywork modifications. The front crossmember, a bolted-on component, could not withstand the torque of the more powerful engine. An upgrade was approved – but only that one change; the engineers were prohibited from diving deeper into the chassis. So the engine output increased, but not the car's rated towing capacity. The instant a trailer was hitched to the car, the engine management system automatically reduced power output to 230 hp in order to avoid additional loads on the engine.

This idea was so new and so good that Porsche took out a patent on it. The two marques made their first joint appearance in June 1993. Porsche and Audi announced the Avant RS2, product of the Audi/Porsche working group (official manufacturer: "Arge Audi/Porsche"), for the Frankfurt Auto Show (IAA) of that year. The heads of the two companies announced that the car would have "more than 220 kW (300 hp)" and would be available beginning in spring 1994. A while later, the respective press departments added that Audi dealerships would handle sales. In a move that was as unusual then as now, Porsche and Audi agreed to split the meager profits.

A car like the RS2 could build brands, generate stories and legends, but not huge profits.

The first, near-production study was displayed at the Frankfurt International Auto Show. The press kit cited a few preliminary specifications: 315 hp, 400 Nm (295 ft-lbs) of torque, 9:1 compression ratio, acceleration to 100 km/h (62 mph) in 5.8 seconds, and a top speed of 262 km/h (163 mph).

Later, the manufacturers revised some of these numbers upward, for at the auto show premiere, the Avant RS2 was still a long way from being finished; it still lacked the final polish. In cold-weather testing, it became apparent that dense air would raise engine torque excessively. Extreme rocking movement overloaded the engine mounts. Reacting quickly, the team eliminated these faults before production got underway.

Always near at hand, Ferdinand Piëch had meanwhile (1993) risen to the post of CEO at Volkswagen. The RS2 remained his project. During model approval drives, typically conducted on the same day with multiple vehicles, he saved the fast Audi for last. Hölscher always stayed in the car, to directly receive any criticism

PRODUCTION IN ZUFFENHAUSEN

The superfast Audi was assembled in Porsche's "Rössle-Bau" in the Zuffenhausen factory – the same facility that produced other special cars for various manufacturers, and Porsche's own 959. As production got underway, Audi delivered painted body shells and all parts carried over from the base models (rear bench seat, instrument panel, and most ancillary equipment) to the assembly line in Stuttgart-Zuffenhausen. There, Porsche added all the things that made up the RS2. Components such as the combination instrument and the Recaro seats came from suppliers. Mirrors, turn signals, wheels, brakes, and other parts came out of Porsche's own production lines, and carried appropriate part numbers.

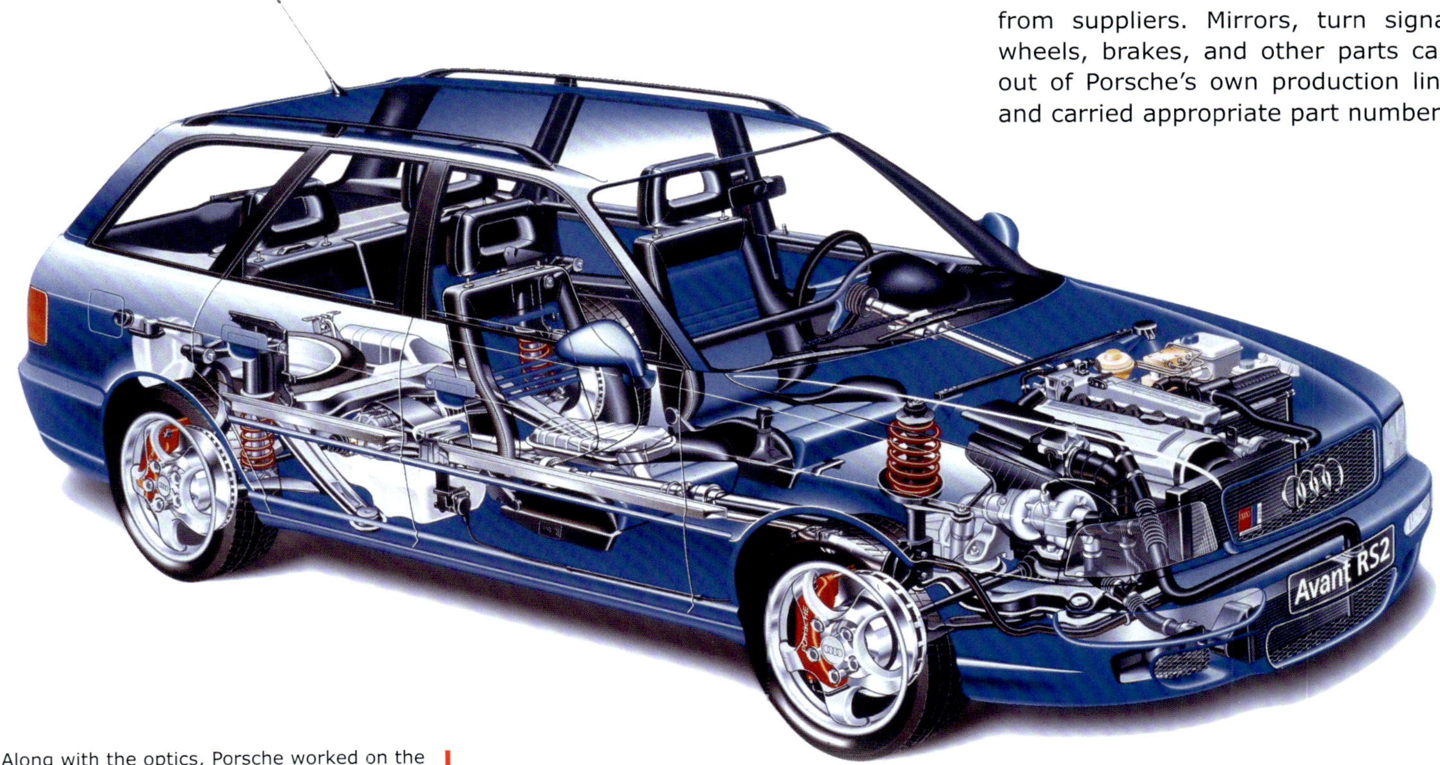

Along with the optics, Porsche worked on the Audi Avant RS2's engine, transmission, axles, suspension, brakes and wheels.

By today's standards, the top end of the B4 model line appeared decidedly restrained. But at its debut, in the button-down world of Audi, the RS2 came across as especially daring.

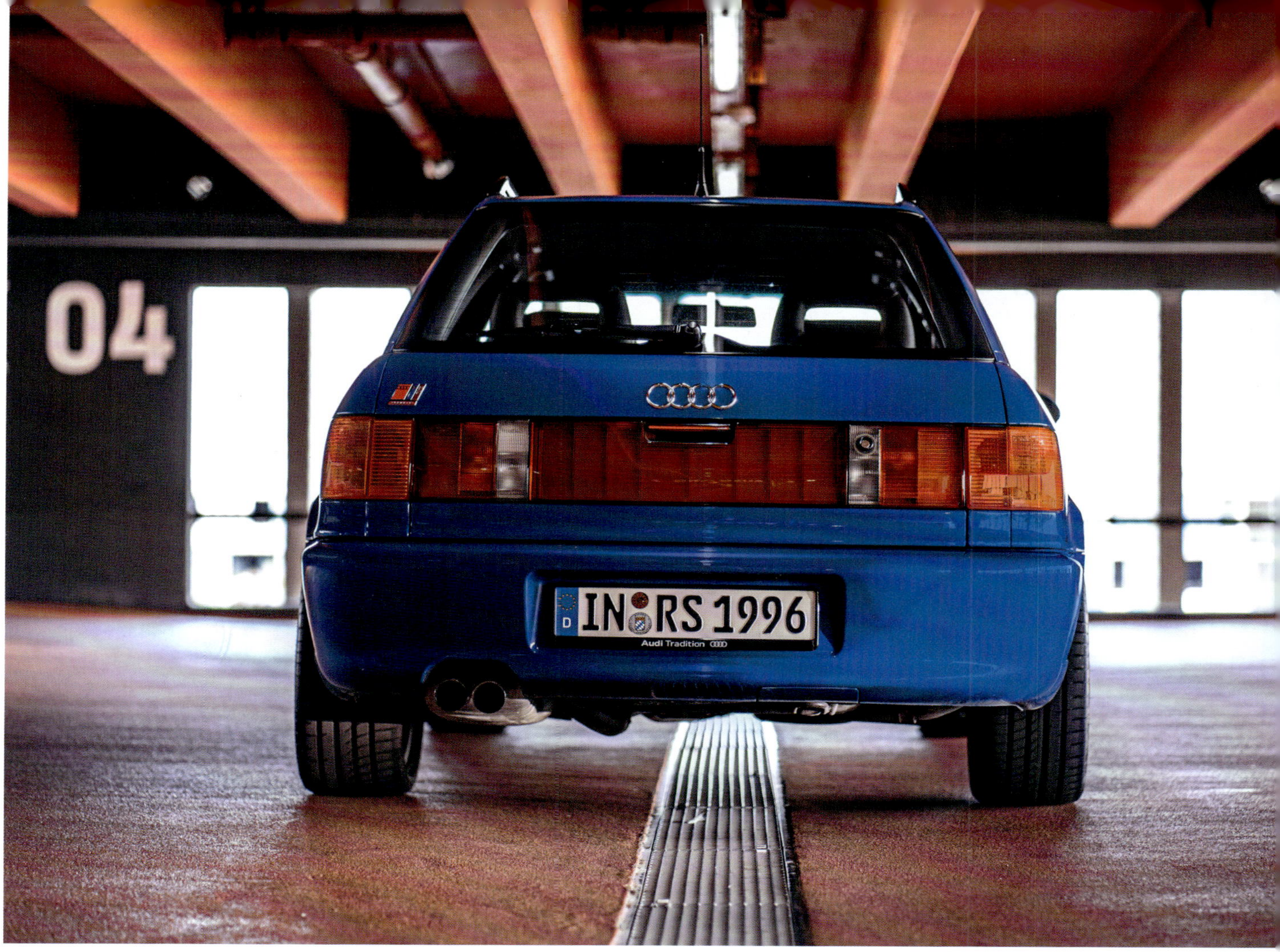
04
IN RS 1996
Audi Tradition

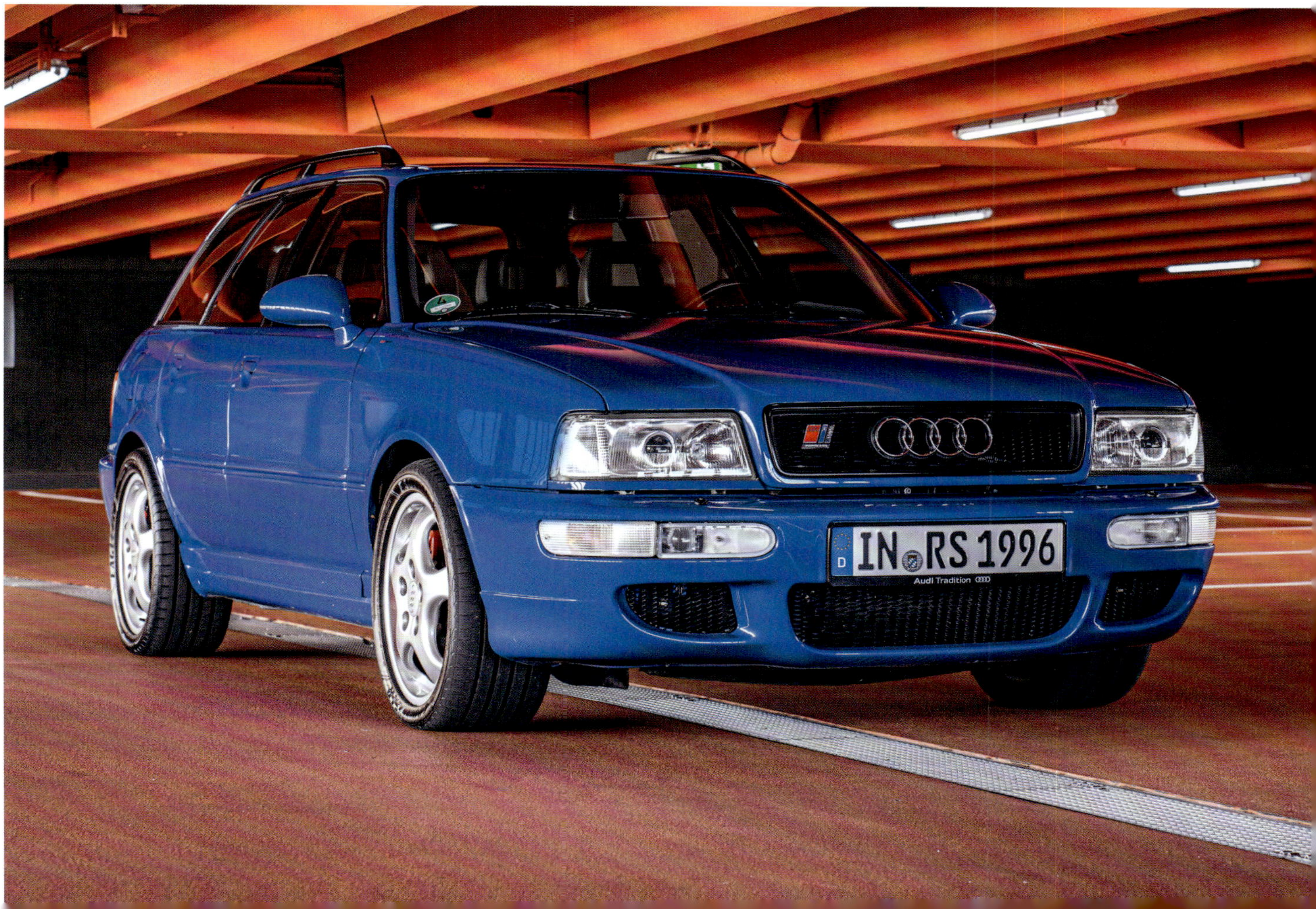
IN RS 1996
Audi Tradition

Project leader Michael Hölscher (far left) and a fleet of RS2s at Porsche's Weissach research and development center.

Sales of the Avant RS2 kicked off on March 19, 1994. It was not the world's first high-performance wagon; BMW's M5 Touring had started two years earlier. But in its mid-range segment, the RS2 was a pioneer. Starting in 1997, Mercedes built its own entry, the C43 AMG T-Model, with 306 hp. BMW would not introduce its first M3 Touring until 2022.

WALTER RÖHRL ON THE RS2

Wiedeking saw the Avant RS2 as an expansion of the Porsche spectrum. He could approach customers who would have loved to buy a sports car built in Zuffenhausen, but needed space for the family and luggage. Internally at Porsche, there were plans for a roomy front-engined sedan, but the Panamera would not appear until fifteen years later. For the time being, there was just the RS2.

The intent was for customers of the RS2 to experience the "Porsche feeling" from their first minute with the car. The February 1994 press release included a separate chapter with quotes by rally legend and (as of 1993) Porsche brand ambassador Walter Röhrl. He found the car "very good-natured and wonderfully easy to drive." Further, he described it as an "absolutely stress-free vehicle." In the official text, Röhrl praised the brakes, engine performance, and handling of the RS2. In particular, he praised the spontaneous response of the engine, "above all from low engine rpms." The German trade magazine *auto motor und sport* contradicted this, and complained about the very obvious turbo lag – especially in comparison to the less powerful but very lively normally-aspirated inline six-cylinder of the BMW M3. Porsche house magazine *Christophorus* summarized: those who like turbo technology "would also like to feel the turbo, and will be overjoyed with this vehicle." All others "might find less favor" with delayed thrust. According to *Christophorus*, the response of the RS2 recalled that of the top of the Porsche 911 line, the 911 Turbo.

Just over 25 years after its presentation, Röhrl agreed with this assessment. "First there's nothing, then the hammer, just like the Porsche Turbo of 1977," he enthused, adding "You feel the power more." Great praise indeed from the man who is connected to the Audi five-cylinder like no other.

The RS2 was only sold in Avant form. Porsche and Audi, however, visually and technically converted two or three S2 sedans into RS2 sedans.

"Powered by Porsche." The development engineers in Zuffenhausen thoroughly reworked the Audi five-cylinder, and raised its power output from 230 to 315 hp.

THE ENGINE OF THE AUDI RS2

This engine achieved its final and most powerful performance level in the Avant RS2. Hölscher described the engine modifications thus: "In principle, nothing changed; on individual parts, nearly everything changed." His team enlarged the turbocharger and intercooler, reworked the cylinder head from intake to exhaust, and modified the intake and exhaust manifolds, downpipe, catalytic converters as well as the exhaust system.

At full load, the fuel injectors delivered the maximum possible amount of fuel into the RS2 intake manifold. The engineers called this mode "continuous line." In this mode, the injectors are constantly open. It was the only way to provide enough fuel to the combustion chambers to match the large volume of air pumped by the turbocharger, and to adequately cool the components. Speed, as well as fuel consumption, were enormous. Even before the market introduction of the RS2, the test driver of a major German automotive newspaper covered the roughly 250 km (155 miles) between Berlin and Hamburg in one hour. The contents of the 64-liter (16.9 U.S. gallons) fuel tank were barely sufficient.

To ensure that the five-cylinder engine was up to the power output, Porsche reinforced one crankshaft bearing and optimized the oil supply. After all, the basic engine design was a child of the 1970s. In the course of the production run, the manual six-speed transmission was given a reinforced first-gear set.

In contrast to the custom of the time, Audi did not adhere to the German auto industry's voluntary self-imposed top speed limit of 250 km/h (155 mph). The fastest Audi topped out at 262 km/h (163 mph). From a standing start, the then-new Porsche 911 Carrera (Type 993) was just able to keep up, but its price in 1994 was 125,750 Deutschmarks. By comparison, the RS2 seemed like a real steal. In the price lists, the base price was given as 98,900 DM. For many years after its production ended, it counted as Porsche's only station wagon.

THE AUDI RS2 AS A SEDAN

The manufacturing consortium with the rather complex name, Arge Audi/ Porsche, built the RS2 only in Avant form. The model's the type certification listed the wagon (with and without sunroof) as the only available body style. The cooperating partners did not stamp chassis numbers with their manufacturer code, WAC, into any other automobile. Nevertheless, during the production run of the Avant RS2, several sedans bearing the same technology were created at Audi and Porsche.

In Weissach, Porsche converted an S2 sedan. The car was equipped with prototype parts and the RS2 drivetrain. The car was sent to Audi, after which its trail has been lost. In the same way, Audi itself modified at least one, very likely two S2 sedans. One of these, a black, now rather worn example with more than 100,000 kilometers (62,000 miles) on its odometer, is in the Audi Tradition collection. Due to lack of documentation, the disposition of the other vehicles is unknown.

Two additional RS2 sedans were built for customers in Saudi Arabia. Neither Audi nor Porsche were responsible, but rather an unknown private company. Visually, the cars appear different from the works conversions.

Neither manufacturer considered series production of the sedan. Originally, they had planned only 2,000 examples of the Avant RS2. In the end, they built 2,900 production cars and eight prototypes. Production was terminated only because the base vehicle's run had ended. An RS2 sedan would have represented additional effort and expense, but no economic advantage.

PAINT CHOICES (EXCERPT)

Solid colors: Laser Red
Metallic: Polar Silver, Ragusa (green), Brilliant Black, Brilliant Blue
Pearl effect: RS Blue, Volcano Black, Amethyst Grey, Indigo

STANDARD EQUIPMENT (EXCERPT)

Exterior:

- 17-inch aluminum Porsche Design wheels with 245/40 tires
- Porsche Design outside mirrors, electrically adjustable and heated
- Rear valance with light design
- Front bumper with pronounced spoiler, rear bumper with integral license plate frame
- Dual exhaust tips, 65 mm diameter

In all, eight prototypes and 2,900 production examples of the Audi RS2 were built, the examples shown here are among the last.

Late in the process, Porsche and Audi decided that the car should have a black radiator grille surround. At Porsche, the continuous light bar at the back is a characteristic of all-wheel drive models.

Recaro sport seats were standard equipment in the roomy Audi RS2.

INTERIOR

- Recaro sport seats, covered in silk nappa leather and Alcantara
- Carbon fiber inserts in door panels and instrument panel
- Single-piece leather shift knob and bellows with aluminum plaque, leather-covered steering wheel and Alcantara-covered center section. At no added cost: airbag steering wheel or sport steering wheel, black
- Black chrome door handles

FUNCTION

- Sport suspension
- Porsche brake system
- Headlamp cleaning system
- Rear limited slip differential
- Ellipsoid headlamps
- On-board computer

An early predecessor of the RS2 engine, Audi built a powerful five-cylinder with the intake manifold of the Sport quattro. It differed from the "Revo S" engine developed by SMS.

THE UNKNOWN STUDY: AUDI COUPE RS2

Long before Porsche calculated camshafts for Audi's five-cylinder engine, SMS carried out important groundbreaking work for the Avant RS2. Located in Cadolzburg, near Nuremberg and about 110 kilometers (70 miles) north of Audi headquarters in Ingolstadt, SMS created a prototype at Audi's request – the engineers at SMS converted a Coupe S2 into a sports car.

Nobody at Audi, not even Piëch, knew what would come out of this project. At its center was the powerful five-cylinder engine reworked by SMS. With a large K27 turbocharger, reduced compression ratio, sport exhaust and a special intake manifold, power was increased by about 70 percent, to 375 hp. Later, SMS offered its customers this conversion under the designation "Revo S." The turbocharger and exhaust manifold of the project more or less represented what would later appear in the production vehicle.

Along with the drivetrain, SMS worked on the body. The car was fitted with aluminum sheetmetal parts in order to reduce vehicle weight. For series production, however, this would be too expensive. The front valance was based on the part used in the S2, but included modified air inlets below the license plate. A black lip expanded the standard production rear spoiler.

Fate was not kind to the hot S2; on the day it was to be presented to Audi, it was involved in an accident. SMS repaired the damage and handed the car over to Audi, after a slight delay.

The client built at least one tuned variant of the Coupe S2 on its own. The Audi vehicle differed from the SMS creation above all in the design of the front valance. Two different wheel designs were under discussion: the Audi "Bolero" rims, and an aftermarket wheel from AZEV, their "A" design, each 17 inches in diameter. The manufacturer never showed or drove these cars in public. The only evidence that they ever existed is a handful of photographs.

Many elements of these cars found their way into series production. The colors of the studies appeared to be early variants of RS Blue (later, Nogaro Blue), worn by the Avant RS2 in the sales brochure. The production car also adopted the matching upholstery in the center portion of the sport seats, but in Alcantara instead of leather.

In the course of the RS2's production run, interested parties inquired at Audi whether they could obtain the powerful drivetrain in a coupe body. The manufacturer felt that the car would deviate from the concept of the Avant RS2. It was supposed to be all about the combination of space and sportiness. Some customers had their Coupe S2s reworked by Konrad Schmidt Motorsport to incorporate the technology of the RS2 or the engine performance level of the Revo S.

A coupe version was indeed under discussion while the RS2 was being conceived. Audi would have liked to lay on a series of 999 examples, at a price point below 100,000 Deutschmarks. The idea was that the car would be to the Coupe S2 what the erstwhile Sport quattro was to the quattro – and thereby underscore its slim bodywork. Porsche, however, feared that such a car would compete too strongly with its own models. Porsche, as a service provider, insisted on a large car as the basis of its efforts – and was ultimately able to prevail.

1999–

Audi RS4 Avant (B5)

quattro GmbH's first RS Audi

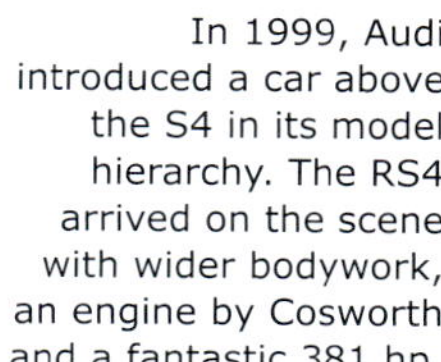

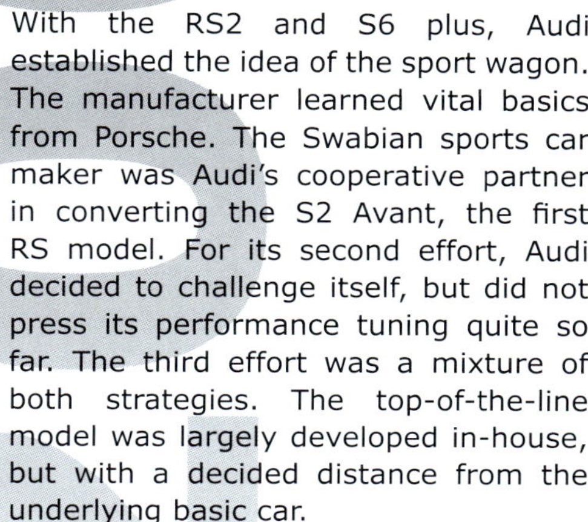

In 1999, Audi introduced a car above the S4 in its model hierarchy. The RS4 arrived on the scene with wider bodywork, an engine by Cosworth and a fantastic 381 hp.

With the RS2 and S6 plus, Audi established the idea of the sport wagon. The manufacturer learned vital basics from Porsche. The Swabian sports car maker was Audi's cooperative partner in converting the S2 Avant, the first RS model. For its second effort, Audi decided to challenge itself, but did not press its performance tuning quite so far. The third effort was a mixture of both strategies. The top-of-the-line model was largely developed in-house, but with a decided distance from the underlying basic car.

Audi established a working group tasked with creating a concept study. Their mission: to determine what a car, slotted above the 1997 Audi S4, would look like. Ulrich Hackenberg, responsible for concept definition at Audi, led the team. Audi's engineering development department provided engine and chassis experts. Quattro GmbH sent chief engineer Stephan Reil. They consulted experts from the Tom Walkinshaw Racing team, and Audi's then-subsidiary, Cosworth Technology.

In 14 months, the team developed a car in a form that had not yet existed. With its 381 hp, the first RS4 exceeded the imagination of Audi's marketing department. Because no other manufacturer had such a powerful wagon in its model line, it was difficult for them to prognosticate sales numbers. Not long before, this performance class had still been the domain of sports cars like the Ferrari F355.

Reil countered that it should not be Audi's goal to lag behind the competition. With his first car, he wanted to show what was technically possible. His argument convinced the bosses. The concept turned into a development order, assigned to quattro GmbH in Neckarsulm. The car carried the name RS4 Avant, and became a legitimate successor to the Avant RS2.

ASSEMBLY LINE PRODUCTION AND HAND CRAFTSMANSHIP

Manufacturing the RS4 was a challenge for the little subsidiary, quattro GmbH. As much as possible was to be carried out on the regular A4 assembly line. The extensive changes to powertrain and body, however, were at odds with the tight schedules of volume production. Audi did not have the capacity to make many of the specific parts unique to the quattro model. Audi's plant in Győr, which would henceforth be the production site of components for limited series, had no space for RS4 special assignments; it was preparing for production of the first Audi TT.

Cosworth Technology provided the turbocharged V6 engine from its facility in Wellingborough, England, after the cylinder heads had been made in Worcester. Audi sourced the wide front fenders from supplier Grau. Audi had the rear side panels modified; standard production A4 side frames were taken off the regular production line and sent to Horst Matzner AG in Osnabrück. There, metalworkers cut into the panels and welded on fender flares. The finished, 3.5 cm (1.4-in.) wider panels went back to Audi and rejoined the body assembly process.

It did not end there. Audi only partially assembled the RS4 on the standard model production line. While the less powerful models rolled off the line in completed form, the sport model left the line almost naked. Missing were all model-specific plastic parts such as valances and side skirts, as well as the intercooler system. At this point in its production process, the RS4 was only fitted with so-called short-circuit intake runners, to allow it to drive under its own power with a closed supercharging system. It still rolled on temporary wheels, used only in the manufacturing process. The standard 255 series tires on 18-inch rims could not be accommodated on the regular assembly line.

Reil called the Ingolstadt-built RS4 an "80 percent car." They were sent by truck to Neckarsulm, where quattro GmbH put them on a hoist and applied hand craftsmanship to complete the process. At quattro, fitters carried out all the tasks that were too involved to be done on the regular assembly line. On as many as 20 cars per day, they installed the intercooler and final intake tract, installed valances, skirts, and the correct wheels. The work took about fifteen hours. The cars were subjected to all necessary inspections and their first

The standard 255 tires are too wide for the conveyor system of the production line. During assembly, the RS4 carries narrower rotating gears.

Two important features of the first Audi RS4: the honeycomb radiator grille and the 2.7-liter twin-turbo V6 engine.

Officially, the Audi RS4 was governed to a top speed of 250 km/h (155 mph). In fact, it would go faster. To cover the possibility, the speedometer was calibrated up to 310 km/h (193 mph).

road tests, after which they were sent to the dealers. The removed, temporary short-circuit runners and narrow production wheels were shipped back to Ingolstadt in crates, only to reappear in Neckarsulm a few weeks later in the continuing stream of new cars.

PREMIERE AT THE 1999 FRANKFURT AUTO SHOW

The RS4 appeared in public for the first time at the 1999 IAA, the International Auto Show, in Frankfurt am Main, strictly speaking still as a near-production study. As with the S6 plus, quattro GmbH emphasized, happily and often, that the most powerful A4 was a product of its own development. It was not until page two that the press kit mentioned that it would be sold under the Audi RS4 name. Before that, the text simply said "RS4" or "RS4 by quattro GmbH."

The RS4 made a fabulous impression in Frankfurt. Quattro chief Werner Frowein reported a resounding resonance. The RS4 exceeded all preceding Audi models in performance and acceleration, even the powerful Audi S8.

The RS4 was aided by the fact that it offered more power than its market competitors, and over a longer timespan. At the same time as the RS4's premiere, BMW released the first information or its new M3, with 343 hp. Mercedes suggested that a six-cylinder supercharged 400 hp engine for the C-Class was in the works, but it never happened. And even if it had... Frowein said the V6 turbo in the RS4 could easily keep up. There was even some headroom in top speed. Ungoverned, the RS4 could reach about 290 km/h (180 mph), as reported by journalists driving the first production cars. The RS4 speedometer was numbered up to 310 km/h (193 mph).

To counter such speeds, the RS4 was given an 18-inch brake system with dual-piston calipers at the front. Quattro GmbH installed ventilated composite rotors, with aluminum rotor hats and cast iron friction rings, on the aluminum steering knuckles. A stiffer, 20 mm lower sport suspension improved roadholding at high speeds.

Of course, nothing could be allowed to go wrong on the brand's top model. Before the start of production, the RS4 covered 8,000 kilometers (5,000 miles) on the Nürburgring north circuit, and drove at full throttle over 26,000 kilometers (more than 16,000 miles) on the high-speed oval test track at

Audi shipped A4 side panels to the Matzner company in Osnabrück, where metal fender flares were added, extending the width by 3.5 cm on each side.

Nardo, in southern Italy. The press response rewarded these efforts. The editors of *sport auto* praised their long-term test car after 100,000 kilometers (62,000 miles) of use, saying it satisfied everything ever desired of an automobile. "I never want to drive another car again," wrote the author. The RS4 was "wonderful" and "sensational." The effusive summary: "A car by crazies, for crazies. Goes like a sports car, drives like a sedan. It's the egg-laying wool-bearing whole milk sow of automobiles."

Along with its many fine qualities, the first Audi RS4 also ushered in new internal standards. Soon most RS models sported fat fenders and big rims. Its oval exhaust tips were bequeathed to its successors; only size and location varied. Along with its measure of visual individuality, the car defined the advancement of an RS compared to an S model. Although the Audi Avant RS2 and S6 plus before it had made forays into the sporty market segment, it was the RS4 that laid the foundation of the modern RS era.

Audi opened its order books in March 2000. Cars arrived at the dealerships two months later. Initially, quattro planned a production run of 3,000 examples. Ultimately, according to internal Audi documents, 6,046 cars were built. The last one left the factory on July 31, 2001.

THE AUDI RS4 ENGINE

For the RS4, Cosworth Technology built a new engine based on the S4 powerplant. Aside from the number of cylinders and displacement, the two had little in common. The Britons selected a different aluminum alloy for the cylinder heads, made using the so-called rollover casting method. This involved pumping molten aluminum into a zirconium sand mold, sealing the mold, then turning it 180 degrees, and finally warm hardening the resulting casting. This resulted in better microstructure, giving the component improved load-bearing ability. The intake runners retained their shape and the "tumble" principle of the S4 runners, in which the intake air swirled into the chambers through three intake valves. Cosworth optimized their flow and reduced the diameter of the exhaust runners. Improved coolant routing and new valve seats reduced thermal loads on the exhaust valves. During assembly, the hydraulic lifters were individually matched to their bores to compensate for manufacturing tolerances.

In order to improve the rigidity on the basic engine, as well as to reduce stresses in the component, the developers changed several design details of the engine block. The main bearing caps were reinforced, and ventilation passages between the cylinders were made smaller. The normal crankshaft of

Working together, Audi subsidiary Cosworth Engineering and quattro GmbH developed the powerful powerplant of the RS4 on the basis of the S4 engine.

the 2.8-liter normally-aspirated gasoline engine (S4) was replaced by a unique part with ten percent greater strength.

Reinforced pistons with appropriate valve pockets reduced the compression ratio from 9.3:1 (S4) to 9.0:1 (RS4). Piston wristpins and connecting rod bolts were enlarged compared to the regular production items. All parts were designed to withstand 7,200 rpm and peak cylinder pressure of 115 bar (1,670 psi).

New turbochargers with a larger compressor (51 instead of 46 mm) and turbine wheel (50 instead of 45 mm) raised boost pressure from 0.9 to 1.2 bar (13.0 to 17.4 psi). An intercooler with 16 percent greater area and an aluminum plenum were used, along with optimized exhaust mufflers. Compared to the S4, torque increased from 400 to 440 Newton-meters (295 to 325 ft-lbs) while power output climbed from 265 to 381 hp. To ensure that the driver

The RS4 brake system included dual-piston calipers and composite brake rotors, with aluminum rotor hat and cast iron friction ring.

would feel the increased performance in short sprints, quattro shortened the six-speed transmission's third and fourth gear ratios by seven percent each.

During the two-year production run of the RS4, an important drivetrain detail was changed. Beginning with the 45th calendar week of 2000, the car met the new Euro 3 exhaust emissions standard. To achieve this, the engine was given a second pair of lambda (oxygen) sensors behind the catalysts, and an expanded diagnostic capability. Henceforth the engine identifier was changed from ASJ to AZR. Mechanics and output remained unchanged.

AUDI RS4 SPORT

The fastest mid-range car significantly outshone the competition, but also had to meet Audi's own requirements. These included certain comfort characteristics, which resulted in compromises in the car's high-performance class. RS, after all, signifies *Rennsport* – racing sports. Customers who did not wish to sacrifice maximum hardness, did not have to. For them, quattro offered optional performance accessories beyond the standard RS features, with installation prior to delivery. Equipped with the complete package, the RS4 turned into the RS4 Sport.

The Audi RS4, lowered, with bucket seats, sport exhaust, suede-covered steering wheel and grippy Pirelli tires, was the sportiest of the sport version.

Conversion of the sport version to the even more sporty version posed new logistical challenges. With shorter springs, the RS4 was so low that it would not fit onto the loading ramps of normal car transporter trucks. Audi ordered special vehicles to transport the Sport. The payoff was an appreciable improvement of the RS4's road dynamics. Even while endurance testing was still underway, *sport auto* had its Imola Yellow RS4 converted. At the end of the long-term test, the magazine's editors argued about who would get to buy the Audi.

Along with a sport suspension lowered by an additional 15 mm, and a stiffer anti-roll bar at the rear, quattro offered a sport brake system with cross-drilled rotors and grippier, but noisier, brake pads, a catalyst-back sport exhaust system with a smaller center muffler and matte black exhaust tips, sport seats (Recaro Pole Position), sport steering wheel, and a shift knob with reversed leather ("rough side out"). The price list also offered floor mats with the RS4 logo and color edge binding. All told, these options added up to 6,730 Euros. In addition, Pirelli sport tires (P Zero Corsa, in the standard size) were available.

PAINT CHOICES (EXCERPT)

Solid colors: Imola Yellow, Brilliant Black
Pearl effect: Nogaro Blue, Misano Red, Goodwood Green, Avus Silver

STANDARD EQUIPMENT (EXCERPT)

Exterior:

- 18-inch aluminum wheels with 255/35 tires
- Xenon headlamps with cleaning system
- Flared fenders, door sills, roof edge spoiler
- Outside mirrors, roof rail, window frames and radiator surround in matte aluminum-look
- No decorative trim on doors

Wide fenders, special rocker panels and skirts, as well as deleted side trim, differentiated the RS4 body from that of the S4.

Xenon lamps, 18-inch rims, and aluminum outside mirror housings were standard equipment on the RS4.

Restrained sportiness, 1999: the standard production RS4 incorporated a high level of comfort. Spartan restrictions were added-cost options.

INTERIOR

- Leather or leather/cloth combination sport seats
- Piano black or carbon décor
- Sport steering wheel with leather or Alcantara cover
- Door handle, handbrake knob, shift gate ring and glovebox lock in matte black

FUNCTION

- Electrically adjustable and heatable seats
- Automatic climate control
- "Concert" radio with Bose sound system
- RS sport suspension (20 mm lower)
- RS brakes
- RS exhaust system

2005–

Audi RS 4 (B7)

odies three

The new RS 4 Avant took its time arriving. Audi and quattro GmbH presented the RS 4 sedan before unveiling the wagon.

After a strong serve, Audi's fast mid-range models took a breather. When the A4 model line (the B5 platform) and with it the first RS4 reached the end of production in 2001, quattro GmbH concentrated on the RS 6 project. The operation still did not have sufficient capacity to develop two cars simultaneously. Before a new RS 4 design could be handed over to Neckarsulm for final assembly, production of the A4 platform known internally as the B6 had already begun and ended.

Audi called the successor A4 the B7. Strictly speaking, this was not a new car, but rather a comprehensive product revision (in other words: a facelift). At the time, RS models did not appear until the second half of a model cycle. The impression that quattro GmbH was skipping an entire A4 generation is erroneous. The fault lay solely with Audi's model politics.

There were lengthy discussions on how the new RS 4 would be powered. Theoretically, a new V6 turbo based on the recently introduced engine family could be used. The 3.2-liter gasoline engine would, however, have to undergo extensive modifications to withstand the desired power level. The webs between its cylinders were too narrow for a 400-horsepower turbo. Adapting the block would significantly reduce displacement. The V6 was not an option.

Instead, quattro GmbH built RS 4 prototypes using two different engines. One was powered by the predecessor's six-cylinder turbo, the other with a new, high-revving, normally-aspirated V8. In this way, the decision makers compared the driving feel of both concepts. The emotional characteristics of the big engine even convinced dyed-in-the-wool turbo advocates, including development chief Stephan Reil. With that engine choice, the RS 4 was in line with some of the non-turbocharged, freely aspirating competition.

SEDAN, AVANT AND, FOR THE FIRST TIME, CABRIOLET

For the first time in the history of the RS series, the Avant did not play the leading role. In the summer of 2005, Audi and quattro GmbH presented the RS 4 sedan – the first officially distributed RS notchback in the mid-range. The wagon did not follow until a year later. At the same time, another body variant entered the market – the A4 Cabriolet was also offered as an RS model. Audi's first all-wheel drive convertible was an appropriate basis for the RS conversion. Together, the three variants were intended to appeal to a

Audi contested the 2007 DTM (German Touring Car Championship) with ten drivers, male and female. Before the season opener, nine of them posed with the new Audi RS 4.

The open RS 4 was fitted with sport seats as standard equipment, with bucket seats a no-cost option, the Cabriolet being the exception. On the Avant and sedan, it was the other way around.

broader, international public. With a view to the U.S. market, Audi presented the RS 4 at the 2006 Detroit Auto Show. The Sedan and Cabriolet went on sale in the North American market.

Audi built the tin-roofed A4 derivatives in Ingolstadt. They were given their wider side panels on the assembly line, along with aluminum front fenders and engine hoods. As on the predecessor, the wider tires of the sports models were not compatible with the plant's assembly lines. Some steps in the production process were too complex to be integrated in the normal assembly process. For this reason, the sedan and Avant versions of the RS 4 left the line unfinished and traveled by truck to final assembly in Neckarsulm. There, quattro GmbH added all composite body parts, as well as wheels and tires, and assembled the engines.

The A4 Cabriolet was built at a different location. Audi had it assembled in partnership with Karmann in Osnabrück. The differences between the open-top car and the classic variants precluded assembly of the Cabriolet on the same production line. Setting up a separate assembly line in Ingolstadt would have been prohibitively expensive. Audi instead chose to outsource the soft-topped niche model.

Karmann's cabriolet experts at the company's plant in Rheine were more flexible than Audi in Ingolstadt. The open RS 4 was assembled in its entirety at this location, and not partially finished in Neckarsulm. Karmann built the A4 and RS 4 Cabriolets on the same line, and delivered completed cars to their customer, Audi. This was a preview of what was to come, because in the long term, Audi would also complete the RS models on the regular production line.

THE FIRST AUDI RS WITH CERAMIC BRAKES AND ASYMMETRICAL ALL-WHEEL DRIVE

The second RS 4 generation was intended to have more sporting character than its predecessor. To this end, Audi carried out fundamental changes to the all-wheel drive system. Previously, a Torsen center differential had evenly split torque to both axles. In the new car, the manufacturer utilized a new, third-generation Torsen design, the Type C. Its construction, a planetary transmission with sun and ring gears, provided a 40/60 front to rear torque split. At Audi, the greater torque was sent to the rear wheels for improved driving dynamics.

Overall, the B7 iteration of the RS 4 brought with it an expanded performance package, greater than had previously been within the scope of quattro GmbH. For an additional 5,950 Euros, ceramic brakes could be fitted to the front axle. Cross-drilled carbon fiber reinforced composite brake rotors were better able to deal with heat than conventional steel discs. They resisted brake fade, which in practice is primarily encountered on the race track. The sporty Dynamic Ride Control (DRC) suspension, introduced a few years earlier in the RS 6 C5 and only optionally available on that model, was part of the RS 4's standard equipment. The body was lowered by 3 cm (1.2 in.) compared to the A4.

The new and modern RS 4 engine of the B7 generation started at the push of a button.

In addition, quattro GmbH installed a "sport mode." At the push of a button, the engine control unit switched to a more direct throttle pedal characteristic. This made the engine response feel more spontaneous. At the same time, flaps in the final exhaust mufflers opened for a more intense sound. The (standard) RS bucket seats fit the driver more snugly, and provided additional support in aggressive cornering. Electronic safety

Major sporting aspirations have become obvious – the RS 4 wore wide fenders, oval exhaust tips and various RS logos.

systems incorporated in sport mode permitted such maneuvers.

On its first drive, German car magazine *auto motor und sport* found that with its neutral power distribution, the RS 4 almost moved like a rear-drive car. Later, the magazine explained that without being provoked by load changes, the sportster departed from its neutral behavior only with reluctance. Audi paid close attention to weight, and put the body, suspension, seats and wheels on a diet. This did not make it a lightweight car, but a more agile one.

In a comparison of the different model lines, drive moderator Chris Harris described the B7 generation as "the definitive RS 4" because it did not feel like the usual Audi. Steering, suspension, and brakes would make it the most powerful competitor to its own successor.

INTERNET MARKETING VIA MICROSITE

To express the fascination of the RS 4 to customers, Audi provided its dealers with various tools. These included classic displays for their showrooms, posters, brochures, photographs and fan items. Via direct mail, prospective customers received illustrative materials showing the RS 4 on the Circuit de Barcelona-Catalunya race track, poetically underscoring its qualities. Potential buyers might be invited to a VIP event.

Audi was also thinking about "new media." The manufacturer dedicated a special web site to the RS 4. It strictly covered the sporty A4 derivative, emphasized its advantages, provided technical specifications, images, and 360° interior and exterior views. A brief video introduced each chapter. Today, such marketing is regarded as normal, a part of our lives, but the YouTube platform went live only two weeks before the RS 4 microsite was activated.

The RS 4 B7 was the first RS model to distribute most of its power to the rear wheels.

THE RS 4 ENGINE: DIRECT-INJECTION V8

Audi retired the old five-valve engines and developed an all-new powertrain generation: direct-injected gasoline engines in V configuration, modular and scalable from six to ten cylinders. For the new RS 4, Audi and quattro GmbH chose an eight-cylinder. In contrast to the V6 of its predecessor, the engine was not supercharged. Its power came from free, natural induction and high rpm. This represented a fundamental change of concept for the model line.

The first appearance of the new engine was in an SUV. The 4.2-liter aluminum V8 debuted in the Audi Q7, where it developed 350 hp and 440 Newton-meters (325 ft-lbs) of torque. For the RS 4, Audi applied a closely related but independent, more powerful and more exciting variant. In the sport engine, maximum engine speed rose to 8,250 rpm.

In contrast to previous practice, Audi designed a two-part engine block. The lower part, the "bedplate," reinforced the engine like a ladder frame. Cast iron main bearing caps reduced crankshaft bearing clearance at high temperatures.

The high-revving version was given special treatment in many details. Before honing the cylinder walls, the entire block was torqued to eliminate distortion in service. Heavy metal counterweights in two crankshaft cheeks counteracted high-speed vibrations in the RS 4 engine. In addition, Audi used stronger connecting rods, forged pistons, modified crankcase ventilation and different timing chains.

The RS 4 combination instrument, seen here in the U.S. version, was clearly organized, generously scaled and without extraneous frills.

Optimized passages, lighter intake valves, modifications to the injector nozzles, camshafts, roller rocker arms, cooling system and camshaft phasing prepared the cylinder head for the anticipated high loads. Increased engine speed and output also meant increased weight. The RS 4 engine weighed 212 kg (467 lbs), 14 kg (31 lbs) more than the SUV version.

A special intake manifold, with large runner cross sections, as well as an exhaust header system with individual exhaust runners and controlled flaps in the final exhaust mufflers completed the engine. Its design shifted the torque curve toward higher rpms. The payoff: power output rose to a little over 100 hp per liter (1.63 hp per cubic inch).

Great praise for the paradigm shift in the engine bay came from *auto motor und sport*. The magazine compared the high-revving V8 with BMW's inline six and Ferrari V12 engines. In a time of high gasoline prices and torquey diesel engines, the Audi motor represented pure "powerplant luxury."

Of course, this came at a price. Owners complained of a loss in power after years of service. Specialist firms identified oil deposits in the intake tract as a basic problem of the V8 – a problem shared with most direct-injection gasoline engines. Usually, a thorough cleaning restored the original power output, but was not a permanent solution.

PAINT CHOICES (EXCERPT)

Solid colors: Imola Yellow
Metallic: Light Silver
Pearl effect: Misano Red, Sprint Blue, Avus Silver, Mugello Blue, Daytona Gray, Cambridge Green, Phantom Black

STANDARD EQUIPMENT (EXCERPT)

Exterior:

- 18-inch aluminum wheels with 255/40 tires
- Xenon plus headlamps with daytime running lights
- Flared fenders, door sills, rear or roof edge spoiler
- Outside mirrors and roof rail in matte aluminum-look
- No decorative trim on doors

For the first time, Audi installed all-wheel drive in Cabriolets of the B6 and B7 A4 generations. There was no reason not to offer the same in the open RS models.

The RS 4 bodies again wore aluminum trim as a sporty contrast.

Snug bucket seats gave the RS 4 B7 a high level of sportiness. All around: A4 ambiance and several stylish details.

INTERIOR

- Sport bucket seats with pneumatic side bolsters; no-cost option: electrically adjustable sport seats
- Carbon fiber decorative inlays
- RS sport steering wheel, flattened bottom, with aluminum-look inserts and perforated leather

FUNCTION

- Comfort automatic climate control
- Front and rear acoustic parking warning system
- "Concert" radio with Bose sound system
- DRC sport suspension (30 mm lower)
- RS brakes
- RS exhaust system with flap control

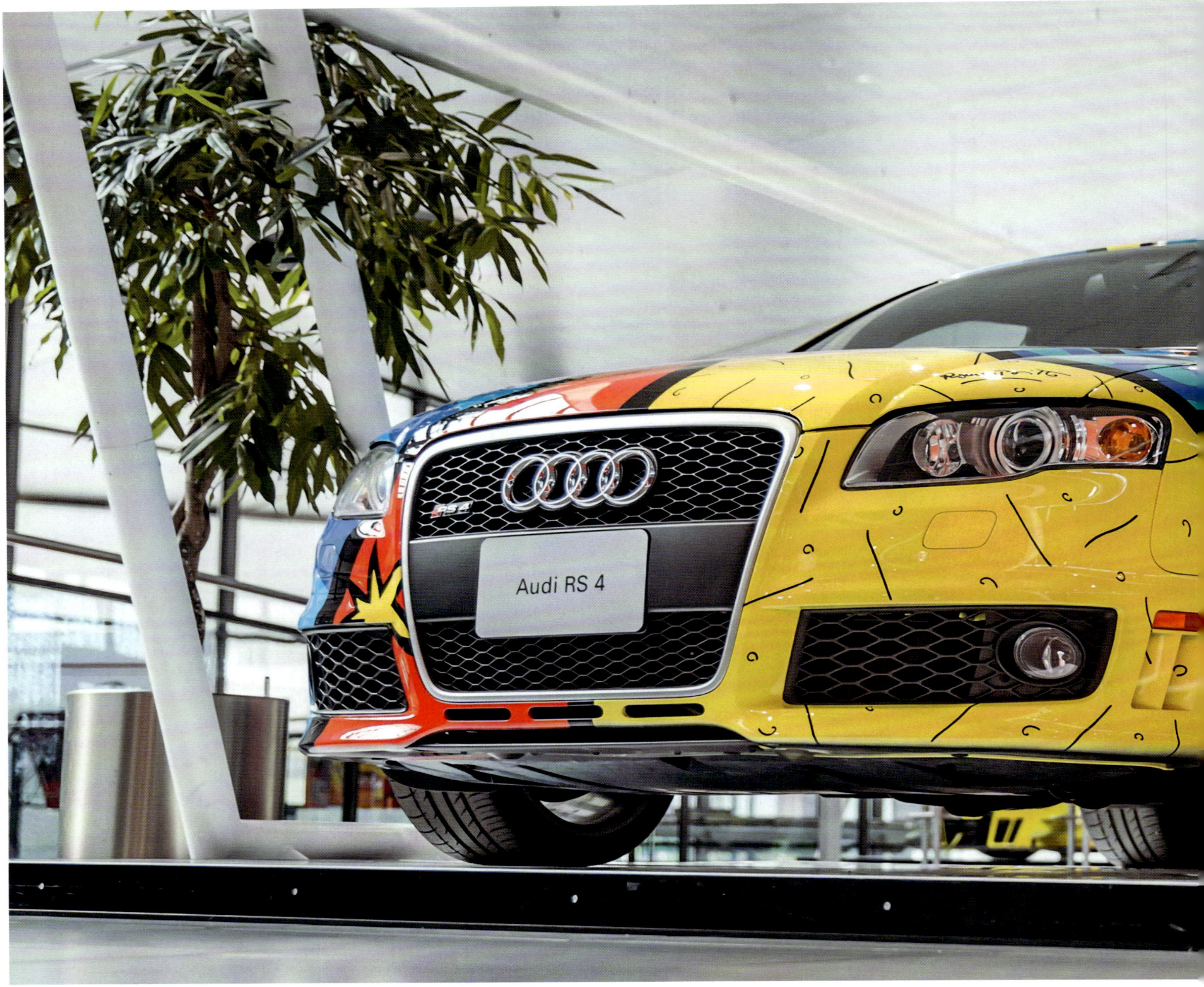

RS4

Audi felt that the beautiful RS 5 coupe deserved a place in motorsports, so it converted it into a pace car.

In March 2010, Audi celebrated a special anniversary: the Audi quattro turned thirty. The quattro ushered in everything that is still important to Audi today – from all-wheel drive to motorsports. On the anniversary day, the manufacturer gave itself the best gift of all. At the Geneva Motor Show – scene of the original quattro premiere in 1980 – Audi presented the RS 5. The attractive coupe paid obvious homage to its progenitor, with wide fenders, full-time all-wheel drive, and an immensely powerful engine.

The RS 5, however, was not based on Walter Röhrl's legendary works rally car, but rather on a much more recent platform. The Audi A5 had joined the A4 in the product lineup in 2007. It would be the basis of the more exciting body variations in Audi's middle-class range. Two of these variations were all new to the program. Audi offered the A5 as a Coupe, Cabriolet and Sportback. The German Design Council, a nonprofit foundation, awarded the 2010 German Design Award in the "Product Design Gold" category. Audi chief designer Walter de Silva called the car the most beautiful he had ever created.

The A5 was not only beautiful, but also a technology showcase. Internally at Audi, it was called the "snowplow for the MLB" (Modularer Längsbaukasten, the Modular Longitudinal Platform), meaning, it was the marque's first car to be based on the new company-wide modular platform for longitudinal engines and front- or all-wheel drive. In this capacity, it paved the way for additional models with identical architecture.

BETTER WEIGHT DISTRIBUTION

The new platform provided a wealth of new technology not previously available, or that could only be realized with great effort. These included rather mundane features such as an electric parking brake or shift reminder, safety-relevant details such as multi-stage airbags, and comfort features such as driving profile selection. In addition, its new suspension design (five-link at the front, trapezoidal link at the rear, largely made of aluminum), provided better rolling and ride comfort. Most important, however, the materials used to build the chassis were changed.

To optimize body weight and stiffness, Audi applied various materials. The body of the A5 consisted of conventional deep-drawn steel (doors, hoods), high-strength steel (A- and C-pillars), higher-strength steel (roof, floorpan), ultra-high-strength steel (door sills) and hot-formed steel (longitudinal members, B-pillars), in appropriate thicknesses. Audi formed the front fenders out of aluminum.

An especially important innovation was the platform's available transmissions. In these, Audi switched the position of torque converter and drive flange. Previously, the classic configuration had forced engineers to locate the drive far in the front of the car. This was detrimental to weight distribution. With the new layout, engine and transmission were moved back by 15.2 cm (6 in.). This changed everything: the engine

The RS 5 was the first RS Audi to be based on the Modular Longitudinal Platform. This architecture improved overall balance and weight.

With less weight on the front axle, the RS 5 was especially agile in tight turns.

no longer hung far in front of the axle, but rather mostly directly above. This yielded an enormous improvement in the car's balance.

RS 5 AND A5 ON A SINGLE ASSEMBLY LINE

In developing the top-of-the-line RS 5, quattro GmbH adopted everything that made the A5 better than previous Audi models. The car was based on a light, rigid chassis, supported by newly designed suspension, and distributed its weight more evenly than any previous RS model. For the engineers in Neckarsulm, the production car provided a base with plenty of freedom for sports-oriented optimization – technically, as well as visually.

Big wheels were already fitted to the normal production A5. For the RS 5, though, quattro GmbH wanted more autonomy, and widened the bodywork. New fenders ensured that the outside door handles no longer represented the widest points of the car; quattro GmbH widened the car by 3 mm (1/8-inch) beyond the door handles on each side. With their elegant form, the new fenders provided space for 265- and 275-series tires, wheels with less offset, and larger hubs at the rear.

Audi had the new body parts pressed in Győr. The Hungarian plant produced the front fenders, rear side panels, as well as a specific rear hatch with an electrically deployed spoiler. The coupe took its roof, engine hood and doors from the regular production model. In Ingolstadt, Audi assembled the RS 5 on the same production line as the A5. The RS 5 left the Audi assembly line in completed form; unlike many sport models before it, the A5 did not have to be shipped to Neckarsulm for completion. This saved resources.

ALL NEW, FROM ALL-WHEEL DRIVE TO THE CYLINDERS

For the drivetrain, quattro GmbH again went for high engine speeds. As expected of an emotional normally-aspirated engine, the V8 delivered its maximum power at the upper end of its rev range. All of 450 horsepower were available, at an impressive 8,250 rpm. The concept came from the now discontinued RS 4 (B7), but the mechanicals were all new. Extensive changes to the intake manifold, valvetrain and crankshaft increased power output by 30 hp over its predecessor. But the car would only become more dynamic as a result of additional measures.

Instead of a manual transmission, Audi bolted a seven-speed dual-clutch automatic to the eight-cylinder engine. The automatic went through the gears more quickly than even expert hands could work a manual-shift lever. Audi specified the car's 0-100 km/h (62 mph) time at 4.6 seconds. In tests by the German magazine *sport auto*, the RS undercut the factory's own claim by 0.2 seconds. *Auto Zeitung* even measured a time of 4.3 seconds.

The large "Singleframe" radiator grille was part of Audi's design language, the honeycomb was characteristic of the RS models.

Optional brakes for higher loads. At extra cost, Audi installed ceramic brake discs on the RS 5.

Also contributing to these values was the all-wheel drive system, an inseparable feature of Audi's RS models since 1994. In the RS 5, however, Audi changed the engineering concept. Instead of the proven Torsen principle, the drivetrain now used a crown gear center differential. The self-locking, maintenance-free component sent up to 70 percent of the engine torque to the front axle, or 85 percent to the rear. Its greatest benefit was that it weighed only 4.8 kg (10.6 lbs), 2.1 kg (4.6 lbs) less than its predecessor. Audi augmented the mechanical torque distribution with a dynamic, controllable component. The brake system of the RS 5 was capable of targeted braking of individual wheels, diverting torque to other wheels. This so-called wheel-selective torque control assisted turn-in into corners by sending more power to the outside wheels.

Optionally, a sport differential at the rear axle further assisted in cornering. It sought the same goal: depending on the driving situation, it forced the outside rear wheel to turn at higher speed. In this way, the RS 5 would lay into any corner in a more agile manner. The control software took into account steering wheel and yaw angle, speed, and lateral acceleration.

The more dynamically a car moves, the more authoritative its brakes need to be. In the RS 5, Audi installed eight-piston aluminum calipers and two-piece brake rotors at the front, measuring 365 mm in diameter. As on many RS models, the rotors consisted of an aluminum hat and steel friction ring. Optionally, Audi also offered ceramic brakes for the RS 5. In testing by *sport auto*, these decelerated the RS 5 from 200 km/h (124 mph) to a full stop in 5.3 seconds.

THE RS 5 CABRIOLET APPEARS FOR THE FACELIFT

When the A5 was given a modest facelift in July 2011, the RS 5 also changed. Audi modified the radiator grille and headlamps, redrew the creases in the engine hood, and swapped the round brake discs for "wave design" components for better heat transfer and lower weight. After some delay, a second body variant was introduced: the RS 5 Cabriolet debuted in 2012. The open version employed the same drivetrain technology as the coupe.

On any convertible, the manufacturer must solve a fundamental problem. A roofless body, with only half a B-pillar, lacks stiffness. To counteract this, Audi installed a transverse reinforcement under the rear seat, and reinforced the A-pillars, door sills and other floorpan parts. At the front and rear, diagonal braces supported both axles against the floorpan. Győr again delivered special RS parts, and the Audi plant in Neckarsulm built "civilian" and sporty Cabriolets on the same assembly line. The reinforcements, however, exacted a toll on vehicle weight; with its comprehensive stiffening, the RS 5 Cabriolet weighed about 200 kg (440 lbs) more than the coupe.

The effort paid off, however. *Auto Zeitung* confirmed that there were no creaks or rattles in the open RS 5. The added weight did exact a toll on top speed. With its soft top, the car could sprint to 100 km/h (62 mph) in "just" 4.9 seconds, but still topped out at 250 km/h (155 mph) in standard trim or 280 km/h (174 mph) in optional form. For the Cabriolet, Audi offered the same options that made the coupe faster: sport differential, adjustable DRC (Dynamic Ride Control) suspension, and ceramic brakes were in the options lists for both models. An inherent feature was only available on the Cabriolet: with the top down, the engine sound was even more impressive inside the car.

The RS Cabriolet first appeared in 2012. At that time, the coupe had been on the market for two years.

With its open top, the Cabriolet offered the better sound experience. The enclosed variant, however, still provided a more performance-oriented drive.

The RS 5 remained the more sporty choice, thanks to lower weight, and was ultimately safer. The German enthusiast magazine *sport auto*, as part of its "supertest," lapped the Nürburgring north circuit in 7:59, and the short course at Hockenheim in 1:14.3. Their conclusion: "Engine and transmission, in their entertaining cooperation, are a force to be reckoned with. The sophisticated all-wheel drive is, in every regard, an insurance policy. And Audi's annoying braking problems are, at least in this case with the ceramic brakes, no longer an issue." The fact that Audi only provided the full potential of the coupe in exchange for a considerable optional upgrade did harvest criticism. On the RS 5, the vehicle dynamics-related extras added up to another 15,000 Euros.

THE ENGINE OF THE AUDI RS 5

The new high-revving V8 of the Audi RS 5 shared many details with the engine of the RS 4 B7. It retained the bedplate design, with a two-piece cylinder block, made of an aluminum-silicon alloy, displacing 4,163 cc (254 cu in.) with an undersquare layout, with longer stroke than bore dimension – 84.5 mm bore, 92.8 mm stroke. The most important change to the block was that quattro GmbH reduced friction between pistons and cylinder walls, and in the chain drive to the camshafts.

New aluminum pistons reduced compression ratio from 12.5 to 11:1. Use of lighter materials and weight reduction in the valvetrain enabled higher engine speeds. Instead of revving to 8,250 rpm, the RS 5 engine could turn to 8,500. A newly-designed, dual induction system of composite material, with two (instead of one) throttles, provided the engine with even more combustion air. Tumble flaps in the intake manifold, managed by the engine control module, improved engine efficiency in the part-load regime. In addition, Audi optimized exhaust flow in the stainless steel headers.

The payoff was that between 4,000 and 6,000 rpm, the new engine delivered 430 Nm (317 ft-lbs) of torque. Its power output rose by 30 hp, to 450 hp. For Audi, in view of ever-tightening CO_2 emissions requirements, its improved fuel economy was just as important; consumption in the standard test cycle dropped by about 20 percent, to 10.7 liters per 100 km (22.0 miles per U.S. gallon). The powerplant was able to achieve this in part by means of a demand-controlled oil pump and intelligent generator strategy ("recuperation"). The engines were built in the same plant that provided all of the RS 5 – specific sheetmetal; specially-trained workers at the Győr plant hand-assembled the latest evolutionary stage of Audi's 4.2-liter eight-cylinder. The finished powerplant weighed 216 kg (476 lbs) – four kg (8.8 lbs) more than its predecessor.

The new 4.2-liter V8 was based on the engine of the RS 4 B7, but major parts had been redesigned.

PAINT CHOICES (EXCERPT)

Solid colors: Ibis White, Nardo Gray
Metallic: Suzuka Gray, Monza Silver, Glacier White, Mythos Black
Pearl effect: Misano Red, Sepang Blue, Daytona Gray, Phantom Black
Crystal effect: Prism Silver, Panther Black
Top colors (Cabriolet): Black, red, gray, brown

STANDARD EQUIPMENT (EXCERPT)

Exterior:

- 19-inch aluminum wheels with 265/35 tires
- Xenon plus headlamps, LED taillamps
- Rear spoiler, rocker panel skirts, RS-specific front and rear valance
- Matte aluminum -look outside mirror housings, trim strips and radiator grille surround

The power-operated top of the RS 5 Cabriolet could be opened in less than 15 seconds.

In converting the A5 to the RS 5, the bodywork was widened by 3 mm (1/8-inch) per side. The reason was that on the standard model, the door handles were the widest part of the car.

Bucket seats were on the option list for the RS 5. Slotted door openers and carbon clips are part of the standard equipment.

INTERIOR

- Front sport seats with black Alcantara/leather combination, electrically adjustable and heatable
- Three-spoke multifunction sport steering wheel with shift paddles
- Carbon fiber décor inserts
- Slotted interior door latches

FUNCTION

- Automatic climate control
- "Concert" audio system
- 18-inch steel brake system (as of facelift, Cabriolet: wave design)
- Parking assistant
- Sport suspension

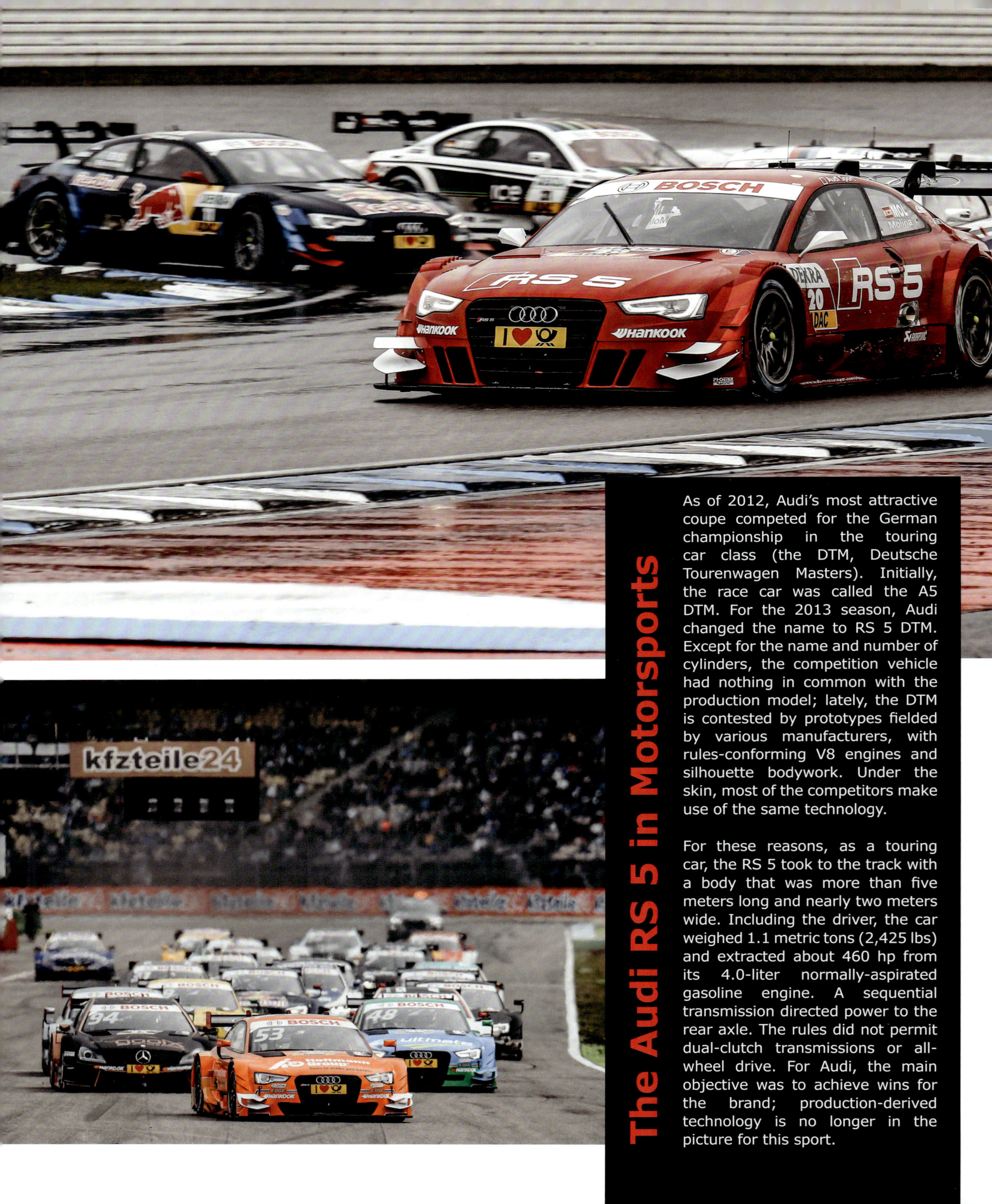

The Audi RS 5 in Motorsports

As of 2012, Audi's most attractive coupe competed for the German championship in the touring car class (the DTM, Deutsche Tourenwagen Masters). Initially, the race car was called the A5 DTM. For the 2013 season, Audi changed the name to RS 5 DTM. Except for the name and number of cylinders, the competition vehicle had nothing in common with the production model; lately, the DTM is contested by prototypes fielded by various manufacturers, with rules-conforming V8 engines and silhouette bodywork. Under the skin, most of the competitors make use of the same technology.

For these reasons, as a touring car, the RS 5 took to the track with a body that was more than five meters long and nearly two meters wide. Including the driver, the car weighed 1.1 metric tons (2,425 lbs) and extracted about 460 hp from its 4.0-liter normally-aspirated gasoline engine. A sequential transmission directed power to the rear axle. The rules did not permit dual-clutch transmissions or all-wheel drive. For Audi, the main objective was to achieve wins for the brand; production-derived technology is no longer in the picture for this sport.

For the 25th anniversary of the TDI engine, Audi examined whether RS and diesel could go together. Two concept cars were created, one of them focused on the race track.

The Diesel Experiment

Audi RS 5 TDI concept and RS 5 TDI competition concept

Diesel and motorsports go together like pizza and pineapple; it works, but may not be to everyone's liking. At the classic Le Mans endurance race, Audi captured eight titles with TDI engines, and was even thinking openly about an R8 diesel. So it was only logical to try combining TDI and RS. On the 25th birthday of the TDI engine, an unusual test was initiated, with a diesel engine in an Audi RS 5. At that time, its character could not have been farther removed from the original. The RS 5 hood usually covered a normally-aspirated engine that loved high revs. For the diesel experiment, Audi swapped the gasoline V8 for a triple-supercharged, six-cylinder, compression ignition powerplant, which, on principle, should only offer a narrower rev band.

Instead, it offered gobs of torque: 750 Newton-meters (553 ft-lbs), and 385 hp. By RS standards, this power level was not noteworthy, but for a diesel with three liters of displacement, it was fantastic. In production, the output was dialed back to 326 hp.

THREE SUPERCHARGERS IN THE RS 5 TDI CONCEPT

The secret of the sport diesel: the engine was fitted with an electrically-driven compressor. In the blink of an eye, this could accelerate to 72,000 rpm, shoveling ambient air into the intake tract – precisely when the two mechanical turbochargers were still trying to climb out of the rpm cellar. These, on the other hand, did not have to react especially quickly, so they could be sized larger and therefore provide top power output. The system generated 2.4 bar (35 psi) of boost pressure.

The result convinced the motoring press. After a test on the Hockenheim race track, *auto motor und sport* titled its report, "The first really sporty diesel." The V6 pulled strongly, without interruption, to 5,500 rpm. On the track, it lapped just under a second slower than a production Audi RS 5 – although this was much more powerful and weight a good 80 kg (176 lbs) less. The RS 5 TDI also provided a sound experience: actuators set the intake tracts into resonance, and simulated the auditory effect of an engine of the original's caliber under the hood. In view of the car's driving performance, an RS diesel was indeed a valid topic within quattro GmbH.

RS 5 TDI COMPETITION CONCEPT: A SECOND ATTEMPT, WITH 435 HP

The diesel experiments did not end with just one study. Audi built a second variant, as further proof that motorsport is not dependent on the type of fuel being used. In the RS 5 TDI competition concept, a V6 diesel generated 435 hp and 800 Nm (590 ft-lbs). This nearly matched the performance level of the gasoline engine.

With a Spartan interior and lightweight body components, the car weighed just 1,619 kg (3,569 lbs). During a record attempt, the RS 5 TDI competition concept lapped the Sachsenring track in 1:35.35 minutes – a record in the diesel category. This put the one-off study on a par with the Porsche Cayman 718 GTS in its four-cylinder form – an impressive display of muscle, but without any lasting effect on the RS series.

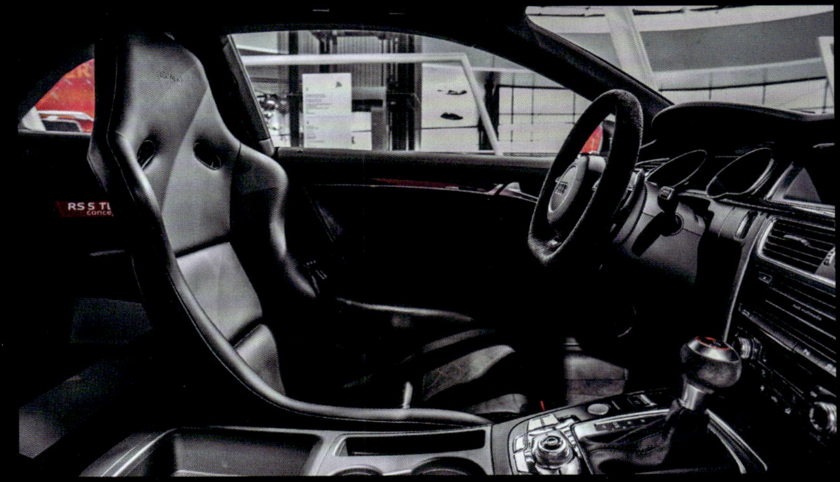

For better power-to-weight ratio Audi deleted the rear seats in the RS 5 TDI competition concept, which made for a spartan interior.

Audi RS 4 Avant (B8)

The practical mid-range models

2012–

The RS 4 returned to its classic body shape. In the B8 generation, Audi built it only as an Avant – a wagon.

The introduction of the RS 5 allowed Audi to reduce the proliferation of models in the established RS 4 line. The new strategy, with two power models in the mid-range, had its own advantages: this returned the oldest RS model line back to its roots. The new RS 4 got more room at the back, more power at the front – a "high-performance Avant." What the marketing people decided, with their farsightedness and red pencils, was sold by Audi as a recollection of "the good old days" – according to Audi, the new RS 4 was a "modern classic," aligned with the brand's history. And so it was. In homage to the RS2, Audi later even issued a special edition, in traditional colors.

In all, Audi's fast mid-range models continued to offer three variants, only they were spread across two model lines. This was made possible by a new modular platform concept. Synergies and components shared between the various models lowered development and production costs. This increased the variety of models offered. Audi introduced the concept in the spring of 2007, in the A5. When the Audi A4 arrived on the scene in the fall of that same year, it also took on all the new features of the coupe. Technically, both models were closely related: anything that made the A5 efficient, rigid and light, also benefited the A4.

There was, however, one important difference. For the A4 Avant, Audi did not copy the coupe chassis, but rather built a new one for the wagon. The architecture allowed each model to have its own, individual material mix. Audi assembled the A4 using high, higher, and highest-strength and hot-formed steels, as well as aluminum, but applied the materials differently. So the roof and fenders of the A4 were made of conventional steel, while many floorpan components were of high-strength steel. Audi used aluminum for the front crossmember.

Audi took its time with the top-of-the-line RS 4; first, the RS 5 would have to acclimate itself to the market. For two years, the RS 5 served alone in its segment. In June 2012, it was finally joined by the hot wagon with its broad shoulders, standard all-wheel drive, and 450 hp out of 4.2 liters of displacement.

CARGO SPACE AND ENGINE DISPLACEMENT

In converting the staid family wagon into the RS 4, quattro GmbH laid it on more thickly than on the coupe. The base body was narrower, which allowed more room for outward expansion. Wider fender flares added a total of two and a half centimeters (one inch) to its width. Again, the Győr plant stamped the fenders, side panels, and rear doors to RS-specification, and delivered these to Ingolstadt. There, the A4 and RS 4 alternated production on a single assembly line.

Audi's platform and model strategies meant that the RS 4 would be the engineering twin of the RS 5. Again, quattro GmbH installed the high-revving normally-aspirated V8, coupled to the same dual-clutch transmission, with power distributed power to both axles through the same crown gear center differential. The same brake system slowed it down. Drivetrain-relevant differences could only be found in the track, wheelbase, and weight.

Still, the RS 4 could do something that its coupe siblings could not. It was the only variant that combined the qualities of large engine displacement and ample cargo capacity. Product manager Rolf

The RS 4 Avant scored points for its large cargo capacity, which was almost as important as engine displacement.

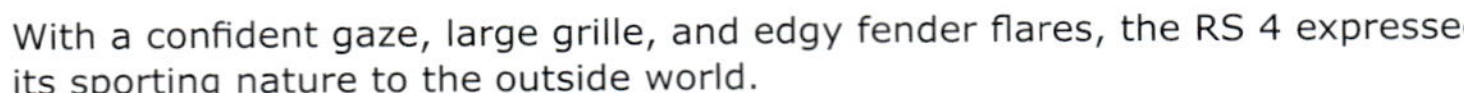
With a confident gaze, large grille, and edgy fender flares, the RS 4 expressed its sporting nature to the outside world.

All-wheel drive is part of the RS tradition. The RS 4 adopted the crown gear center differential technology of the related RS 5.

Michl called his RS 4 an "everyday sports car." What he meant was that the car could blast along on a race track – after hauling the entire family and its gear there. He was well-aware that most customers valued the latter quality far more than the former. Yet the combination made the RS 4 something special. It gave a little bit of freedom back to otherwise staid, upright family men.

DIFFERENT DRIVING MODES, DIFFERENT DRIVING NEEDS

The new RS 4 continued the traditional qualities of its predecessors, but also introduced new features. Naturally, it was faster than the old models – a key point in the catalog of development targets. It exceeded their performance (barely) in the sprint, and, optionally, achieved a stop speed of 280 km/h (174 mph). Above all, however, in the B8 model line, Audi realized a wider spread between comfort and sport. Various driving modes matched the tuning to the actual driving situation.

Audi called this variability "drive select." Henceforth, the driver could choose three modes – "Comfort," "Auto," and "Dynamic" – from the infotainment menu. These activated pre-programmed maps for steering (optional), throttle response, transmission characteristics, exhaust flap control, sport differential behavior (optional), and shock absorber damping (optional). In the "individual" mode (only available with a navigation system) the various characteristics could be freely combined. For example, an RS 4 driver might select "sport sound" combined with a comfortable suspension setting.

With these available choices, the RS 4 expanded its spectrum and did an even better job of bridging the chasm between family transporter and sports car. It could move with sporty tautness, or swallow uneven roads, wind out through the gears of shift early. By this means, Audi expanded the car's target audience. Still, at its introduction, this modern technology harvested considerable criticism. *Drive* moderator Chris Harris faulted the growing complexity of the car; its predecessor still functioned without such wide-ranging adjustments and settings. Purists struggled to accept the adaptive possibilities. Only later did selectable driving modes become widely accepted in the broader market.

GREAT ENGINE, MEDIOCRE STEERING

In general, the testers concentrated less on the new possibilities and more on the old school. *Auto Zeitung* praised the engine: "The manner in which the highly complex, turbo-less V8 responds to throttle, sprints up to 8,000 rpm without hesitation, all while belting out its loud song, is something that has almost been forgotten in these times of politically correct, downsized turbos – this is automotive theater on a grand scale." In many segments, the marketplace was showing a trend toward smaller, turbocharged engines, but most of the top mid-range models held fast to the old concept.

Trade magazine *auto motor und sport* emphasized the benefits of improved weight distribution: "Fear of understeer is left at the gate as the RS 4 grabs the line through a turn with a neutral attitude and holds it without sliding, until it rushes out of the corner neutral or even with a bit of emphasis on the rear, depending on throttle." As in the RS 5, inside the RS 4 transmission, the clutch pack and drive flange traded places. The front axle moved a few centimeters forward, thereby redistributing decisive kilograms. In the opinion of the road testers, only the adaptive steering did not satisfy the car's sporting aspirations. *auto motor und sport* described it as "rubbery and artificial," and that it "did not connect the pilot as directly with the front axle as one might wish." *Auto Zeitung* added, "In addition, the continuous adaptation of steering forces and steering wheel

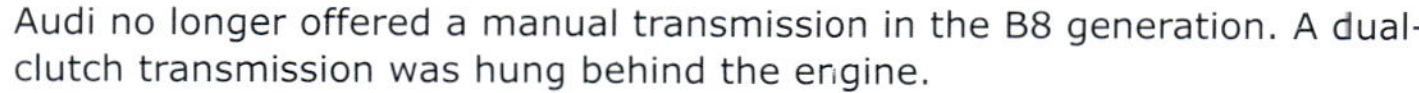
Audi no longer offered a manual transmission in the B8 generation. A dual-clutch transmission was hung behind the engine.

To underscore its motorsports connection, Audi presented the RS 4 on the Red Bull Ring in Austria.

angle does more to irritate than to help. The steering unit works best if the linear sport steering mode is selected in the vehicle menu." The 1,000 Euro added cost for the "dynamic steering" option would be better applied toward the ceramic brakes (6,000 Euros).

Especially when fitted with the optional brake package, the RS 4 returned stellar test results. In *auto motor und sport* testing, the RS 4 braked from 100 km/h (62 mph) to a full stop in just over 35 meters (114 feet) regardless of condition – hot or cold brakes, empty or fully laden car. In the sprint to 100 km/h, the car exactly matched the factory claim (4.7 seconds). Moreover, it negotiated the slalom test at 140.9 km/h (87.6 mph) nearly as quickly as a Porsche 911 Carrera S. Overall, the wagon packed quite a lot of sport in its luggage.

On the other hand, the RS 4 could not quite avoid the usual compromises associated with a sports car, not even with trendy digital driving profiles. Nor was it intended to. But in all modes, its suspension was decidedly taut, and its brakes squealed during stops. Audi would address these criticisms in the succeeding model.

THE SPECIAL EDITION: AUDI RS 4 NOGARO SELECTION

At their first contact with the RS 4, Audi sought to communicate to the automotive press the appropriate awareness of its corporate tradition. For the press event at the Red Bull Ring in Spielberg, Austria, Audi brought out the car's predecessors. Parked alongside the race track were three generations of RS 4 and an RS2. Two years later, that early progenitor, with its Porsche DNA, served as inspiration for a special edition. For the 20th anniversary of the RS2 premiere, Audi laid on a special edition, the RS 4 "Nogaro selection." Nogaro referred to its blue paintwork. On the RS2, this had served as a communication color, at the time still called RS Blue. It was not until 1996 and the premiere of the S6 plus that Audi changed the designation to Nogaro Blue. This name commemorated two wins by Audi driver Frank Biela in touring car races on the track at Nogaro, France.

As on its 1994 inspiration, Audi painted the RS 4 Nogaro selection's radiator frame and roof rails black, the outside mirror housings in body color, and the brake calipers red. Seat center sections and door panels were optionally upholstered in Alcantara to match the body color; standard seat color was black. Décor panels in carbon fiber rounded out the homage.

Technically, little changed in the special edition. It was powered by the same 4.2-liter normally-aspirated V8 coupled with a dual-clutch transmission and crown gear center differential fitted to the regular production car. Audi installed the driving profiles, 20-inch wheels, and higher 280 km/h (174 mph) top speed as standard equipment. Added-cost options included sport differential, DRC suspension and ceramic brakes. The package, steeped in Audi history, raised the RS 4 price by about 10,000 to 87,300 Euros. Audi built only 100 examples of the Nogaro selection.

RS 4 options included ceramic brakes.

Oval exhaust tips are a recognition feature of RS models. With most generational changes, their dimensions continued to grow.

Inspiration and homage – the RS 4 Nogaro selection quoted the RS2.

The eight-cylinder normally-aspirated engine of the RS 4 B8 revved to 8,500 rpm.

Nogaro Blue seat centers were only available on the limited-edition model.

PAINT CHOICES (EXCERPT)

Solid color: Ibis White
Metallic: Suzuka Gray, Mythos Black
Pearl effect: Misano Red, Sepang Blue, Daytona Gray, Phantom Black; Nogaro Blue (Nogaro selection only)
Crystal effect: Prism Silver, Panther Black

STANDARD EQUIPMENT (EXCERPT)

Exterior:

- 19-inch aluminum wheels with 265/35 tires
- Xenon plus headlamps, LED taillamps
- Rear spoiler, rocker panel skirts, RS-specific front and rear valance
- Matt aluminum-look outside mirror housings and roof rails

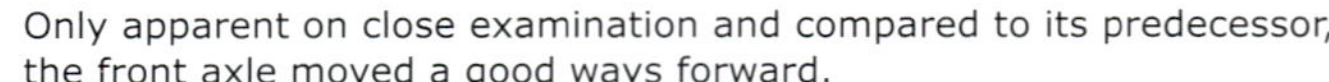

Only apparent on close examination and compared to its predecessor, the front axle moved a good ways forward.

The RS 4 adapted to the driver: selectable driving modes could make the car softer or stiffer. Snug bucket seats were optional on the RS 4 B8.

INTERIOR

- Front S sport seats with black leather, electrically adjustable
- Three-spoke multifunction sport steering wheel, flattened at bottom, with shift paddles
- Carbon fiber décor inserts
- Slotted interior door latches

FUNCTION

- Automatic climate control
- "Concert" audio system
- 18-inch steel brake system (as of facelift: wave design)
- Parking assistant
- Sport suspension

Audi RS 5 Coupe & Sportback (B9)

The fast touring car

2019-

2015

Avoiding more venom and fury, the second-generation RS 5 was softer and more compliant.

Audi reoriented the RS 5. For the 2017 model change, the sportster would become a more comfortable cruiser. In its press kit, the manufacturer described it as "the gran turismo of the RS models." Within the car itself, many changes were inevitable, regardless of GT or sport orientation. The normally-aspirated V8 engine was history, due to more demanding CO_2 hurdles. European Union noise limits reduced its sound output. Not least, many customers wished for something a little less hectic. All of these factors prompted Audi Sport to round a few edges and corners off the car. Nevertheless, these measures did not slow down the RS 5.

Still, early reactions to the car were restrained. Audi chose Andorra for the first journalist test drives. The test route featured winding roads and tight turns in the mountains, with long straight ribbons of asphalt on the way. The testers praised its good manners on the long drive, but criticized its tame behavior in the twisty bits. Where was the sport? The RS 5 had long lost its erstwhile wild side. In his speech, brand boss Stephan Winkelmann enthused about new RS models to come, but many a journalist present wished for more aggressiveness.

Many trade media were in agreement: the RS 5 lacked edginess. But the motoring press consists first and foremost of purists, and less so of customers. The lack of performance was attributable to a deliberate strategy: Audi Sport had consciously chosen new points of emphasis, in keeping with the car's new market positioning. Audi's development and marketing staff had reached this joint decision. They reduced the sharp, sporty orientation in favor of a greater bandwidth and more comfort. In this way, the RS 5 functioned better in most situations as far as the target audience was concerned, a group for whom rare moments on the race track were of less value.

LESS ATHLETICISM DESPITE IDENTICAL POWER

From an engineering perspective, this conceptual shift represented a new beginning for the RS 5, especially in the engine compartment. Audi Sport disposed of the normally-aspirated V8 of the preceding model and replaced it with a V6 turbo. This maintained the 450 hp of its predecessor, but delivered less emotion. Instead of a high-revving concept, it offered a wide, flat torque curve and rather than a growling exhaust, it emitted a restrained hiss. With the engine, transmission and chassis all changed, the entire driving feel of the car was different. The change meant that in the most comfortable driving mode, the RS 5 suspension overshot so much on bumps that *sport auto* described its behavior as "nautical." In its most aggressive mode, however, it was not excessively stiff – a known weak spot in its predecessor.

So much regard for passenger comfort cost the coupe its position as a sporty Audi superlative. And the purists did not hold back. The Swiss online portal radical-mag.com described the RS 5 as "colorless." It drove fast and with precision, "but the wild spectacle is missing." *sport auto* went even farther and recommended the predecessor or the less powerful S model for the race track. Such was the price Audi paid for the new gran turismo layout.

The RS 5 Cabriolet fell victim to the model change. Instead, Audi built a fast Sportback.

Flared fenders widened the RS 5 Coupe and Sportback by 1.5 cm (0.6 in.) per side.

European Union regulations limited the sound of the RS 5 and the powerful roar was gone.

In modern form, the RS 5 sporting digital instrument panel permitted different, selectable displays for speedometer and tach.

From time to time, there were internal debates at Audi regarding a more aggressive variant of the RS 5. Using the RS4 Sport (B5) as an example, added-cost options could be offered for more performance. One source might be suspension specialist Eibach. The company offered a special handling kit consisting of springs and rear stabilizer bar. In testing by *sport auto*, an appropriately converted RS 5 lapped the short course at Hockenheim 1.2 seconds faster than the stock example. For the time being, however, Audi's priorities lay elsewhere.

DIE-CAST ALUMINUM AND CARBON FIBER

The new layout of the second-generation RS 5 was deeply rooted in the car, but not bound to the exterior sheetmetal. Beginning in 2016, the A5's B9 platform was built on a revised architecture. Audi called the optimized longitudinal engine platform the "MLB evo." This introduced new materials into the predecessor's mix, in order to lower weight and increase stiffness. One major influence, for example, was front strut mounts made of die-cast aluminum. These weighed 8 kg (nearly 18 lbs) less than steel components, and more rigidly connected the upper suspension arms to the body.

In building the conversion to the top model, Audi Sport also revised one other material. For the first time, visible carbon fiber played a role different from mere decoration. At added cost, the regular production steel roof panel could be replaced by one of carbon fiber – a well-received option in market competitor BMW M3. In the RS 5, this innovation saved 3 kg (6.6 lbs) or 40 percent at the highest point of the car. Audi sourced the component from Wethje Carbon Composite in Bavaria.

Other items followed the usual RS logic: wide fender flares (one and a half centimeters per side), honeycomb grille at the front, oval exhaust tips at the rear, and between them all, the most powerful drivetrain in its market segment. Torque output, however, exceeded the capability of the Audi dual-clutch transmission. Audi Sport therefore installed a conventional eight-speed torque converter automatic transmission from ZF. A further developed Torsen differential distributed torque to the axles. This component had greater sensitivity than the crown gear solution, and weighed less to boot. At the rear axle, the RS 5 offered the sport differential of the concurrent Audi S5 as an option. Compared to the previous generation, this saved another kilogram (2.2 lbs) of weight.

Audi Sport got to work on the RS model early. There was less than a year between presentation of the A5 (June 2016) and that of the RS 5 (March 2017). Since the mid-2000s, the Audi performance subsidiary pushed for earlier market introduction of its cars. No other top model in the marketplace could match their development pace.

SPORTBACK INSTEAD OF CABRIOLET

The second RS 5 generation dispensed with the Cabriolet model. An open-topped two-door had been allowed to carry the RS logo, but now the RS 5 roof remained fixed. In its place, Audi Sport offered a larger Sportback model. The reason for these changes was the U.S. market. Audi wanted to score points in the North American market, and so, for the time being, had all its new model introductions in the New World. It debuted at the New York Auto Show in April 2018. The home market did not get the roomier RS 5 variant until a year later.

The strategy worked. With the RS 5 Sportback, Audi found a new niche. BMW was not building an M4 Gran Coupe. Mercedes in general did not offer four-door, mid-range coupes. The Audi had no competition in the marketplace; it set the standard. For this privilege, Audi gladly sacrificed the rather modest Cabriolet sales – especially since the model lineup still contained an open performance car in the form of the TT RS roadster.

FACELIFT COSMETICS

Audi affirmed that it took the often harsh criticism of the "tame" RS 5 to heart. The manufacturer said that the polarizing opinions regarding the suspension had been received. Yet for the 2020 facelift, nothing technical was changed on the car. The RS 5 carried

The new focus of the RS 5 ensured that anyone could drive quickly with it. Purists, however, wished for a less filtered experience.

its existing suspension, steering, and powertrain into the new model year. Accordingly, the performance also remained unchanged, with its strengths and weaknesses. Audi did install a particulate filter before the update.

In the year 2020, sportiness no longer played first violin in the company. Other accents were more important to Audi. The manufacturer switched the entire fleet over to a new infotainment system. For the marketing launch of the 2016 A5 generation, a rotary/push dial still controlled most functions. Since introduction of the A8 D5 (2017), the focus shifted to touch surfaces. To ensure that this functioned well, the monitor on the RS 5 dashboard was enlarged. In addition, it moved a bit farther into the interior, so that the driver would not have to stretch quite as far.

In the cockpit, aside from the operating concept, only a few details changed. The shift paddles now showed a higher level of workmanship. Instead of an individual driving mode, the RS 5 offered two definable RS modes, selectable by a new button on the steering wheel. Outside, the lamps, diffuser, grille and bumpers were modified. Subjectively, the model maintenance seemed to come a bit early, as the A5 Sportback had only been available on the German market for two years. The high-volume model showed the way, the sport version followed.

SPEED FOR ALL IN THE 95 PERCENT CAR

Despite all carping about the lack of firmness, the softer chassis tuning gave the RS 5 new qualities. With this sporty Audi, anybody could drive fast. "Audi has added engineering upgrades to the fastest A5, as if they want to go to war with the laws of physics," wrote *Auto Bild*, and summarized "Is this fun? Yes, because now Joe Average can clip apexes and tear around corners. And no, because with all this, you wish for a less filtered driving experience."

auto motor und sport called the RS 5 "a great 95 percent car." It offered speed, lapped Hockenheim faster than its predecessor, and was quicker through the 18-meter slalom. It strenuously objected to tight curves by understeering. And maximum-effort stops were accompanied by considerable nose dive.

What remained, satisfied the internal development targets: a proper model suitable for the masses. *sport auto* found that "it is a fascinating car, almost up to the limit – not as rock-hard as its predecessor, with plenty of kick at the top and handling that not only suggests extreme agility but also offers up more lateral dynamics than one needs in real life." Only at the absolute limit did this break down.

THE ENGINE OF THE RS 5: TURBOS INSTEAD OF CYLINDERS

The turbocharged engine of the RS 5 was part of a new powertrain family. Audi called it "KoVOMo" – Konzern-V-Otto-Motoren, or Corporate V Gasoline Engines. These would serve many models, from mid-range to SUV, at Porsche, Audi, and VW. Ultimate authority for the six-cylinder lay with Audi. Porsche was responsible for the eight-cylinder versions. Both marques worked together on development.

Initially, a 3.0-liter turbocharged variant of the V6 covered the performance class between 330 and 354 hp. Among others, this engine powered the S5. In the RS 5, Audi installed a more powerful derivative. Two identical turbochargers – one per cylinder bank – generated 1.5 bar (21.8 psi) of boost. To handle the increased power, Audi enlarged the diameter of the crankshaft main bearings by 2 mm, and shortened the stroke by 3 mm to 86 mm. This reduced the RS engine displacement to 2.9 liters.

All engines employed a 90° bank angle and 93 mm cylinder spacing. The block consisted of an aluminum/silicon alloy with integral, 1.5 mm thick steel cylinder liners. The turbochargers sat between the cylinder banks ("hot vee") for shorter gas passages. Camshafts and valve lift were variable.

The most significant feature of the engine was its combustion principle. Audi developed the Miller cycle, familiar from Toyota hybrids, to create its own "B cycle." In this process, the intake valves closed during the intake stroke, before the piston reached bottom dead center. In this way, the engine simulated smaller displacement, and allowed a geometric compression ratio of 11.2:1. A relatively long expansion stroke increased the powertrain efficiency. In numbers, despite an output of 450 hp and 600 Nm (443 ft-lbs), in the standard test cycle the RS 5 used only 9.1 liters per 100 km (25.8 mpg, U.S.).

A new six-cylinder replaced the old V8. Fitted with twin turbochargers, it maintained the power output of its predecessor.

PAINT CHOICES (EXCERPT)

Solid color: Nardo Gray, Turbo Blue
Metallic: Navarra Blue, Florett Silver, Sonoma Green, Glacier White, Mythos Black, Tango Red
Pearl effect: Misano Red, Daytona Gray, Phantom Black
Crystal effect: Prism Silver, Panther Black

STANDARD EQUIPMENT (EXCERPT)

Exterior:

- 19-inch aluminum wheels with 265/35 tires
- Matrix LED headlamps, LED taillamps, all with dynamic turn signals
- Rear spoiler, rocker panel skirts, RS-specific front and rear valance
- Outside mirror housings in body color

In the Sportback variant, the RS 5 was roughly as long as the RS 4 Avant.

For the facelift, Audi gave the RS 5 new light graphics for all lamps.

In the middle of the product cycle, Audi changed the controls: the rotary/push dial on the center console was replaced by touch controls.

INTERIOR

- Front RS sport seats with Alcantara/leather combination, black/Cliff Gray, electrically adjustable and heatable
- Three-spoke multifunction plus sport steering wheel, with shift paddles
- Aluminum Race décor inserts
- Slotted interior door latches

FUNCTION

- Automatic climate control
- MMI radio plus with dab+ and Bluetooth interface, eight speakers
- 18-inch steel brake system
- Parking assistant
- Audi drive select
- RS sport suspension

In the thinned-down field of manufacturers contesting the German Touring Masters (DTM), by 2020 Audi was only competing against BMW.

No relation to the production car, the RS 5 first raced with V8 power, and later with turbocharged four cylinders.

The DTM racing career of the RS 5 ended in 2020. Henceforth, the racing class was limited to GT3 vehicles.

The Audi RS 5 in motorsports

The new RS 5 continued the career of its predecessor. Once again, its name appeared in the grid lists of the DTM – the German Touring Masters racing series. Beginning with the 2017 season, Audi's touring car exhibited the face of the new model, but continued to be powered by the V8 engine, which was not found on the production cars, and the silhouette prescribed by the race sanctioning body. Two years later, the rules changed. A four-cylinder turbocharged gasoline engine replaced the eight-cylinder. Output increased to about 610 hp.

The RS 5's participation in the championship ended with the 2020 season. All subsequent races were carried out with vehicles conforming to the FIA's GT3 class. In the final accounting of the 2019 and 2020 seasons the RS 5 won 28 of 36 races; Audi pilots took 95 of 108 podium positions. At the end, Audi was competing against a greatly decimated opposition. In 2020, their only opponent was BMW.

Audi RS 4 Avant (B9)

Return to the V6 Turbo

20

In developing the new RS 4, its ancestor of the B5 generation served as an inspiration.

Starting in 2017, the RS 4 demonstrated that technically similar cars could feel very different. Although Audi Sport equipped it with the mechanicals of the RS 5, the result was something very different, because it carried a great deal of tradition. In the RS 4, the new turbo V6 did not represent downsizing, but rather a reminiscence of its origins in 1999. On the other hand, Audi Sport was able to create a genuine work of art. The wagon drove and sounded more dynamic than the coupe.

When engines in sporting cars get smaller, the result is rarely a more interesting car. It is even worse when the loss of displacement and cylinders is accompanied by a more muted sound. This is precisely what happened to the RS 5, when it was converted to the V6 engine. Road testers and fans mourned the loss of the big, boisterous V8. Few, however, took offense to the RS 4's switch to a smaller turbo engine, because after 18 years and four generations, Audi could proudly point to the car's history. And that RS 4 history began with a twin-turbo V6.

This legendary powerplant was the role model for Audi Sport as they carried out the acoustic tuning of the 2.9-liter engine. The development engineers concentrated on the ancestor's sonic image and gave the 2017 RS 4 a similar exhaust note. In this, the cargo area of the wagon assisted the designers. Its large volume acted as a resonance chamber and transmitted the exhaust sound waves more clearly to the driver's ears. The result: more sound in the Avant than in the coupe.

Audi did not stop there. The RS 4 not only sounded better, but also drove better. This in itself was curious, because the coupe should have felt sportier, but it did not. While Audi had gotten a restrained response after the first media test drives, the trade journalists' reaction to the Avant was more positive. This was more of a mental exercise for the test drivers, because the cars were as identical to one another as a pair of rings in the Audi logo. Within the framework of the platform strategy, they shared more elements than their already very similar predecessors.

DIFFERENCES DESPITE THE PLATFORM

The objective of Audi's platform principle was to develop as few specific components as possible for each model. As a result, in the B9 platform, the RS 4's character moved a good bit closer to the RS 5. The front end and cabin were, apart from the obvious differences in size and shape, nearly identical. Both cars used the same materials and manufacturing processes for their longitudinal members, suspension strut mounts, A- and B-pillars and door sills.

The same applied to the powerplant. Audi developed a single V6 engine, eight-speed automatic transmission, Torsen differential, axles and brake systems for both model lines. Only one detail represented a significant engineering difference to separate the RS 4 from the RS 5: to ensure that its larger cargo area did not cause handling problems when fully loaded, Audi Sport gave the RS 4 stiffer rear springs.

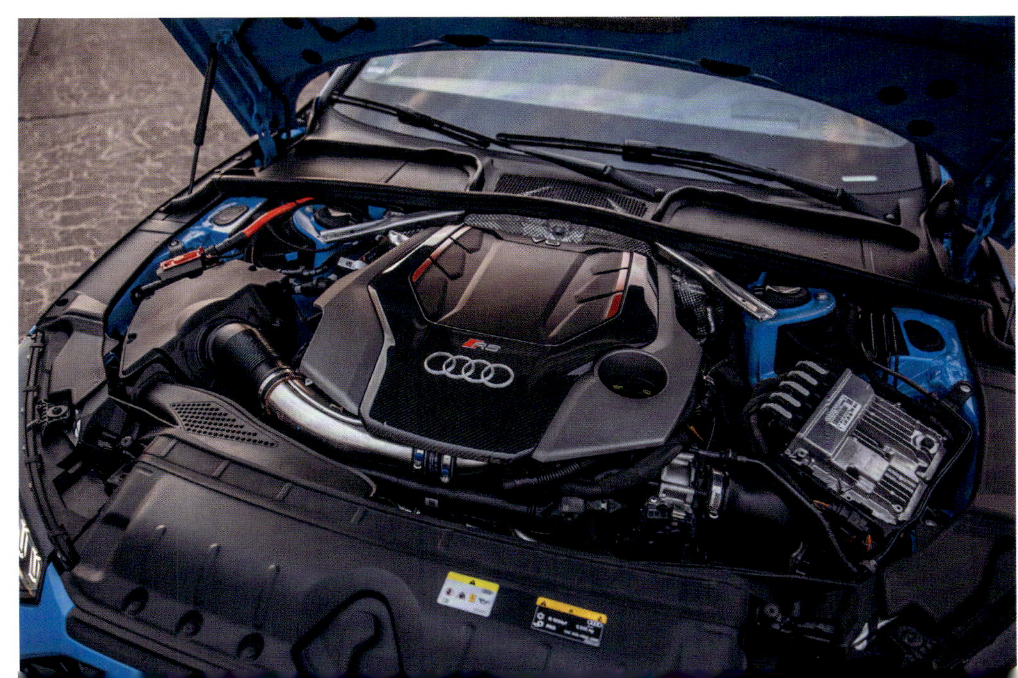

For the premiere of the newest edition, Audi built a bridge to its ancestor, and communicated the downsizing theme as a historically-relevant decision.

Precisely this measure, rather conventional in the industry, significantly improved the RS 4's turn-in behavior, driving feel, feedback and agility. In testing on the race track, *sport auto* even perceived a bit of well-metered anarchy: "... for a production wagon, the RS 4 rear pushes astonishingly hard when the load changes." The powerful wagon was fast, too. On the Hockenheim short course, the car magazine recorded a lap time of 1:13 minutes. For comparison, the 65 kilogram (143 lb) lighter coupe, running on the same tires (275/30 Hankook R20) took a second longer. So the tauter chassis tuning of the RS 4 had a measurable effect at the track.

SMOOTH, BUT FAST

The character of the RS 4 changed as well. Like the RS 5, it sacrificed some of its ability at the limit in exchange for better functionality in everyday use. *sport auto* summed it up: "... the RS 4 Avant has the most trade-offs among the middle-class power wagons," because it wants to be all things to all people. Sport differential, dynamic steering, adjustable suspension and ceramic brakes were available as performance upgrades. Nevertheless, in the interest of greater sales potential, Audi Sport ended its efforts to make every RS 4 generation a bit hotter than the one before.

On the road, the softer tuning manifested itself less dramatically than on the race track. *auto motor und sport* praised the engine above all else: "The car is an executioner. Cool and buffed out, even without a full beard and acres of tattoos, dressed in fine fabric the RS 4 flexes its muscles, speaks only when spoken to, otherwise keeps its exhaust flap shut. The RS 4 sneaks through residential developments, exercises on country roads, slurs the shifts of its eight-speed torque converter automatic, and even skimps on fuel consumption under part throttle, thanks to its so-called B-cycle [Budack cycle, a modified Miller cycle] engine, with its unusual valve timing, valve duration and compression and expansion strokes. All this without having the octane vegan feel like a normally-aspirated Miller cycle engine. Variable valve timing and the twin turbos help."

Many automotive media put the RS 4 to the test, to tease out its hard and soft sides. In the standard performance tests, it returned stellar numbers. To reach 100 km/h (62 mph), it took 3.7 seconds (*Auto Zeitung, Auto Bild*) to 3.8 seconds (*sport auto, auto motor und sport*) instead of the official works number of 4.1 seconds. As an option, Audi limited its top speed to 280 km/h (174 mph), but in practice allowed a bit more; the speedometer would show nearly 300 km/h (186 mph).

In the press kit for the car (December 2017), the manufacturer emphasized its sporty qualities as well as its practical features. For the first time, an RS 4 could be fitted with a towing hitch. A towing capacity of 2,100 kg (4,630 lbs) presented a unique offer for more performance-oriented travel trailer fans, something that had been missing in this class since Audi ended production of its RS2.

As part of the 2020 model year facelift, the kink at the bottom edge of the headlamps disappeared. In addition, Audi modified the front and rear valances.

For the debut, a new rotary/push dial on the center console controlled the RS 4 infotainment system. In 2020, this was eliminated in favor of a touch system.

The RS 4 of Audi's B9 generation was given a new, smoother character. Still, it moved more dynamically than its sibling, the RS 5.

FACELIFT: NEW EYES FOR 2020

In October 2019, Audi presented a reworked version of the RS 4. The basic car underwent a thorough transformation as a result of the facelift. Finally, Audi gave the middle-class car the independence from its predecessor, which had been lacking at the original market introduction. The A4 received new body panels and an extensively modified front. In the RS 4, the modifications were more limited, although it did adopt the new headlamps, without a kink at the lower edge, and was given an appropriate front valance. There was also some spice for the fans – the bottom edge of the hood hinted at an air scoop, a design feature of the 1984 Sport quattro.

Analogous to the RS 5, Audi equipped the interior with a new infotainment system. The rotary/push dial disappeared from the center console, replaced by a large touchscreen monitor which moved a little farther into the interior.

At this time, no changes were made to the drivetrain. This had already been done, in secrecy, months before. In early 2019, Audi adapted the six-cylinder to the conditions imposed by the new Euro 6d Temp Evap ISC exhaust emissions standard. Particulate filters now scrubbed the exhaust stream from the direct-injection engine. Power and performance remained unaffected. The new WLTP test cycle now defined fuel economy, and made the RS 4 appear thirstier by one liter per 100 km. This was a huge difference in test numbers, which had no effect on real-world economy.

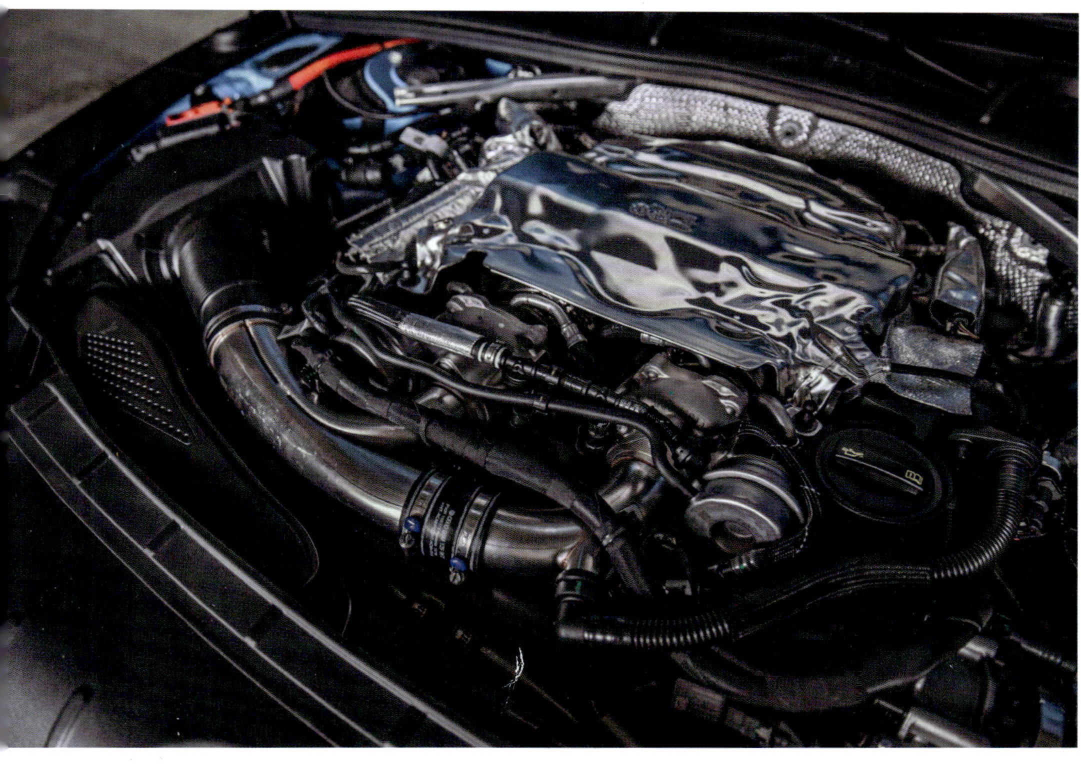

The turbochargers of the V6 engine in the RS 4 were mounted between the cylinder banks. This arrangement shortened the intake runner lengths and improved throttle response.

VOLUME-PRODUCTION ENGINE

What was hardly noticed in the RS 4 was that its new engine marked the end of an era. This was not a switchover from high-revving normally-aspirated engines to a turbo powerplant, but rather the positioning of RS engines in general. In the early years, each powerplant powering an RS model was strictly the province of quattro GmbH or Audi Sport. The interaction with Bentley began in 2013, with the introduction of the new V8 twin turbo. Now, the sphere of activity grew.

The EA 839, as Audi called the new six-cylinder engine family, was generously distributed within the VW group. In 3.0-liter V6 form, the engine, with three available performance levels, powered a total of twelve different cars. The more powerful 2.9-liter version found five customers, of which only two cars had an RS in their names. Porsche installed the engine in more cars than Audi. And the Zuffenhausen marque got it sooner. As of 2016, the V6 could be found in the Panamera. Audi's only consolation was that the 450 hp version was only installed in the RS models.

From a business perspective, this made sense. The costs of an engine development program increase in keeping with the demands made on its exhaust emissions. Especially performance-oriented powerplants have to stretch to satisfy tight emissions standards. It is therefore only logical to refinance development through wide distribution. Still, this cost the cars a certain measure of their individuality.

THE ANNIVERSARY PACKAGE: AUDI RS 4 25 YEARS OF RS

In 2019, Audi celebrated a sporting anniversary: the first RS model had debuted twenty-five years previously. For its birthday, the manufacturer offered a special equipment package. This contained many "citations" of the 1994 RS2. However, this version was not appointed as exclusively as the 2014 "Nogaro selection".

The package encompassed paintwork in Nogaro Blue (alternatively Mythos Black, Nardo Gray or Glacier White) and various add-on parts in a combination of black and matte aluminum. Inside, Audi upholstered the seats with black leather and cobalt blue Alcantara. Along with the RS 4, Audi offered the package for the RS 5, RS 6, RS 7 and TT RS.

Anniversary package for the 25th anniversary of the RS models: as an option, RS models were available in the traditional color, Nogaro Blue.

PAINT CHOICES (EXCERPT)

Solid color: Nardo Gray, Turbo Blue
Metallic: Navarra Blue, Florett Silver, Sonoma Green, Glacier White, Florett Silver, Mythos Black, Tango Red
Pearl effect: Misano Red, Daytona Gray

STANDARD EQUIPMENT (EXCERPT)

Exterior:

- 19-inch aluminum wheels with 265/35 tires
- LED headlamps, LED taillamps, all with dynamic turn signals
- Rear spoiler, rocker panel skirts, RS-specific front and rear valance
- Outside mirror housings in matte aluminum-look, black roof rails

Once again, the Audi RS 4 was only available as an Avant. Its engineering twin, the RS 5, was available in other body configurations.

The scoop at the leading edge of the engine hood quoted a design feature of the 1984 Audi Sport quattro.

In the RS 4, sporty details enliven the business-like A4 cockpit and sport seats and steering wheel are included as standard equipment.

INTERIOR

- Front RS sport seats with Alcantara/leather combination, black/Cliff Gray, electrically adjustable and heatable
- Three-spoke multifunction plus sport steering wheel, with shift paddles
- Aluminum Race décor inserts
- Slotted interior door latches

FUNCTION

- Automatic climate control
- MMI radio plus with Bluetooth interface, eight speakers
- 18-inch steel brake system
- Parking assistant
- Audi drive select
- RS sport suspension

TECHNICAL

		Audi Avant RS2 (P1)		Audi RS 4 (B5)	Audi RS 4 (B7)		
MODEL	Body style	Avant	Sedan	Avant	Avant	Sedan	Cabriolet
	Production timeframe	1994-1996		1999-2001	2006-2008	2005-2008	2006-2009
ENGINE	Engine configuration	Longitudinal front-mounted inline five-cylinder Otto cycle engine		Longitudinal front-mounted V6 Otto cycle engine	Longitudinal front-mounted V8 Otto cycle engine		
	Engine designation	ABY		ASJ, AZR	BNS		
	Displacement, cc	2,226		2,671	4,163		
	Bore x stroke, mm	81x86.4		81x86.4	84.5x92.8		
	Power output, hp (kw) @ rpm	315 (232) at 6,500		381 (280) at 6,100 - 7,000	420 (309) at 7,800		
	Torque in Nm (ft-lbs) @ rpm	410 (302) at 3,000		440 (325) at 2,500-6,000	430 (317) at 5,500		
	Valvetrain, valves per cylinder	Timing belt, dual overhead camshafts, four valves per cylinder		Timing belt, four overhead camshafts, variable intake timing, four valves per cylinder	Timing chain, four overhead camshafts, variable intake and exhaust timing, four valves per cylinder		
	Fuel delivery	Multi-point fuel-injection, dual knock sensors, turbocharged, intercooled, electronic boost control, regulated catalytic converter, Bosch Motronic 2.3 engine control system		Twin turbocharged, multi-point fuel-injection with air mass sensor, map ignition with static high-voltage distribution, Bosch Motronic ME 7.1 engine control system	Direct fuel-injection, map ignition with static high-voltage distribution, Bosch MED 9.1 engine management system		
	Compression ratio	9.3		9	12.5		
POWERTRAIN	Transmission	Six-speed manual		Six-speed manual	Six-speed manual		
	Drivetrain	All-wheel drive, Torsen Type A center differential, manually lockable rear differential		All-wheel drive, automatically locking Torsen Type B center differential, electronic differential lock (EDS) via brake application	All-wheel drive, automatically locking Torsen Type C center differential, electronic differential lock (EDS) via brake application, ESP		
CHASSIS AND SUSPENSION	Front suspension	McPherson struts, lower A-arms, gas pressure shock absorbers, anti-roll bar		Four-link suspension, twin-tube gas pressure shock absorbers, anti-roll bar	Four-link suspension, monotube shock absorbers, coil springs, anti-roll bar, radius link		
	Rear suspension	Dual-link rear axle, gas pressure shock absorbers, anti-roll bar, control links		Dual-link rear axle, gas pressure shock absorbers, anti-roll bar	Trapezoidal link rear suspension, anti-roll bar		
	Steering	Power-assisted rack and pinion		Power-assisted rack and pinion	Power-assisted rack and pinion		
	Turning circle, m (ft)	11.4 (37.4)		11.4 (37.4)	11.1 (36.4)		
	Brake system	Dual-circuit brake system with brake booster, ABS, four-piston calipers and ventilated discs		Dual-circuit brake system with brake booster, ABS, Electronic brake force distribution (EBV), two-piston calipers at front, ventilated discs front and rear (Optional: cross-drilled discs)	Dual-circuit brake system with brake booster, ABS, Electronic brake force distribution, eight-piston calipers at front, ventilated and cross-drilled discs front and rear		
	Brake discs	Front: 305x32 mm, Optional: 322x32 mm; Rear: 299x24 mm		Front: 360x32 mm; Rear: 312x22 mm	Front: 365x32 mm, Optional: 380x38 mm ceramic; Rear: 324x24 mm		
	Wheel size, in.	7x17		8.5x18	8.5x18		
	Tire size	245/45		255/35	255/40		
DIMENSIONS & WEIGHTS	Length/width/height, mm (in.)	4,510/1,695/1,386 (177.6/66.7/54.6)		4,525/1,799/1,386 (178.1/70.8/54.6)	4,586/1,816/1,415 (180.6/71.5/55.7)	4,589/1,816/1,415 (180.7/71.5/55.7)	4,555/1,814/1,391 (179.3/71.4/54.8)
	Wheelbase, mm (in.)	2,597 (102.2)		2,607 (102.6)	2,651 (104.4)	2,648 (104.3)	2,650 (104.3)
	Track, front/rear, mm (in.)	1,448/1,474 (57.0/58.0)		1,549/1,530 (70.0/60.2)	1,559/1,569 (61.4/61.8)		
	Empty weight, kg (lbs)	1,595 (3,516)	1,530 (3,373)	1,620 (3,571)	1,710 (3,770)	1,650 (3,638)	1,845 (4,068)
	Trunk volume, liters (cu ft)	370-650 (13.1-23.0)	430-712 (15.2-25.1)	390-1,250 (13.8-44.1)	442-1,354 (15.6-47.8)	460-720 (16.2-25.4)	246-315 (8.7-11.1)
	Fuel capacity, liters (U.S. gal)	64 (16.9)	62 (16.4)	62 (16.4)	63 (16.6)		
PERFORMANCE	Top speed, km/h (mph)	262 (163)					
	Acceleration, 0-100 km/h, sec (62 mph)	5.4		4.9	4.9	4.8	4.9
	Fuel economy, liters/100 km (U.S. mpg)	10.4 (22.6)		12 (19.6)	13.5-13.6 (17.4-17.3)	13.7 (17.2)	13.9 (16.9)
MISC.	Number built, by year	1993: 4 1994: 2,021 1995: 875		1999: 3 2000: 2,530 2001: 3,513	2005: 12 2006: 2,666 2007: 2,191 2008: 330	2004: 4 2005: 544 2006: 4,384 2007: 2,401 2008: 320	2005: 13 2006: 589 2007: 700 2008: 201
	Total number built	2,900	ca. 2-3	6,049	5,199	7,653	1,503
	Price at market introduction	98.900 DM	Not sold	127.000 DM	71.300 €	69.900 €	82.900 €

SPECIFICATIONS

		Audi RS 4 (B8)	Audi RS 4 (B9)	Audi RS 5 (B8)		Audi RS 5 (B9)	
MODEL	**Body style**	Avant	Avant	Coupe	Cabriolet	Coupe	Sportback
	Production timeframe	2012-2015	since 2017	2010-2015	2012-2015	Since 2017	Since 2019
ENGINE	**Engine configuration**	Longitudinal front-mounted V8 Otto cycle engine	Longitudinal front-mounted V6 Otto cycle engine	Longitudinal front-mounted V8 Otto cycle engine		Longitudinal front-mounted V6 Otto cycle engine	
	Engine designation	CFSA	DECA	CFSA		DECA	
	Displacement, cc	4,163	2,894	4,163		2,894	
	Bore x stroke, mm	84.5x92.8	84.5x86.0	84.5x92.8		84.5x86.0	
	Power output, hp (kw) @ rpm	450 (331) at 8,250	450 (331) at 5,700-5,600	450 (331) at 8,250		450 (331) at 5,700-5,600	
	Torque in Nm (ft-lbs) @ rpm	430 (317) at 4,000-6,000	600 (443) at 1,900-5,000	430 (317) at 4,000-6,000		600 (443) at 1,900-5,000	
	Valvetrain, valves per cylinder	Timing chain, four overhead camshafts, variable intake and exhaust timing, four valves per cylinder	Timing chain, four overhead camshafts, Audi Valvelift on intake side, variable intake and exhaust timing, four valves per cylinder	Timing chain, four overhead camshafts, variable intake and exhaust timing, four valves per cylinder		Timing chain, four overhead camshafts, Audi Valvelift on intake side, variable intake and exhaust timing, four valves per cylinder	
	Fuel delivery	Direct fuel-injection, map ignition with static high-voltage distribution, coordinated Bosch MED 9.1 engine management system	Twin turbocharged, direct fuel-injection, map ignition, Bosch MDG1 engine management system. As of 2/2019: gasoline exhaust particulate filter	Direct fuel-injection, map ignition with static high-voltage distribution, coordinated Bosch MED 9.1 engine management system		Twin turbocharged, direct fuel-injection, map ignition, Bosch MDG1 engine management system. As of 2/2019: gasoline exhaust particulate filter	
	Compression ratio	11	10	12.5		10	
POWERTRAIN	**Transmission**	Seven-speed dual-clutch automatic (S-tronic)	Eight-speed torque converter automatic (tiptronic)	Seven-speed dual-clutch automatic (S-tronic)		Eight-speed torque converter automatic (tiptronic)	
	Drivetrain	All-wheel drive, self-locking crown gear center differential, ESP with wheel-selective torque vectoring	All-wheel drive, automatically locking Torsen Type CSM center differential, ESP with wheel-selective torque vectoring	All-wheel drive, self-locking crown gear center differential, ESP with wheel-selective torque vectoring		All-wheel drive, automatically locking Torsen Type CSM center differential, ESP with wheel-selective torque vectoring	
CHASSIS AND SUSPENSION	**Front suspension**	Five-link suspension, upper and lower transverse arms, solid anti-roll bar	Five-link suspension, tubular anti-roll bar	Five-link suspension, upper and lower transverse arms, solid anti-roll bar		Five-link suspension, tubular anti-roll bar	
	Rear suspension	Trapezoidal link rear suspension, anti-roll bar	Five-link suspension, tubular anti-roll bar	Trapezoidal link rear suspension with elastically mounted subframe, anti-roll bar		Five-link suspension, tubular anti-roll bar	
	Steering	Electromechanical rack and pinion	Electromechanical rack and pinion	Electromechanical rack and pinion		Electromechanical rack and pinion	
	Turning circle, m (ft)	11.9 (39.0)	11.7 (38.4)	11.4 (37.4)		11.7 (38.4)	
	Brake system	Dual-circuit brake system with tandem brake booster, ABS/EBV and ESP with braking assistant, eight-piston front brake calipers, ventilated front and rear discs; optional ceramic brakes with six-piston calipers	Dual-circuit brake system with brake booster, ABS/EBV and ESP, hydraulic brake assistant, six-piston front calipers, ventilated front and rear discs	Dual-circuit brake system with tandem brake booster, ABS/EBV and ESP with braking assistant, eight-piston front brake calipers, ventilated front and rear discs; optional ceramic brakes with six-piston calipers		Dual-circuit brake system with brake booster, ABS/EBV and ESP, hydraulic brake assistant, six-piston front calipers, ventilated front and rear discs	
	Brake discs	Front: 365x34 mm (wave design); Optional: 380x38 mm ceramic; Rear: 330x22 mm (wave design)	Front: 375x36 mm; Optional: 400x38 mm ceramic; Rear: 330x22 mm	Front: 365x34 mm (wave design); Optional: 380x38 mm ceramic; Rear: 330x22 mm (wave design)		Front: 375x36 mm; Optional: 400x38 mm ceramic; Rear: 330x22 mm	
	Wheel size, in.	9x19					
	Tire size	265/35					
DIMENSIONS & WEIGHTS	**Length/width/height, mm (in.)**	4,719/1,850/1,416 (185.8/72.8/55.7)	4,782/1,866/1,438 (188.3/73.5/56.6)	4,649/1,860/1,366 (183.0/73.2/53.8)	4,649/1,860/1,380 (183.0/73.2/53.8)	4,723/1,866/1,372 (185.9/73.5/54.0)	4,783/1,866/1,399 (188.3/73.5/55.1)
	Wheelbase, mm (in.)	2,813 (110.7)	2,826 (111.3)	2,751 (108.3)	2,766 (108.9)	2,766 (108.9)	2,826 (111.3)
	Track, front/rear, mm (in.)	1,599/1,586 (63.0/62.4)	1,580/1,575 (62.2-62.0)	1,586/1,582 (62.4-62.3)		1,598/1,588 (62.9/62.5)	
	Empty weight, kg (lbs)	1,795 (3,957)	1,745 (3,847)	1,715 (3,781)	1,920 (4,233)	1,707 (3,763)	1,742 (3,840)
	Trunk volume, liters (cu ft)	490-1,430 (17.3-50.5)	495-1,495 (17.5-52.8)	455-829 (16.1-29.3)	320/380-750 (11.3/13.4-26.5)	465 (16.4)	480-1,300 (17.0-45.9)
	Fuel capacity, liters (U.S. gal)	61 (16.1)	58 (15.3)	61 (16.1)		58 (15.3)	
PERFORMANCE	**Top speed, km/h (mph)**	250 (governed); optional 280 (governed) (155; 174)					
	Acceleration, 0-100 km/h, sec (62 mph)	4.7	4.1	4.5	4.9	3.9	
	Fuel economy, liters/100 km (U.S. mpg)	10.7 (22.0)	8.8 (26.7)	10.5 (22.4)	10.7 (22.0)	8.7 (27.0)	9.2 (25.6)
MISC.	**Number built, by year**	2011: 13 2012: 1,611 2013: 2,466 2014: 2,143 2015: 867	2016: 4 2017: 953 2018: 3,815 2019: 3,647	2009: 32 2010: 2,323 2011: 2,688 2012: 2,559 2013: 2,703 2014: 2,282 2015: 886	2012: 58 2013: 1,367 2014: 860 2015: 433	2016: 83 2017: 2,719 2018: 3,321 2019: 1,383	2017: 24 2018: 2,566 2019: 3,611
	Total number built	7,100	8,419	14,473	2,718	Still in production	
	Price at market introduction	76,600 €	79,800 €	77,700 €	88,500 €	82,700 €	82,700 €

Source Audi AG

M

UPPER MID-RANGE MODELS

Big sedans and wagons hold special meaning for quattro GmbH, for it is in this segment that the Audi subsidiary first ventured to build a car on its own. On the pilot project, the letter R was still absent – the car was simply called the S6 plus. Overall, it stayed quite close to the base model. Still, it allowed the newly minted carmaker to demonstrate its abilities (with some help from its corporate parent).

The successors showed greater independence. And they grew. This was readily apparent in the RS 6 wheels. With each succeeding generation, the wheels gained an inch in diameter. In 2002, the C5 model generation rolled on (optional) 19-inch rims. In 2019, the Audi RS 6 C8 could be ordered with optional 22-inch wheels over ceramic brakes. Big boots for a big entrance.

The exclusivity of the RS models was not just apparent from their well-filled fenders. In 2002, visibly flared fenders were a special feature, but not limited to the RS 6. All V8 models in the C5 line, except for the allroad, carried fat fenders. On the succeeding model, only the RS 6 was given a wider track. The C7 generation further distanced itself from the sheetmetal of the regular production A6. And Audi even gave the C8 its own unique face – it sported the headlamps of its attractive twin, the RS 7.

The RS 7 was an independent development. It started reservedly, cautiously and without great risk. Initially it did not get its own bodywork, only wider composite parts. The second generation, however, appeared more self-assured, with broader shoulders. More so than its predecessor, its engineering echoed that of its more voluminous brother. This turned the RS 7 into exactly what its fans desired from the very beginning: a visually independent model, with all of the typical RS insignia.

1996–

Audi S6 plus Avant & Sedan (C4)

quattro GmbH's first car

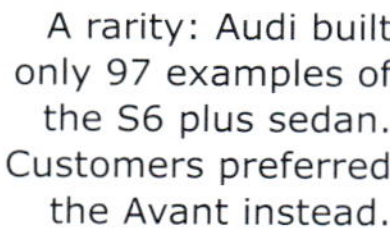

A rarity: Audi built only 97 examples of the S6 plus sedan. Customers preferred the Avant instead.

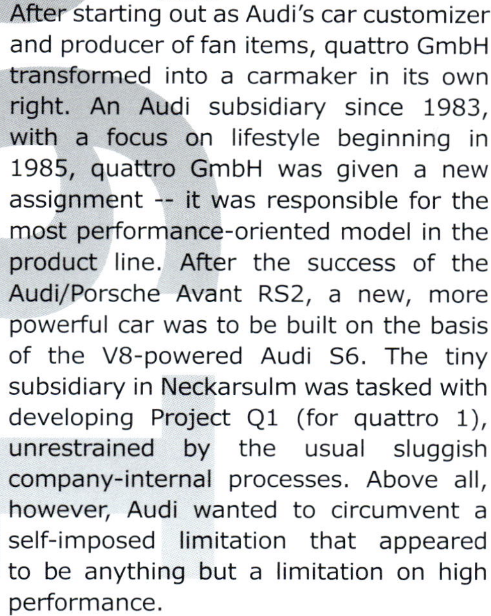

After starting out as Audi's car customizer and producer of fan items, quattro GmbH transformed into a carmaker in its own right. An Audi subsidiary since 1983, with a focus on lifestyle beginning in 1985, quattro GmbH was given a new assignment -- it was responsible for the most performance-oriented model in the product line. After the success of the Audi/Porsche Avant RS2, a new, more powerful car was to be built on the basis of the V8-powered Audi S6. The tiny subsidiary in Neckarsulm was tasked with developing Project Q1 (for quattro 1), unrestrained by the usual sluggish company-internal processes. Above all, however, Audi wanted to circumvent a self-imposed limitation that appeared to be anything but a limitation on high performance.

Beginning in 1987, BMW, Mercedes, VW and Audi all agreed to a self-imposed speed limit. In order to avoid an Autobahn arms race, the manufacturers governed their fastest models to a top speed of 250 km/h (155 mph). Even the powerful V8 models, such as the Mercedes 500 E or BMW 540i were subject to this voluntary limitation. Still, exceptions managed to sneak into the marketplace; in the 1990s, Mercedes' performance subsidiary AMG began to take a less restrictive view of the rule. On paper, the AMG models were limited to 250 km/h, but they managed a few kilometers per hour more than advertised.

Audi did not want to be left behind. To adhere to the industry agreement, quattro GmbH was promoted to the role of carmaker. Henceforth, the vehicle registration papers of the resulting "outsourced" models listed the subsidiary as the official manufacturer, instead of Audi. The VIN numbers of these vehicles began with the letters WUA instead of WAU. In the motor vehicle registration offices, this caused some confusion; clerks noticed the transposed letters, or stated manufacturer, as mistakes and erroneously "corrected" these.

FROM ACCESSORIES TO TUNED ENGINES

Quattro GmbH enjoyed its new status mostly on paper. In terms of personnel, structure and finances, it was not prepared for its new assignment. The little team under quattro boss Rudolf Gölz was entrusted with Audi's accessory business and, from 1995, customization of individual vehicles. But quattro GmbH was not yet in a position to build an entire car using its own resources. Accordingly, on Project Q1, the boundaries between the newly minted carmaker and its parent company became blurred.

Audi's engine development department in Neckarsulm designed a more powerful version of the 4.2-liter V8 that powered the standard Audi S6. Employing classical tuning measures, power rose from 290 to 326 hp. This even exceeded the output of the Audi Avant RS2, which was still getting its power at Porsche.

Along with the engine, Audi and quattro GmbH modified everything that had an effect on the car's driving qualities. The fast S6 was given bigger front brakes with dual-piston calipers, shorter gear ratios as of third gear for its six-speed transmission, and generally stiffer suspension tuning. Each corner mounted 17-inch rims with 255 section tires.
In this form, at the end of 1995

Porsche declined to grant permission to use the RS label. Instead, the sportiest derivative of the C4 model line was called the S6 plus.

The tuned eight-cylinder in the S6 generated 326 hp, 36 more than the powerplant of the normal S6.

Standard equipment of the S6 plus included 17-inch wheels, along with large overhang.

quattro GmbH requested official road certification for the Avant and sedan body configurations. Initially, the papers carried the internal designation "quattro W6." It had not yet been decided under what name the car would actually be sold. An RS 6, analogous to the RS2, was not to be. Porsche claimed the "RS" label as its own. And no wonder. Porsche, as a service provider, was not party to this project and did not want to contribute, even if only in name. Ultimately, the Q1, quattro GmbH's first car, entered the market as the Audi S6 plus.

PREMIERE ON THE QUATTRO DISPLAY STAND

The Audi S6 plus was first shown to the public at the 1996 Geneva Motor Show. Quattro GmbH presented it on its own stand. In this way, it emphasized itself as an entity separate from Audi. Along with its first car, the subsidiary displayed other competencies; quattro was responsible for accessories, fan articles and special conversions. An individualized Audi A8 was displayed alongside the S6 plus, to demonstrate the program's bandwidth.

Quattro GmbH also visually differentiated the tuned S6 from the Audi version. Those familiar with the normal S6 could see that in its color choices. Only the plus model could be had in the special colors, Nogaro Blue and Misano Red. Seventeen-inch aluminum rims were standard equipment; this size was an added-cost option on the base S6. The plus was also given unique emblems on the radiator grille and trunk lid, black window and grille accents, as well as a special rear spoiler. Compared to quattro GmbH's later cars, though, the modifications came across as restrained. Sheetmetal and valances remained unchanged from standard production.

The interior was trimmed with black accents, a unique shift knob, and a speedometer face in blue, gray, or white, calibrated to 300 km/h (186 mph). The sport seats were covered in a combination of leather and Alcantara as standard equipment. *Auto Zeitung* later described the S6 plus interior as "lounge-like."

AUDI LENDS A HAND

Quattro GmbH lacked the personnel to get the car out to customers and to promote it in the press. The colleagues at the parent organization took on these responsibilities. Marketing man Udo Rügheimer produced the brochure, containing a foldout showing both body styles and special colors for the S6 plus. A price list printed on transparent paper was included. The Audi event management team planned a driving event on behalf of quattro GmbH, to be held in Gross Dölln, in the former East Germany. Journalists and dealers were invited to attend. Several potential customers were among the first test drivers.

They experienced a car that felt sportier than other models in the upper mid-range models. The press first had to become accustomed to the added

Seven gauges with white faces in the cockpit of the Audi S6 plus. Audi also offered these in gray or blue.

chassis stiffness. In its comparison test pitting the S6 plus against the Mercedes E 50 AMG, *auto motor und sport* complained that "its suspension only does its job grudgingly." On longer trips, even performance-oriented drivers felt it was overdone; the precise contact with the road was "exaggerated."

At the same time, the S6 plus earned praise from the magazine. It drove "like a genuine sports car, that just happens to have gotten two extra doors." The test emphasized the car's traction, handling, cornering speeds, willingness to rev, and neutral turn-in. Its standard all-wheel drive system with Torsen differential separated it from its market competitors.

All this was not enough to bring forth a sensational report. The Mercedes W210 had come onto the market a year before, and Audi's A6 generation on the C4 platform was scheduled to end in 1997. Compared to the more powerful, more expensive, and more modern AMG product, quattro's first effort crossed the finish line in second place. In the car magazine's overall rating, the S6 plus still collected 100 points, just behind the AMG's 103 points. It was especially lacking in the comfort department. The testers objected in particular to perceptible kicking of the steering, and stiff suspension. These drawbacks could not be compensated by its sporting abilities and better than 30,000 Deutschmark price advantage.

Top speed, such an important topic within Audi, was only mentioned in passing in the road test article. Officially, the S6 would run as fast as its competitors; the registration papers cited the 250 km/h limit agreed upon by the industry. But the homologation papers treated this topic more thoroughly. Without a speed limiter, the car reached a top speed of 262 km/h (163 mph) for the S6 plus Avant, and 269 km/h (167 mph) for the S6 plus sedan. Figuring in tolerances, either body style had a top speed of 274 km/h (170 mph). These numbers were corroborated by the experiences of car owners. With that, the AMG Mercedes lost a bit of its secret advantage.

After just two years, production of the Audi S6 plus ended, along with the entire A6 model line. Audi built a total of 855 Avant and 97 sedan versions of the S6 plus, a total of 952 examples. In 1996, Gölz had announced an expected production run of 1,000 cars. Although the "R" may have been missing from its model designation, the S6 plus counts as the progenitor of all sports cars produced in-house. Its successors would be more powerful, more sporty, and more independent.

THE ENGINE OF THE AUDI S6 PLUS: PLUS 36 HP

The big difference between the S6 plus and later RS models was located directly above its front axle. The V8 engine in the first quattro project produced 36 more horsepower than the regular Audi S6. Later RS models would be even more strongly differentiated from regular production; these exceeded the S versions by at least 90 hp.

To achieve a horsepower gain of at least 12 percent, the development engineers modified the cylinder heads of the eight-cylinder engine. New intake camshafts increased valve lift and overlap. On the intake side, solid lifters replaced hydraulic lifters. Maximum speed of the engine rose from 6,500 to 7,250 rpm. Compression ratio was raised from 10.8 to 11.6 to one.

The reworked engine adopted the variable intake manifold of the Audi S8 that was presented at the same time. Combined with a larger mass air flow meter and optimized exhaust system, this improved gas flow into and out of the engine. With appropriately matched software, the maximum torque of 400 Nm (295 ft-lbs) was available at engine speeds as low as 3,500 rpm, 500 rpm lower than on the S6. The reworked engine, bearing the code AHK, developed its maximum output of 326 hp at 6,500 rpm.

These measures improved the sprint to 100 km/h (62 mph) by 0.3 seconds compared to the S6 and enabled an appreciably higher top speed. Quattro GmbH did not offer an automatic transmission for the S6 plus.

V8
4.2
Audi
VOLKSWAGEN
AUDI
HANNO
SCELTO
Agip
ACHTUNG WARNING ATTENTION

PAINT CHOICES

Pearl effect: Nogaro Blue, Misano Red

STANDARD EQUIPMENT (EXCERPT)

Exterior:

- 17-inch aluminum wheels with 255/40 tires
- Xenon headlamps
- Enlarged rear spoiler
- Black accents on windows, roof rails and radiator grille

Audi sprayed all S6 colors and two exclusive special colors on the top model of the C4 line.

Xenon headlamps were part of the S6 plus standard equipment package.

The auxiliary instruments looked sporty, but were not limited to the S6 plus.

Magazine reports on Audi's sport wagon used the word "lounge-like" to describe the interior.

INTERIOR

- Sport seats covered in leather/Alcantara
- Black anodized door latches and handbrake knob
- Three-spoke sport steering wheel
- Instrument faces in white, blue or gray, speedometer calibrated to 300 km/h

FUNCTION

- Central locking with remote control
- Trunk pass-through with ski sack
- Cargo net (Avant only)
- 16-inch brake system

The Secret Project: The Audi/Porsche RS4

Even long before reaching its zenith as the S6 plus, Audi's C4 model line would be fitted with a premium powerplant. At the end of 1992, the car was still called the Audi 100; the manufacturer called its fastest model to date the S4. In it, the five-cylinder turbocharged engine produced 230 hp. Alternatively, a 280 hp V8 was available. The Audi/Porsche working group considered using the car as the basis for its "P1" project, which would later become the Avant RS2.

Internal Porsche documents describe very concrete plans for an Audi RS4. It was to be powered by a V8 engine; variants displacing 3.6 and 4.2 liters were under discussion. The targets: 325 hp and 5.4 seconds to 100 km/h (62 mph). It is no coincidence that these numbers represent what the S6 plus would later deliver.

The eight-cylinder was intended to appeal to customers in the United States, possibly because that market lacked acceptance for the five-cylinder. Audi imagined a price of $50,000 in the New World, but struggled in a very competitive market. In Germany, the RS4 in sedan form was expected to cost 130,000 Deutschmarks.

Porsche noted that the body needed to lose weight. In a thought experiment, such a diet also lowered the cost of the engine, because less weight meant less power was needed for good performance. On a normally-aspirated engine, every horsepower costs a great deal of money. Fifty kilograms (110 lbs) would have to be lost, by means including an aluminum engine hood. The decision makers quickly discarded any thoughts of additional aluminum components.

Audi planned to lower the car by 40 mm (more than 1.5 in.) through different springs and shock absorbers. Cross-spoke wheels, measuring 8x17 inches, were to round out the visuals. Porsche insisted that Audi's HP2 brakes were inadequate for the planned project; a Porsche brake system would be required.

Porsche designer, Roland Heiler, created renderings for an Audi RS4. The car was given a distinctive radiator grille with the shared logo, a large roof spoiler and a rear valance with molded-in script. The wheels and outside mirrors of this proposal were taken from the Porsche 911.

Both manufacturers discussed how much Porsche would be apparent in the finished car. The motto of the project was "Powered by Porsche." During development, emphasis shifted from scripts to styling themes. Heiler's sketches remained conceptual renderings; Audi and Porsche decided on the Audi 80 as a base platform.

This, however, did not mean the end of the project. After completing work on the RS2, Porsche again took up a car based on the C4 platform. The result was a wind tunnel model with a modified front end. However, Audi did not put this idea into production.

Ingolstadt was also working on the vision of a more powerful Audi 100. The RS4 sedan, sketched in-house, appeared considerably more restrained than the Porsche proposal. Visually, it largely resembled the Audi S4. Only the radiator grille was given a honeycomb insert instead of horizontal slats. In the red portion of the S4 logo, the designers added the letter R below the Audi rings. Audi has never provided technical specifications of the project, only a single photograph.

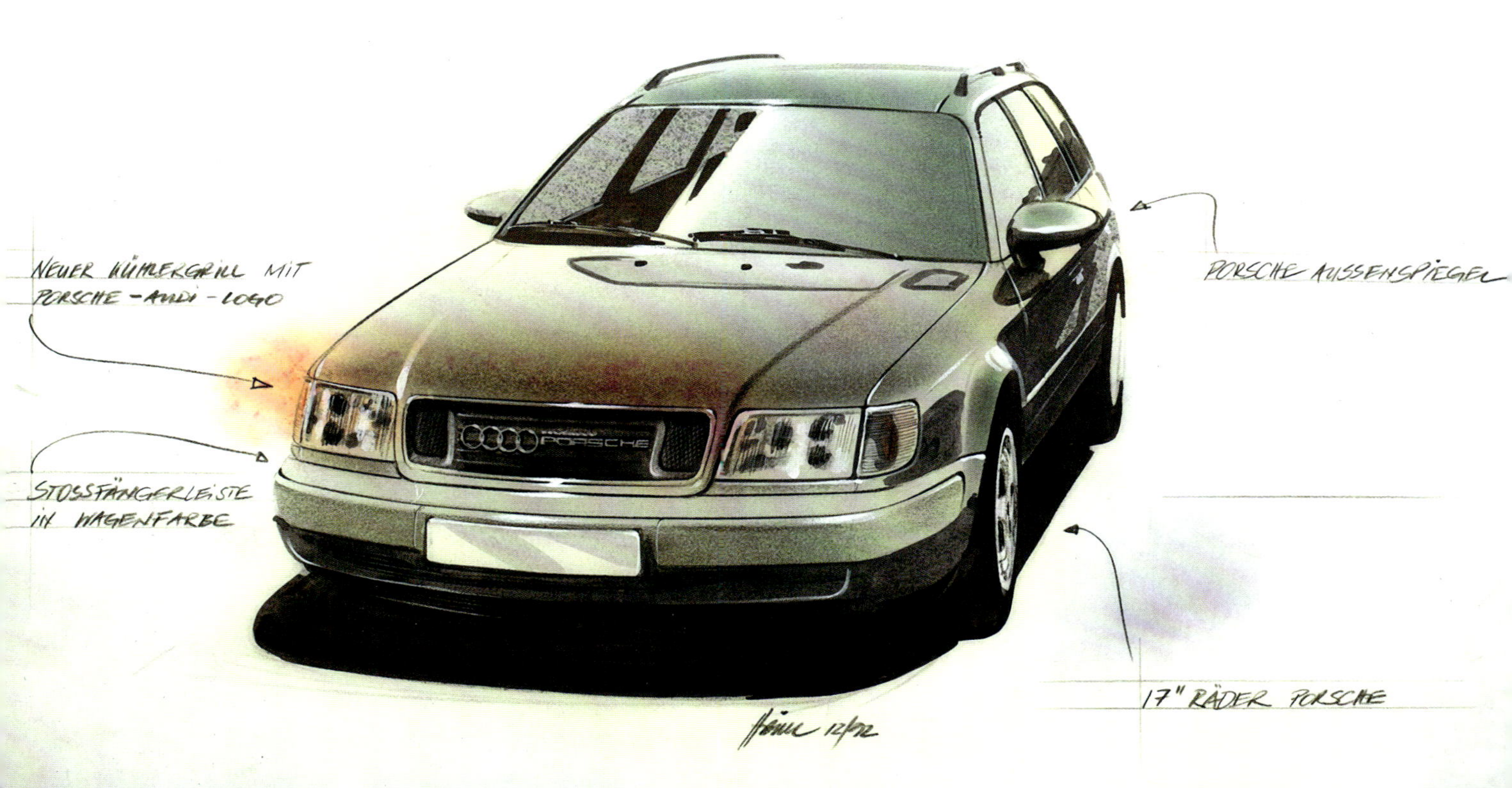

NEUER KÜHLERGRILL MIT PORSCHE-AUDI-LOGO

STOSSFÄNGERLEISTE IN WAGENFARBE

PORSCHE AUSSENSPIEGEL

17" RÄDER PORSCHE

12/92

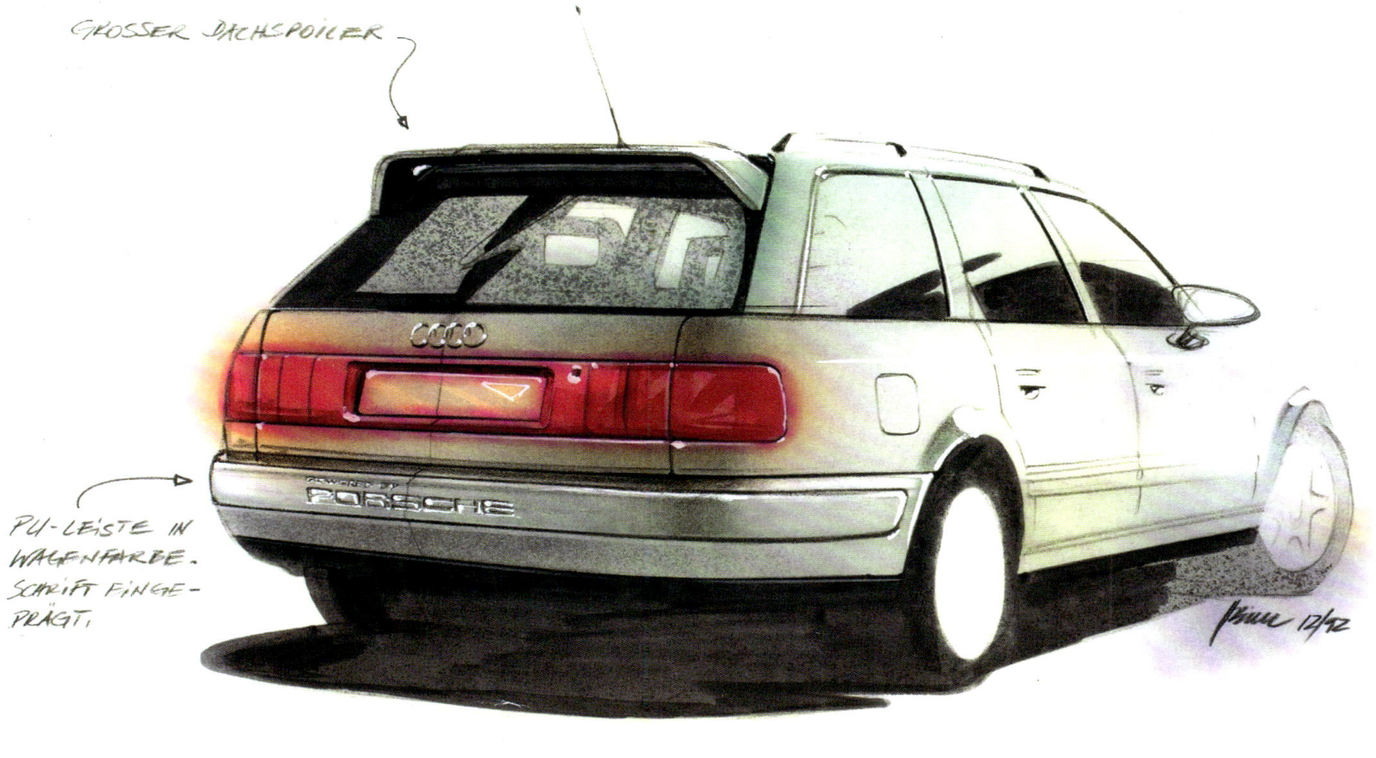

GROSSER DACHSPOILER

PU-LEISTE IN WAGENFARBE. SCHRIFT EINGEPRÄGT.

12/92

Audi RS 6 Avant & Sedan (C5)

2002-

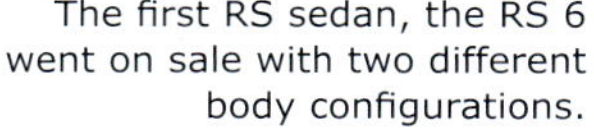
The first RS sedan, the RS 6 went on sale with two different body configurations.

In Neckarsulm, the end of RS4 production freed up capacity for a new sports model. There was no direct successor; the A4 would have to wait a few more years (and half a model generation) for its next transformation into an RS model. But the A6 had reached an appropriate age to justify laying on a high-performance variant. The first Audi RS 6 appeared in January 2002. With it came a new model nomenclature – from that point onward, all RS models carried a space in their names.

Audi itself did vital groundwork on the RS 6 of the C5 model line. The top model in the second A6 model line appeared with wider bodywork, just like the RS4 before it. The widened fenders were not created on the drawing boards of quattro GmbH, but rather at the parent organization.

The reason was Audi's desire for more performance in the upper middle-class market segment. Audi wanted to offer the eight-cylinder gasoline engine of the A8 in the A6 and the sporty S6 variant. However, the bulky engine, with its timing belt driven valvetrain, would not fit in the tight engine compartment of the standard A6 body.

A modified front end solved the problem. Audi created a new front end for the powerful versions. Front valance, engine hood and fenders were wrapped around the larger powerplant. These lengthened the car by almost 4 centimeters (about 1.5 in.). To at least partially compensate for the heavier engine, Audi formed the new fenders out of aluminum. The front hood was already made of the lighter material, even on the regular production models.

As part of the same process, the A6 V8 and S6 were given wider front and rear fender flares, adding two centimeters (almost one inch) per side. These covered 235 and 255 series tires, while the base Audi A6 still rolled on 205 series rubber. The widened A6, with eight cylinders, went into series production even before the RS4 appeared with its wider fenders.

AVANT AND SEDAN

Audi no longer needed to be involved with the sheetmetal work. In contrast to the recently discontinued RS4, for the top-of-the-line A6 model the sports subsidiary adopted normal production bodies – in two different variations, to be precise. For the first time, an RS model, in Avant and sedan form, was officially included in the price lists. The notchback was intended to appeal to American customers. Audi planned on building a total of 860 examples of the RS 6 sedan for the U.S. market. The model lasted for one year in the New World.

Add-on components visually distinguished the RS 6 from the less powerful V8 models. The car was given its own unique valances, wider rocker panel extensions, and its own roof spoiler (Avant) or trunk lip spoiler (sedan). Rub strips were deleted from the doors, while the front carried a unique grille design. Outside mirror housings, roof rails and the radiator grille frame gleamed in matte aluminum. Standard wheels at all four corners measured 18 inches in diameter; 19-inch rims were available as an added-cost option.

In the spring of 2002, *auto motor und sport* felt that the added inch was not enough to be obvious. The showoff effect

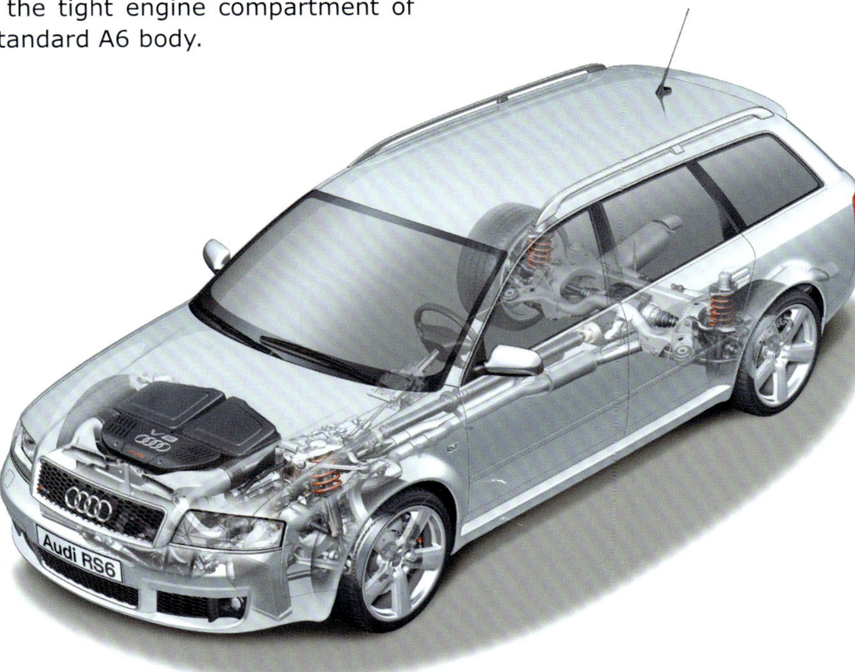

Under the hood of the RS 6, Audi's most powerful production engine to date performed its task with twin-turbo V8-generated 450 hp.

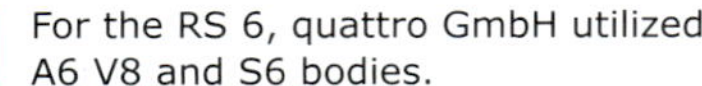

For the RS 6, quattro GmbH utilized A6 V8 and S6 bodies.

of the larger wheels was "essentially zero." Understatement was the RS 6's great strength. Above all, nobody expected this much power in a wagon – because nothing comparable had ever been seen.

THE MOST POWERFUL AUDI TO DATE

When the RS 6 debuted in the spring of 2002 at the Geneva Motor Show, it was the most powerful car in its segment. The soon to be discontinued Mercedes-Benz E 55 AMG (W210 model line, to late 2002) called on 354 horsepower, on the same level as the Audi S6. For the E39 generation, BMW gave its M5 more power, but this was still not enough – 400 hp put it in second place. The RS 6 took the crown, with 450 hp.

Cosworth Technology, which had already been responsible for the RS4 powerplant, teamed with quattro GmbH to develop the engine for the RS 6. Both Audi subsidiaries reworked the five-valve aluminum V8 of the S6, equipped it with two turbochargers, and raised output by 110 hp and torque by 140 Nm (103 ft-lbs). The marque's first turbocharged V8 gasoline engine exceeded the power output of all other Audi engines, by a considerable margin. Not even Audi's own W12 engine, in the A8, could match it.

The manual transmission of the Audi parts bins could not cope with such abundant power; these were not designed to take 560 Nm (413 ft-lbs) of torque. For this reason, the RS 6 was the first RS model to have an automatic transmission. Quattro GmbH adapted the five-speed automatic of the A8 6.0 W12. Reinforced housing, gearing and mounts, as well as faster shifts, matched the component for the more performance-oriented character of the RS 6. Additional cooling fins and special heat transfer paste between the cooling body and housing kept temperatures at the rear differential at acceptable levels.

DYNAMIC RIDE CONTROL TO COUNTER BODY ROLL

A more powerful engine and dynamic looks were not enough to make the wagon a real performer. The RS 6 was intended to throw its 1.9 metric tons around corners with authority – not an easy task for a car with a decidedly nose-heavy weight distribution. Audi's solution for this problem was called DRC, for Dynamic Ride Control. In aggressive driving, this innovative suspension concept reduced body roll and dive. In the sales brochure, Audi joked: "Caution! Sharp left-hand straight!"

The shock absorbers of the DRC suspension were connected diagonally via oil lines. Mechanical central valves

For the first time, quattro GmbH equipped an RS model with an automatic transmission.

Thirty Audi dealers dashed through the "Green Hell" with their brand-new RS 6s in the exhibition run on the Nürburgring.

in the lines controlled how far a shock absorber would be allowed to compress. During turning, acceleration or braking, the flow through the shock absorbers was deliberately adjusted, without any time delay. This made additional shock absorber reserves available, and the car superstructure exhibited less roll. The suspension absorbed road irregularities in a completely normal manner. Only the generally stiffer suspension tuning, compared to the regular production model, affected ride comfort in the RS 6.

Long term, the DRC suspension would become a constant in the RS program. In the first RS 6, it was a 650 Euro option. Journalists opined that it was money well spent. *auto motor und sport*, however, criticized the stiff tuning, and the behavior of the rear axle on wavy surfaces. Later, a weakness of the system would become apparent: if a shock absorber leaked, its opposite number would also suffer from low oil pressure and fail as well. Specialist service shops cited high failure rates and in the case of such failures, recommended retrofitting classic shock absorbers.

In the braking department, quattro GmbH went for size. At the front, the RS 6 was fitted with directional composite brake discs, with aluminum hat sections and gray iron friction rings, combined with eight-piston fixed calipers. At the rear, single-piston calipers and two-piece discs carried out their braking duties. In addition, quattro installed a large-diameter brake master cylinder, measuring 28 mm in diameter. In *auto motor und sport* testing, the sport wagon stopped with a deceleration rate in excess of 10 m/s² (32.8 ft/sec²), just slightly more than 1 g (9.8 m/sec², 32.2 ft/sec²).

Quattro GmbH sought a motorsports aura for the RS 6. For this reason, the manufacturer presented the car at a special event. Thirty Audi dealers started their maiden voyages in their demonstrator cars within the framework of the Nürburgring 24 Hours race. In front of 194,000 spectators, they covered 25,947 kilometers (16,123 miles) of the "Green Hell" with brand-new cars which they had taken possession of just minutes before. The exhibition race excited the fans as well as quattro boss Werner Frowein. He well knew the value of this demonstration.

AUDI RS 6 SPORT: FACTORY-ORIGINAL ACCESSORIES

Despite all efforts, the big wagon still did not feel convincingly sporty. To remedy this, Audi offered racy options for the

Audi did not completely build the RS 6 on the A6 assembly line. Quattro GmbH employed hand craftsmanship to finish each car.

Just before production ended, the most powerful Audi was made even more powerful. In the RS 6 plus, new engine tuning raised engine output to 480 hp.

RS 6. Customers could choose to have their cars equipped with various performance components, right on the assembly line. The program was less comprehensive than on the RS4 Sport, but covered the most important areas. In the RS 6 price lists, the subcategory "Sport" carried several options, generally affecting driving dynamics.

The offerings included cross-drilled brake rotors, a sport exhaust system with altered mufflers and black exhaust tips, as well as the DRC suspension. In addition, the list included floor mats, aluminum pedals and suede leather-covered automatic transmission selector lever and steering wheel. Audi advised that signs of wear might appear on the steering wheel. The complete package was priced at 3,800 Euros. Neither grippy performance tires nor bucket seats were offered.

With or without the sport package, the differences between the RS 6 and the regular A6 models were too extensive for the A6 assembly line production process in the Neckarsulm factory. The RS 6 rolled off the line ready to drive, but still incomplete. Thus, the cars were shipped to nearby quattro GmbH, where they were finished by hand craftsman. There, the workers filled the DRC suspension with oil, installed all composite parts to the body and completed the engine.

280 KM/H (174 MPH) TOP SPEED IN THE AUDI RS 6 PLUS

The RS 6 was not able to maintain its lead over the competition for long. In May 2002, it was still decidedly ahead, but in October of that year the new Mercedes-Benz E-Class (W211) closed the gap. In the E 55 AMG, a supercharged gasoline V8 yielded 476 hp. *auto motor und sport* compared both cars and named the Mercedes the winner. Deciding factors were acceleration and comfort.

Shortly before its model line ceased production, the RS 6 once again elbowed its way to the top. Quattro GmbH laid on a limited special edition, with sporting aspirations and a decent power increase. Optimized engine control increased the rev limit of the RS 6 plus, and stretched the torque curve. Power output rose by 30 hp to 480 hp. The hardware of the eight-cylinder remained unchanged; boost pressure was still 0.8 bar (11.6 psi), torque was also unchanged at 560 Nm (413 ft-lbs). To avoid any thermal problems, the RS 6 plus was fitted with two additional radiators, originally intended for export models shipped to hotter climes.

One key feature of the RS 6 plus was that for the first time since the RS2, an Audi officially topped out in excess of 250 km/h (155 mph). Quattro GmbH pushed the speed governor to 280 km/h (174 mph), making it the fastest sport wagon. In practice, its predecessors accomplished the same feat, but now it was officially stated in the car's papers. Ungoverned, the RS 6 plus could exceed 300 km/h (186 mph).

A large portion of the sport package was included as standard equipment on the RS 6 plus. Cross-drilled brake rotors and sport exhaust system were always included; the DRC suspension

The RS 6 plus offered interesting equipment options. The intent was to limit production to 999; in fact quattro GmbH only built 564 examples.

The twin-turbo engine of the RS 6 was based on the normally-aspirated V8 of the Audi S6. Cosworth Engineering developec and manufactured the top-of-the-line powerplant.

was a no-cost option. In addition, the car rolled on 19-inch wheels and special combinations of exterior paint and interior trim. Choices included "Blue" (exterior: pearl effect Sprint Blue, interior black leather with Alcantara silver seat center sections and carbon trim); "Silver" (Light Silver Metallic with black leather and black Alcantara center sections, matte aluminum décor trim) and "Black/Cognac" (Ebony Black Metallic, Cognac leather with black accents and piano black décor trim). Audi limited production to 999 Avants, but the RS 6 plus failed to meet this target; only 564 examples were built.

THE ENGINE OF THE AUDI RS 6

For the powerplant of the RS 6, quattro GmbH once again teamed with Cosworth. After production of the RS4 ended, Audi's British subsidiary converted its works in Wellingborough to production of the new engines. Based on the normally-aspirated gasoline V8 (engine code ANK), familiar from the S6, Cosworth created the turbocharged variant (code BCY). Twin turbochargers and intercoolers raised power output of the 4.2-liter five-valve engine, initially to 450 hp, then in the RS 6 plus to 480 hp. Cosworth used the crankshaft of the S6, with modifications. To withstand greater forces, in the RS 6 it was given ten instead of eight holes on the transmission side. Newly designed pistons lowered the compression ratio from 11:1 to 9.8:1. Modified cylinder heads improved combustion chamber cooling, while sodium-filled exhaust valves helped withstand high thermal loads. Between the block and cylinder heads, Cosworth installed head gaskets with four instead of three plies to ensure longer-term durability. A combination oil cooler lowered lubricant temperatures in the drivetrain. Two-thirds of its surface area served to cool the engine oil, while the remainder cooled the transmission oil. Both circuits also employed oil/water heat exchangers to quickly bring the lubricants to operating temperature. Two electric fans replaced the viscous-clutch fan of the base engine. An electric "run-on" water pump forced coolant through the engine after shutdown to prevent localized overheating in the vicinity of the turbochargers.

PAINT CHOICES (EXCERPT)

Metallic: Light Silver (RS 6 plus only)
Pearl effect: Avus Silver, Daytona Gray, Ebony Black, Goodwood Green, Mugello Blue, Sprint Blue (RS 6 plus only)

STANDARD EQUIPMENT (EXCERPT)

Exterior:

- 18-inch aluminum wheels with 255/35 tires
- Xenon plus headlamps
- Rear spoiler, rocker panel skirts, RS-specific front and rear valance
- Matte aluminum accents on window frames, roof rails and radiator grille

Decent conversion: valances, rocker panel skirts and deleted rub strips differentiated the RS 6 from the less powerful Audi S6.

Inside, only subtle details marked the RS 6 as the top-of-the-line model.

A whiff of motorsports in a production car: shift paddles on the reverse side of the steering wheel were reminiscent of Formula 1 practice.

INTERIOR

- Front leather sport seats
- Three-spoke sport steering wheel with shift paddles
- Décor inserts in carbon, poplar burl wood or piano black

FUNCTION

- Automatic climate control
- Concert CD radio with Bose speaker system
- Head airbag system
- 18-inch brake system

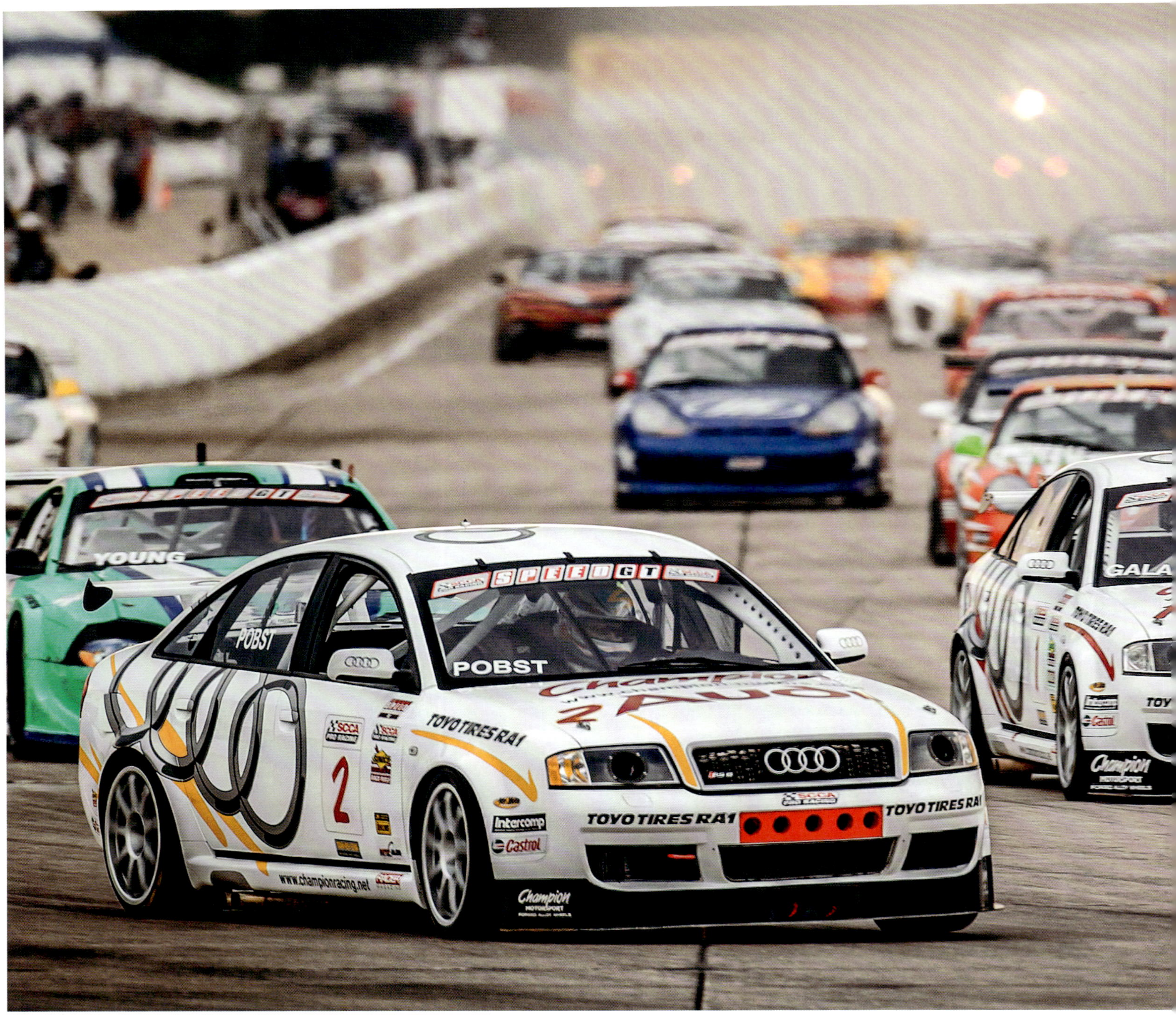
YOUNG
POBST
POBST
TOYO TIRES RA1
TOYO TIRES RA1
TOYO TIRES RA1
Intercomp
Castrol
www.championracing.net
2
GALA

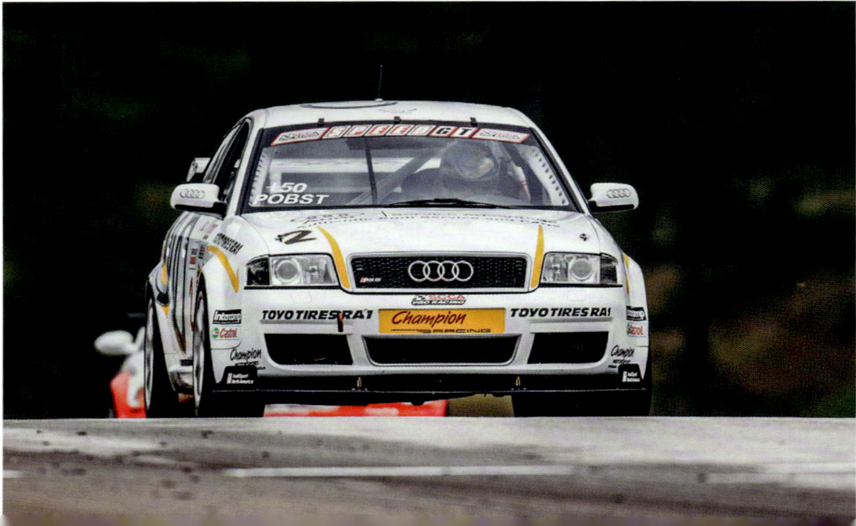

POBST
TOYO TIRES RA1
Champion
TOYO TIRES RA1

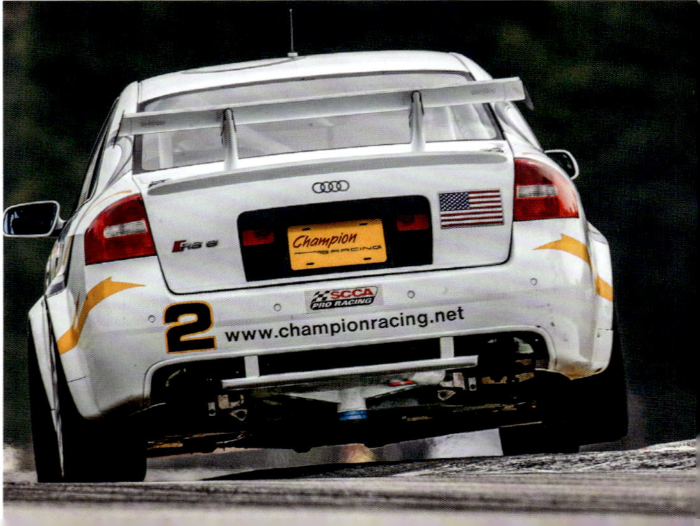

Champion
2
www.championracing.net

For the Speed GT racing series, Audi's heavy sedan was turned into a trim athlete at 1,383 kilograms, 475 hp and was immediately successful.

Randy Pobst drove the RS 6 to the championship in the car's motorsports debut. In the second season, his teammate Michael Galati finished second overall.

The Audi RS 6 C5 in motorsports

In the marketing-speak of the German press release, the Audi RS 6 was hailed as a production sports car. In North America, it truly became one. Champion Racing, the racing team fielded by the American Audi and Porsche dealership Champion Motors of Pompano Beach, Florida, entered the RS 6 sedan in the Speed World Challenge Series. In the 2003 and 2004 seasons, the car competed in the GT class within the framework of the American Le Mans Series (ALMS).

In the space of fifteen weeks, Champion Racing, with support from Audi, built the RS 6 racing version, the RS 6 Competition. The race car weighed 1,383 kg (3,049 lbs) – the minimum weight prescribed by the rules. Its biturbo V8 produced 475 hp and transmitted its power through a three-plate Tilton clutch, the six-speed manual transmission used in the Audi S4 and a modified drivetrain powering all four wheels. Adjustable anti-roll bars, Eibach springs, Öhlins shock absorbers, optimized brake system and a 100-liter (26.4 U.S. gallon) fuel tank made the car fit for competition.

Race drivers Michael Galati and Randy Pobst piloted the two entered vehicles. Pobst won the championship in the car's first season – an incentive for Audi to invest more resources. In the following season, the team was called the "Audi Certified Champion RS 6 Team." In keeping with rules changes, the cars now raced with reduced boost pressure, more power (525 hp) and more weight (1,400 kg, 3,086 lbs). Galati finished second in the final standings, Pobst fourth. Audi withdrew from the series to concentrate on the customer sports R8. The second-place car of the second season is now owned by New German Performance, an independent repair shop with locations in Maryland and Virginia.

2008–

Audi RS 6 Avant & Sedan (C6)

For the first time, 300 km/h (186 mph)

The fastest production wagon bore Audi rings. During its production run, no competitor could catch the RS 6 C6.

The second-generation Audi RS 6 started production in April 2008. For quattro GmbH, the new top model represented both a pinnacle and a departure. Its five-liter V10 was clearly a superlative engine, the biggest RS engine ever built. With its 580 hp, it made its predecessor – itself the most powerful Audi of its day – come off like an ordinary S model. After the V10, quattro GmbH restructured its production and turned over more tasks to Audi.

Above all, this car marked a truly unusual situation. The C6 was the last car for which Audi would develop an engine that would power an RS model exclusively. All succeeding powerplants would be distributed among several different models. In addition, quattro GmbH increasingly assigned production of its RS models to the same plants that built the more mundane models bearing the A and Q designations. Partial assembly in the main plant, followed by complex custom manufacturing at quattro GmbH, would no longer be carried out on such a large scale.

Until that condition was achieved, however, RS final assembly in Neckarsulm would still be full up with work. Previously, a model changeover at quattro GmbH meant that one RS model departed the scene, as another took its place. Now, two model lines were being built simultaneously. Production of the RS 6 started before RS 4 production finally ceased at the Neckarsulm factory. For a few months, final assembly of both cars was carried out side by side. The assembly processes were flexible enough that this posed no problem.

WIDE FENDERS AND A TIGHT ENGINE COMPARTMENT

Tradition played a vital role in the new RS 6. Its edgy fenders were intended to mimic the 1980 Audi quattro – a styling feature that Audi would often quote in the course of the following years. Together, the wider fender flares added 3 cm (1.2 in.) in width, on top of the regular production car's width of 1.86 meters (73.2 in.)

Still, the regular production body just would not do for the RS 6. It needed to carry larger wheels and attract attention. Accordingly, Audi pressed new quarter panels with extended fender flares, altered rear doors, wider aluminum fenders and a modified cargo area floor, all produced in the Hungarian plant at Győr. In addition, the rear inner fenders and jacking points on the rocker panels were different. The sedan was given its own unique trunk lid with an integrated ducktail spoiler.

This catalog of changes was nothing unusual for Audi's logistics. In the Neckarsulm plant, special sheetmetal components alternated with regular production parts on the A6 assembly line. The shells of the fastest sport wagons came together among businessmens' diesels and family sedans, but there was insufficient time to install the complex engine. Again, partially completed RS models rolled off the line and went to quattro GmbH. Located at the same facility, this represented a mere relocation within the plant. The work that needed to be done in quattro's assembly shops was hardly any different from the scope of previous projects. The bodies still lacked model-specific composite parts, along with several engineering elements. However, the unique characteristics of the RS 6 C6 and its huge engine made final assembly more difficult. Quattro chief developer Stephan Reil said that he was not aware of a tighter engine bay than that of this car.

Even in the S6, space limitations made it difficult to work on the normally-aspirated V10. Working on the twin-turbo ten-cylinder of the RS 6 was more like wallpapering a room – through the mail slot. It took up to 25 hours to turn the basically drivable, but naked car, into a completed Audi RS 6. This process was too complex to be continued long term, but was necessary to build the world's fastest wagon.

ADAPTIVE SHOCK ABSORBERS AND CERAMIC BRAKES

This superlative applied above all on straight roads. There, the RS 6 showed the world the meaning of speed. With ten cylinders, five liters of displacement, two turbochargers and 580 hp, it could theoretically reach 315 km/h (196 mph). The manufacturer put a lid on things at 250 km/h (155 mph) or, optionally, 280 km/h (174 mph). In terms of power output, it overshadowed all competitors and even the Audi R8. When the RS 6 was finally knocked off its throne, it enjoyed a long retirement on the used car market. In view of these specifications, *Autocar* tester Chris Harris asked the question: "How much is too much?"

To transfer this power to the wheels, Audi converted a special version of the A8

Ten cylinders, twin turbochargers and 580 hp; quattro GmbH would never again install so much engine in an RS model.

W12 six-speed automatic transmission, with the internal designation 09E. The changes improved its durability, cooling, shift speeds and power distribution. With heat exchangers for both oil circuits, the mechatronics of the modern A4 transmission (type 0B6) and rearward power distribution, the gearbox was a good fit for the RS 6 concept. Although more modern alternatives to the classic torque converter automatic had already established themselves in the market, the transmission enjoyed favorable comments from the automotive media.

To ensure that the massive propulsion lump at the front of the car did not throw the RS 6 into the weeds, quattro GmbH again reached for its DRC suspension. After its debut in the C5 model line, this design, with its shock absorbers connected diagonally via oil lines had become an RS standard. This was fitted to the new model as standard equipment. In addition, adaptive shock absorbers were listed as options. These permitted ride characteristics ranging between soft comfort and firm sporting character.

Size, power and technology all represent additional weight. Compared to its predecessor, the super Audi gained 140 kg (308 lbs); in base trim, it was the first to break the two (metric) tonne barrier. Six-piston calipers grabbing 39 cm discs slowed its considerable mass, converting kinetic energy into friction and heat. For an additional 8,200 Euros, Audi could install eight-piston calipers and 42 cm ceramic rotors. Fitted with the optional brakes, *Auto Bild* measured a stopping distance from 100 km/h (62 mph) of less than 35 meters (115 feet) – "a record," declared the magazine.

According to *Auto Bild*, the major suspension and brake package were a boon to the RS 6 Performance. Despite its nose-heavy weight distribution – 60 percent of its weight hung over the front axle – the magazine praised the Audi after comparing it with the Mercedes-Benz E63 AMG T and the BMW M5 Touring: "Audi builds the fastest racing wagon – it's unbeatable on the track." On a short handling course, it outran the BMW by nearly one second, the Mercedes by two seconds. To be fair, the Audi did enter the fray with an appreciable horsepower advantage.

THE MOST POWERFUL WAGON

Audi and quattro GmbH saw the car's power as a vital sales argument. They presented the RS 6 as the world's most powerful wagon. The manufacturers packaged the full opulence of the engine compartment in one modest sentence: "A supercharged ten-cylinder is the ideal engine for sporty dynamics." Their reasoning: it is lighter, smaller and more efficient than a twelve-cylinder. That much was true – but it still weighed 278 kg (613 lbs) and most of that was hung out ahead of the front axle.

This had little effect on longitudinal dynamics. Several car magazines measured its 0-100 km/h (62 mph) acceleration times and got values between 4.3 and 4.4 seconds. That the RS 6 could have a wild side was signaled at the press introduction. A sport mode for the active safety systems "... allows experienced drivers to execute magnificent drifts on low-traction surfaces." But when it came to

tight corners, the Audi came up against its limits. Shortly after the end of its production run, *sport auto* compared the RS 6 with the new Mercedes-Benz E63 AMG T-model. In a tight 180-meter slalom and on the Hockenheim handling course, the well-balanced marque with the star could easily outperform the nose-heavy Audi. Nevertheless, in a straight line, the RS 6 remained untouchable.

AUDI RS 6 PLUS: 303 KM/H (188 MPH) TOP SPEED

In the top speed department, Audi gave the RS a special sendoff. Shortly before the end of production, the manufacturer issued a limited special edition. Five hundred examples of the RS 6 plus were built. In contrast to its predecessors, it was not given extra power; output of the V10 remained at 580 hp. But the manufacturer did install a different speed limiter. The special models could get up to 303 km/h (188 mph). Within Audi, only the R8 was faster.

The 2010 farewell edition could be configured with two equipment packages. The RS 6 plus Sport (added cost of 3,250 Euros) had a leather-covered center console and instrument panel. Audi also offered the RS 6 plus Executive (option price: 8,310 Euros) in a unique color and had more leather-covered interior parts from the quattro GmbH accessory catalog.

Both versions were equipped with 20-inch wheels, the "sport suspension plus," navigation system, driving assistant and the carbon fiber package in the engine compartment. Unlike its predecessor, this time Audi was able to sell the entire planned production run.

THE ENGINE OF THE AUDI RS 6

A special car needs a special engine and this one was exceptional. Audi designed the biturbo setup of the ten-cylinder strictly for the RS 6. It was a member of the company's gasoline V engine family. The cylinder spacing (90 mm) and bank angle (90°) were shared with the 3.2-liter V6 of the A6 and the 4.2-liter V8 of the RS 4. For this, the biggest engine of the family, the manufacturer extended the eight-cylinder block by two more pistons, to an overall length of 685 mm (27 in.).

Audi built three versions of the ten-cylinder. One variation powered the big S6 and S8 sedans; another the R8 and Lamborghini Gallardo super sports cars. The RS 6 was given the most powerful version and the only one to be turbocharged. It shared many components with its siblings, but must be regarded as a standalone engine. About 400 parts were completely new. In general, it had more in common with the sports cars.

As on the normally-aspirated versions, the engine block consisted of two parts, a so-called bedplate design. This construction incorporated all crankshaft main bearing caps into a frame-like component, the bedplate, which reinforced the bottom of the crankcase. Audi cast the parts for all versions using the same aluminum alloys and reinforced the main bearings by using cast iron inserts.

Unlike the engines of the S6 and S8, the RS 6 did not employ a balance shaft. The crankshaft resembled that of the R8. For increased strength, each crankpin carried two connecting rods; on the S6 and S8, the split crankpins had an 18° offset. The RS 6 crankshaft had its stroke reduced by 3.8 mm, to 89 mm. This reduced displacement from 5.2 to 5.0 liters. Audi reduced the turbo motor's compression ratio from 12.5:1 to 10.5:1.

In another parallel to the R8 and Lamborghini Gallardo, Audi gave the RS 6 a dry sump lubrication system. This provided the engine a reliable oil supply, even under extreme lateral acceleration. Due to the engine's altered orientation, the engineers designed a dedicated oil cooler mounted ahead of the engine, in the airstream. The mid-engined sports cars cooled their engine oil using a ventilation duct in the left rear vehicle flank.

An intake manifold without flaps, new exhaust manifolds, turbochargers and intercoolers completed the RS 6 power unit. Retained were the direct-injection system, four-valve technology and variable timing for all valves. With 0.7 bar (10 psi) boost pressure, the engine produced 650 Nm (479 ft-lbs) of torque in the band from 1,500 to 6,250 rpm. Between 6,250 and 6,700 rpm, 580 hp were on tap. *auto motor und sport* summed it up: "The turbochargers were provided by IHI, which sounds like hee hee, and feels like it, too." The engine propelled the car in a "downright arrogant" manner and allowed it to move like a much lighter model.

PAINT CHOICES (EXCERPT)

Metallic: Monza Silver
Pearl effect: Misano Red, Sepang Blue, Daytona Gray, Monterey Green, Mugello Blue, Phantom Black

STANDARD EQUIPMENT (EXCERPT)

Exterior:

- 19-inch aluminum wheels with 255/40 tires
- Xenon plus headlamps with adaptive cornering lights
- Rear spoiler, rocker panel skirts, RS-specific front and rear valance
- Matte aluminum accents on window frames, roof rails and radiator grille

Box fender flares recalled the design of the 1980 Audi quattro. On the RS 6 C6, these covered factory-installed 19- or 20-inch rims.

Audi built its last RS 6 sedan with the C6 generation. Soon, a Sportback would replace the classic notchback.

In the C6 generation, the MMI (Multi Media Interface) controls moved to the center console. This made it easier to operate the rotary/push knob while driving.

INTERIOR

- Integral power adjustable front leather sport seats
- Three-spoke multifunction sport steering wheel, flattened at bottom, with shift paddles
- Décor inserts in carbon
- Slotted interior door latches

FUNCTION

- Automatic climate control
- MMI Radio plus with Bose surround sound and Bluetooth interface
- 19-inch brake system
- Parking assistant
- DRC sport suspension

THE STUDY: AUDI NUVOLARI QUATTRO

Audi announced the 2008 RS 6 as early as 2003. At the Geneva Motor Show, the manufacturer presented the Nuvolari quattro styling study. The big coupe introduced the firm's new design vocabulary, with its single frame radiator grille. The interior resembled the later C6-platform A6 model line.

Even at the Geneva show, Audi chief Martin Winterkorn said that the study would be too expensive to put into production. But the engine would come. The concept car contained a 5-liter twin-turbo ten-cylinder developing 600 hp, in other words roughly what would later propel the RS 6.

2013–

Audi RS 6 Avant (C7)

Downsizing in the 600 hp class

With less weight and better weight distribution, the RS 6 got even faster after the model changeover even though it lost some power.

The C6 generation RS 6, with its *übermotor,* was succeeded by a more understated car – at least, understated by RS standards. In the just discontinued RS 6, quattro GmbH showed how much engine could be packed into an upper mid-range car. The engineers were able to squeeze ten cylinders into the engine bay, and still bolt two turbochargers to the manifolds. The RS 6 C7, on the other hand, put an end to the philosophy of massive powertrains. For the first time, the era of downsizing had begun for an RS model. Accordingly, the new RS 6 was given a 4-liter powerplant, the smallest engine of its model line to date.

In view of the new product orientation, many a fan of the power-by-mass philosophy might have wept an oil-stained tear or two. Still, the RS 6 did not necessarily have to represent pure power and size. Naturally, a V10 is fast. That does not mean that a V8 cannot be a better alternative. Meet the Audi RS 6, C7 model line. With a smaller engine (V8) and less power (560 hp), yet better dynamics. Especially when going sideways.

How can restraint lead to greater excesses? By means of a more refined overall package. The greatest strength of the preceding model had also been its greatest flaw. The huge, heavy engine extended far ahead of the front axle. In turns, the long nose forced the RS 6 V10 to the outside. In a straight line, it had hardly any challengers, but when the road got twisty, it got in its own way. The main target of the successor model's development program was to make the RS 6 more nimble. There was an urgent need to lose weight, especially over the front wheels.

LIGHTWEIGHT PLATFORM

A new platform helped the RS 6 achieve this goal. In 2007, Audi introduced the "modular longitudinal platform" in the A5 line. Just over three years later, the A6 adopted the new architecture. Moreover, Audi invested more resources in expensive materials for the bodies of its upper mid-range models. On the A6, all bolt-on body parts were made of aluminum. The front strut dome supports and the D-pillar nodes were made of cast aluminum. Aluminum extrusions were used for crossmembers and strut tower braces. All other components were made of steel, formed using various methods.

While the body was made stiffer and lighter by these methods, another change improved the car's balance. This too was a direct benefit of the platform. A new transmission layout moved the torque converter behind the front-axle shafts. In all, this moved the drivetrain a good 15 cm (6 in.) rearward. The engine no longer extended quite so far forward of the axle.

Combined with the shorter, lighter V8 engine of the new RS 6, the result was much better weight distribution. On the preceding model, the front wheels still needed to carry nearly 59 percent of the weight. In the new version, depending on equipment this was reduced to 52 to 55 percent – about 100 kilograms (220 pounds) less. The "little" engine was not just more economical; above all, its improved weight distribution also yielded a positive benefit in handling. After its first drive, *Auto Zeitung* titled its report: "A Statement Against Inertia."

PASSING THE PREDECESSOR – AT 305 KM/H (190 MPH)

Despite all this, the RS 6 had to contend with negative preconceptions. In bench racing sessions, a loss of 20 hp compared to the discontinued model sounded like a major setback. That might be true in terms of peak performance, but in practice things looked quite different. Despite the numbers on paper, the new car was faster in every way. Thanks to

The smallest RS engine to date in the upper mid-range models: a 4.0-liter, twin-turbo V8 developing 560 hp powered the new RS 6.

Launch Control and fast-shifting eight-speed automatic, the RS 6 sprinted to 100 km/h (62 mph) in 3.9 seconds, a good half second faster than the earlier car. In its fastest configuration it topped out at 305 km/h (190 mph). This beat the discontinued RS 6 plus by 2 km/h (just over 1 mph). With the update, the top speed option was available to all RS 6 customers, not just for special editions. The only requirement was that the "Dynamic Plus" package, with ceramic brakes, dynamic steering, sport differential and suspension, LED lamps, automatically dimming inside mirror and higher rear tire pressures had to be ordered.

The performance numbers were impressive, but gave no indication of the new RS 6's most outstanding quality. The specifications sheet only hinted at it; thanks to better weight distribution, finally the car was able to gobble up curves. *sport auto* set a new internal record for sport wagons on the Hockenheim short course, at 1:13.7 minutes, and found some words of praise: "One might have one's own opinion about a two-ton wagon on a race track, but what the new Audi RS 6 Avant delivers is impressive, and not just in its own class. It simply does everything better than its predecessor, is hellishly fast, and despite that, is more economical."

AIR SUSPENSION, CERAMIC BRAKES

Along with the diet, the reworked power distribution was a major contributor to improved performance. A new Torsen differential debuted in the RS 6. It worked on the same principle as that of the RS 4 B7, that is, distributed torque by means of a planetary transmission, 40 percent to the front, 60 percent to the rear. As needed in the event of wheel slip, the differential redistributed the driving torque. In this latest generation (Torsen CSM) the unit weighed only 3.2 kg (7 lbs), less than half the weight of the old version (6.9 kg, 15.2 lbs).

As standard equipment, Audi expanded the system to include wheel-selective torque vectoring – a novelty in connection with a Torsen differential – and optionally offered a rear sport differential. *sport auto* explained the system to its readers as follows: "On snow-covered mountain roads, such as the road from Chur to Arosa in Switzerland, all-wheel drive fun is pre-programmed. The RS 6 scores points

The optional ceramic brakes handled high loads with nary a complaint. They remained up to the task long after the tires had given up.

not only for its outstanding traction; under load, the back end comes out ever so slightly."

In addition, Audi equipped an RS model with air suspension. For the RS 6, the manufacturer programmed a sporty application of its "adaptive air suspension," lowered by 20 mm (nearly 0.8 in.) and immediate, but perfectly usable suspension tuning for everyday use. The traditional DRC suspension, with adaptive damping and stiffer tuning was available as an option; this had been part of the model line since 2002. A more recent addition to the program, but still firmly linked to the RS 6, was the front ceramic brake option, once again measuring 420 mm. According to *sport auto*, in their "super test" which emphasized race track performance, these performed "flawlessly and without fade." Even when the optional 285-section tires reached their limits as they heated up.

In order to fit these wheels and suspension bits under the car, quattro GmbH widened the wagon's bodywork by 6.2 cm (3.5 in.) For the RS 6, only the front doors and roof skin were carried over from the regular production car; the rest of the sheetmetal was designed specifically for the top-end model, along with new valances and door sills. For customers desiring a bit less understatement, Audi offered to place optional "quattro" script at the front.

The RS 6 was built in Neckarsulm, on the same line as the A6. For the complex car, quattro GmbH again employed the familiar, convoluted process. While other RS models rolled out of various other plants in completely finished form, the wagon, just before completion, once again visited the quattro assembly shops. There, among other things, the valances and sills were attached, and the DRC suspension filled with oil.

AUDI RS 6 PERFORMANCE: 605 HP

Beginning in 2015, the RS 6 demonstrated that its V8 did not need to lag behind the old ten-cylinder. Now the RS 6 Performance outdid the old Audi even in the one aspect that had been denied before – power output. With detail modifications to the engine, output rose to 605 hp. For brief bursts, the "Dynamic" driving mode allowed peak torque of 750 Nm (553 ft-lbs) on "overboost."

With this added power, the dash to 100 km/h (62 mph) was accomplished 0.2 seconds faster (3.7 seconds), and 200 km/h (124 mph) was reached 1.4 seconds sooner (12.1 seconds). Depending on equipment, Audi limited top speed to 250, 280 or 305 km/h (155, 174, or 190 mph). Standard equipment included 21-inch wheels; extras to improve driving dynamics were available as added-cost options.

SPECIAL MODEL: 705 HP, RECALLING THE RS2

In early 2018, just before the end of the C7 model line, Audi once again laid on another especially fast and tradition-conscious RS 6. With its color (Nogaro Blue) and seat covers (black/blue), the "Nogaro Edition" mimicked the 1994 RS2. Alternatively, the special edition, based on the RS 6 Performance with 605 hp, could be ordered with black paintwork.

Audi distributed its nostalgia editions generously throughout its model lineup. A similar package graced the 2014 RS 4; another decorated the RS 6 that followed, and other fast models. In the case at hand, the manufacturer limited production to 150 examples, and certified this limitation by a plaque in the interior. An optional highlight for this RS 6 was an available performance package provided by aftermarket tuning company Abt Sportsline. This raised power output of the biturbo V8 to 705 hp and increased top speed to 320 km/h (199 mph). The price: 152,800 Euros.

THE ENGINE OF THE RS 6: A NEW V8 TURBO

The switch from V10 to V8 might sound like a fundamentally new approach. On the engineering side, that was only partially correct, because both powerplants were part of the same engine family. Audi's new 4.0-liter twin-turbo engine was based on the same 4.2-liter normally-aspirated engine from which the manufacturer had derived the ten-cylinder in the first place.

The limited-edition RS 6 in Nogaro Blue took after its predecessors, and was optionally available with up to 705 hp.

RS
V8 TFSI

With improved weight distribution and a new platform, the RS 6 was more agile in curves. It was also quicker on the straights.

Parallels between the engines were, however, limited to the configuration of the engine blocks. The V8 retained the bedplate design with cast iron inserts, the 90-degree bank angle, and the most significant dimensions. The engine family had a 90 mm cylinder spacing and 84.5 mm bore. A 90 mm stroke resulted in a displacement of 4.0 liters. However, there were deviations from the pattern. Even with its cooling passages, the latest evolution differed from its siblings.

The biggest difference from previous Audi engines was that the engineers reversed the cylinder head layout. Previously, the V engines had drawn their air from a bridge between the cylinder heads, and exhausted the burned gases to the side of the engine. The EA 824 engine family now got a so-called "hot V." Using this principle, the exhaust side, with its two turbochargers, was located inside the V of the cylinder banks. This layout shortened the gas passages, for improved turbocharger response, and reduced the overall size of the powerplant.

To save fuel in part-throttle operation, Audi installed a cylinder deactivation system. Whenever the engine was not called upon to deliver more than 250 Nm (184 ft-lbs) of torque and was turning less than 3,500 rpm, the system deactivated cylinders 2, 3, 5, and 8 by means of actuators that pushed the cams for those cylinders aside so that they no longer moved the cam followers, allowing the valves to remain closed. A special program in the engine control software also shut off the spark plugs and fuel injectors to those cylinders.

Thanks to this measure, Audi saved ten to twelve grams of CO_2 per kilometer in the test cycle. Combined with the standard stop-start system, CO_2 emissions were cut by as much as 24 grams. According to the standardized test cycle, the RS 6 used only 9.8 liters per 100 kilometers (24 miles per U.S. gallon). The main drawback of this concept was that four-cylinder operation resulted in excessive vibration. To suppress these, Audi installed active engine mounts. These operated like loudspeakers, setting up counter-oscillations to cancel engine vibrations. By this means, the RS 6 engine achieved near-V8 levels of comfort with half the number of pistons. Whatever remained of the vibration was countered by an intelligent "countersound" system.

The engine premiered in 2012 in the Audi S6, developing 420 hp. For service in the RS 6, diverse details were modified. It was given different turbochargers, pistons, valve timing and an optimized intake manifold. This resulted in 560 hp. For use in the RS 6 Performance, Audi optimized the turbocharger geometry, installed different exhaust valves, and new engine control software to raise output to 605 hp.

With cylinder deactivation and a stop-start system, the RS 6 of the C7 generation had improved fuel economy.

PAINT CHOICES (EXCERPT)

Solid color: Ibis White, Nardo Gray
Metallic: Ascari Blue
Pearl effect: Misano Red, Sepang Blue, Daytona Gray, Mythos Black, Glacier White
Crystal effect: Panther Black, Prism Silver
Matte effect: Daytona Gray

STANDARD EQUIPMENT (EXCERPT)

Exterior:

- 20-inch aluminum wheels with 275/35 tires
- Xenon plus headlamps with cleaning system, LED taillamps; after facelift: LED headlamps
- Rear spoiler, rocker panel skirts, RS-specific front and rear valance
- Matte aluminum accents on window frames, roof rails and radiator grille

The RS 6 carried over only the front doors and roof skin from the standard production model. All other sheetmetal was new.

An eight-speed automatic transmission distributed the V8 engine's power to all four wheels via a Torsen differential.

For the first time, quattro GmbH installed an air suspension in the RS 6, in order to improve ride comfort.

INTERIOR

- RS power adjustable front leather and Alcantara sport seats
- Three-spoke multifunction sport steering wheel, flattened at bottom, with shift paddles
- Décor inserts in carbon
- Slotted interior door latches

FUNCTION

- Automatic climate control
- MMI Radio plus with Bose surround sound and Bluetooth interface
- 19-inch brake system
- Parking assistant
- RS adaptive air suspension
- RS exhaust system

Audi RS 7 Sportback (C7)

The slim twin

2013–

Standard equipment included a steel brake system with wave discs at the hubs of the RS 7. Ceramic rotors were available as an option.

In the summer of 2013, quattro GmbH introduced a new RS model. Henceforth, the RS 7 Sportback would take the place of the RS 6 sedan in the portfolio. The five-door coupe, with the svelte back end, began life as an independent model with lofty aspirations. Audi positioned the car as the only RS in the top market segment, in other words, one level above the RS 6. The manufacturer regarded this goal as achieved, because it combined "the design of a coupe, the space of a sedan, and the variability of a wagon" – and because Mercedes-Benz positioned its competing model, the CLS Shooting Brake, in the same way.

Despite the perceived class difference, Audi built the body of the RS 7 in almost exactly the same way as that of the RS 6. Both cars used the same platform, and a comparable mix of materials. The frame of the passenger cabin consisted of hot-formed steel, the front end and floorpan were made of high-strength steel, and the door sills of ultra-high-strength steel. The strut domes and rear door mounting supports were made of cast aluminum; crossmember, shock tower brace, doors, hood and rear door were made of aluminum – all analogous to the upper mid-range model.

In one aspect, the RS 7 even offered something less. In contrast to its sister model RS 6, the body of the RS 7 did not differ from that of the base model A7. Even the regular production car, part of the Audi lineup since 2010, measured 1.91 meters (75.2 in.) in width, just two centimeters less than the RS 6. If quattro GmbH were to modify the sheetmetal in the same way, the car would be simply too wide for everyday use. In addition, wheels with increased negative offset would adversely affect the driving characteristics. Theoretically, a widened RS 7 would need negative offset purely for visual reasons, otherwise the wheels would be lost deep within the fenders.

A subtle widening, by one centimeter per side, would have been possible, but would not achieve the desired effect. For this reason, quattro GmbH waived the traditional conversion and the associated increase in tire width. Instead of the originally conceived 285-series tires, the car's optional 21-inch wheels carried tires that only measured 275/30. This was a justifiable compromise, which also saved on development costs.

Aside from body changes, on its way to becoming a sports car the A7 had the full RS program applied to it. The front valance directed air to the intercoolers, which Audi mounted on the left and right sides under the headlamps. The rear bumper integrated traditional oval (fist sized) exhaust trim extensions that revealed the (egg sized) exhaust tips. Wide rocker panel extensions and a new radiator grille completed the RS appearance package.

TECHNICALLY AN AUDI RS 6

The RS 7 copied all of its engineering from the RS 6. It took its 4.0-liter, twin-turbo V8 that developed 560 hp (as of 2015 in the RS 7 Performance: 605 hp), its eight-speed torque converter automatic transmission (tiptronic) and Torsen differential, front and rear suspension and brake system (wave discs and six-piston calipers). Once again quattro GmbH benefited from the modular platform principle. Although the nomenclature suggested differences, the mechanics remained unchanged.

The same was true for the optional vehicle dynamics systems. Just as on the RS 6, the options list of the RS 7

For the facelift, Audi switched the standard headlamps of the RS 7 from Bi-Xenon to LED technology.

After the success of the Mercedes-Benz CLS, Audi could not do without a large, five-door coupe.

included a sport rear differential, sport suspension plus (with Dynamic Ride Control), dynamic steering and ceramic brakes. Various option packages increased top speed from 250 km/h (155 mph) to 280 (174 mph) or 305 km/h (190 mph). There were only marginal differences in performance of the technically identical twins; with its flat roof, the RS 7 offered slightly better aerodynamics. Functionally, the RS 7 stood out in the points that made the RS 7 different. Its attractive shape represented, above all, restraint. Rear-seat occupants had limited head- and kneeroom (and this in a luxury car!) and had a limited luggage allowance. Still, Audi did not want to be without this body variant. Mercedes-Benz had been building a four-door luxury coupe since 2004; BMW joined the fray in 2012. With their AMG and M models, both offered direct competition to the RS 7. And then there was the brand sibling, Porsche, with its Panamera.

Auto Bild sportscars compared all four models and declared the Audi the winner. The RS 7 prevailed against the CLS 63 AMG, M6 and Panamera Turbo because it offered the best overall package. The trade magazine determined that in this market segment, it just was not possible to be competitive without all-wheel drive. At Audi, this had been standard equipment on its sport models since 1980. The Porsche was faster, but could not justify its roughly 40,000 Euro higher price.

Somewhat later, *auto motor und sport* confirmed these test results, with a less extensive comparison test of its own. They pitted the RS 7 Performance against the BMW M6 Gran Coupe Competition in the 600 hp class. Audi was the clear winner, collecting 443 points against BMW's 392. The "RS Performance always keeps its power under control, is astoundingly comfortable, very safe, reasonably thirsty, but not a sports car." BMW lost because the M6 promised to be exactly that – a sports car – but came across as too vehement for its class.

PROTOTYPES: AUDI RS 7 PILOTED DRIVING CONCEPTS "BOBBY" AND "ROBBY"

Shape and appeal made the RS 7 a special car. In the fall of 2014, this aura was expanded. Audi converted its luxury coupe into an autonomously driving race car. The prototype, nicknamed "Bobby," lapped the Hockenheimring grand prix course in a demonstration drive during the DTM (German Touring Car Masters) finale weekend, driverless, in just over two minutes, reaching a top speed of 230 km/h (143 mph). "Bobby" was named in honor of American racing legend Bobby Unser, who had won the 1986 Pikes Peak Hill Climb at the wheel of an Audi Sport quattro.

The body and drivetrain of the autonomous RS 7 were equivalent to those of the production car. On this platform, the team around chief development engineer Peter Bergmiller installed a computerized driver. Stereo cameras at front and rear, precision GPS, and a digital accelerometer in the center of the car provided additional

The RS 7 was not the fastest car in its segment. However, it offered the best overall package of performance, drivability and price.

The second autonomous RS 7 prototype ("Robby") outran most human challengers on Sonoma Raceway.

data inputs. A computer in the luggage compartment processed all the incoming data and controlled the car.

Audi and "Bobby" challenged journalists. In December 2014, at the Ascari race track near Marbella, Spain, the robotic car went up against human competition. Although the RS 7 circulated the course briskly with times around 2:15 minutes, it did not beat all human challengers. With too much additional equipment on board, it was significantly heavier.

Bergmiller's team perceived the results as a challenge. "Bobby" turned into "Robby." Named RS 7 piloted driving concept, the car, with a new nickname and red wrap, again stepped up for a comparison contest. It now lacked the rear seats and comfort equipment. Instead, it was fitted with sport seats and a simplified computer architecture. In all, these measures reduced its weight by 400 kg (880 lbs). This made it weigh the same as a regular RS 7 Sportback.

Now, more fleet of foot and with renewed resolve, the car once again measured its abilities against flesh-and-blood drivers, this time at Sonoma Raceway (formerly known as Sears Point), in California. "Robby" circulated in 2:01.01, faster than most of its challengers. Audi announced that only drivers familiar with the track were "marginally faster."

Regardless of what RS fans might think of the rolling contradiction of a self-driving enthusiast car, autonomous driving is one of Audi's great themes for the future. Alongside the sport models, an A7 prototype nicknamed "Jack" conducted autonomous drives on the A9 Autobahn in Germany. The manufacturer trained it to exhibit human behavior so that other road users could better anticipate its actions. Before activating a turn signal, it would move closer to the dividing line in its own lane, and it would allow more space when passing trucks.

Audi announced that it would offer Level 3 autonomous driving as an option in the next A8. The car would drive independently in traffic jams or congested traffic at speeds up to 60 km/h (37 mph). The driver would be able to watch television or read the newspaper. A safety system would sound a warning in plenty of time to take the wheel. If the car were to make a wrong decision, the manufacturer would bear the responsibility. Functional prototypes have validated the advancement of this technology. However, due to lack of approval by regulatory agencies, Audi postponed this topic for a future date.

"Robby" drove autonomously, without a driver, but with stereo cameras, high-resolution GPS and digital accelerometer.

PAINT CHOICES (EXCERPT)

Solid color: Nardo Gray
Metallic: Glacier White, Florett Silver, Mythos Black
Pearl effect: Misano Red, Sepang Blue, Daytona Gray, Prism Silver, Phantom Black
Crystal effect: Panther Black, Prism Silver, Estoril Blue
Matte effect: Daytona Gray

STANDARD EQUIPMENT (EXCERPT)

Exterior:

- 20-inch aluminum wheels with 275/35 tires
- Xenon plus headlamps with cleaning system, LED taillamps; after facelift: LED headlamps
- Rocker panel skirts, RS-specific front and rear valance
- Matte aluminum accents on window frames, roof rails and radiator grille

The body of the first RS 7 was equivalent to that of the A7. If it had gotten the usual sheetmetal add-ons, it would have been too wide for everyday use.

The cockpit of the RS 7 was identical to that of the Audi RS 6.

The options list of the RS 7 provided a multitude of choices for fine upholstery and attractive contrasting stitching.

INTERIOR

- RS power adjustable front leather and Alcantara sport seats
- Three-spoke multifunction sport steering wheel, flattened at bottom, with shift paddles
- Décor inserts in carbon
- Slotted interior door latches

FUNCTION

- Automatic climate control
- MMI Radio plus with Bose surround sound and Bluetooth interface
- 19-inch brake system
- Parking assistant
- RS adaptive air suspension
- RS exhaust system

Audi RS 6 Avant (C8)

The RS Hybrid

20

In its C8 generation, Audi's RS 6 gained weight, yet moved with greater agility and economy than before.

For 25 years, electrification played no role in Audi's RS models. That changed with the C8 generation. Audi Sport designed the new RS 6 as a mild hybrid. Power was not supplied entirely by a combustion engine. Effective immediately, an electric motor supplied some additional torque. The electric motor lacked enough power to make a measurable difference in total power or propulsive effort, but it significantly reduced the car's fuel consumption in that it assisted the gasoline engine or allowed it to shut down when it was not needed.

This represented a paradigm shift in the RS portfolio. Application of hybrid drive showed that Audi was evaluating its drivetrain concepts. Still, Audi Sport did not envision anything more than a "soft" hybridization in the RS 6. A full hybrid, or even a plug-in hybrid, was never under consideration in the concept phase, because customers still expected something else. Therefore, a V8 engine remained at the core of the powertrain. The new 4.0-liter powerplant developed 600 hp and 800 Nm (590 ft-lbs) of torque. With this level of performance, the manufacturer positioned the new car exactly where it had previously slotted only the higher-output "performance" versions.

With nearly identical power output, acceleration was only marginally improved over that of the old RS 6 Performance. The new RS 6 accelerated to 100 km/h (62 mph) a tenth of a second faster (3.6 seconds) and matched it in the sprint to 200 km/h (124 mph) in 12 seconds. Audi continued to limit top speed to 250 km/h (155 mph) in standard trim, and optionally to 280 or 305 km/h (174 or 190 mph). Audi's equipment policy only allowed the highest top speeds to be unlocked if all available vehicle dynamics options ("Dynamic Plus package") were ordered.

While straight-line performance was little changed, the fast wagon's handling improved. The RS 6 offered optional all-wheel steering. At low speeds, the rear wheels steered opposite to the fronts, for a smaller turning circle and easier maneuvering and greater agility in hairpin bends. At higher speeds, they steered in the same direction as the front wheels for more stable handling. Audi Sport also added dynamic steering, sport differential, ceramic brakes and DRC suspension (replacing the standard air suspension) to the list of added-cost options.

The interplay of all these components resulted in a level of agility that few would expect of a car with a curb weight of 2.1 metric tonnes (4,629 lbs). *Motor1 Deutschland* praised the package: "Turn-in, the way the car changes direction, is decidedly snappier and more accurate than on the previous generation." Radical-mag.com of Switzerland was even more enthusiastic: "My God, this grip! Thank you for this steering precision, thank for the really, really good suspension, thank you for the perfectly modulatable brakes." In view of the spectacle offered, the fact that the new RS 6 weighed more than any of its predecessors, including the hefty V10, was only mentioned in passing.

HEAVIER BUT FASTER

More weight follows from more technology. Every new function and every optional extra puts greater load

A digital display replaced analog gauges in the new RS 6.

Audi scattered only a few genuine pushbuttons throughout the cabin of the RS 6. Touchscreens now controlled most functions.

Optionally, 22-inch wheels filled the widened fenders of the RS 6.

on the axles. The only exception: ceramic brakes reduced the unsprung weight by 34 kilograms (75 lbs). But the RS 6 now included new functions requiring additional parts. For example: the auxiliary battery (about 10 kg, 22 lbs) and the DC/DC voltage converter of the mild hybrid system. Audi gladly accepted their weight penalty in exchange for a reduction in fuel consumption of 0.8 liters per 100 km (0.2 U.S. gallons per 62.1 miles).

RS 6 customers expect the same amenities as found in the A6. For this reason, the top-of-the-line model included thirty-eight assistance systems and additional desirable options in its 90-page price list. Frequently, everyday utility took precedence over sheer performance. On the preceding generation, Audi had fitted more than half of all vehicles with a towing package. Now it was available in combination with the DRC suspension.

Due to demands for increased stiffness, Audi was no longer able to find any significant weight reduction areas in the body structure. The new RS 6 was built on a slightly reworked version of the Modular Longitudinal Platform. In its structure and materials, the body resembled that of its predecessor. A composite (steel and aluminum) crossmember and newly designed front end increased stiffness, but did not reduce weight.

A7 HEADLAMPS IN THE RS 6

Although it carried over the roof, front doors and tailgate from the base model, the C8 generation of the RS 6 was distinctive in its own right. Audi Sport widened the fenders by 4 cm (1.6 in.), fitted oval exhaust tips in the rear valance (33 percent larger than on the predecessor), and developed a unique spoiler package. Rim size grew to 21 inches (standard) or 22 inches (optional).

In addition, the wagon was given its own headlamp treatment. The sport model adopted the flatter LED lamps of the Audi A7. Optionally, the RS 6 could be equipped with matrix LED headlamps. At speeds above 70 km/h (43 mph), laser high beams illuminate the road about twice as far ahead and dim automatically when the on-board camera detects oncoming traffic. Audi did not offer this option on the A6.

Inside, the RS 6 was optically and acoustically closer to the A6. New displays in the digital speedometer, additional settings and equipment packages differentiated the sports version from the base model. Above all, the car eschewed acoustic drama. *Auto Bild* wrote that in comfort mode, "the interior was whisper-quiet." This appealed to customers who used the car as a regular means of transportation.

THE ENGINE OF THE RS 6: DEVELOPED BY PORSCHE

Although the eight-cylinder turbo engines of the C7 and C8 model lines appeared similar in many respects, from an engineering perspective they had very little in common. They did not even come out of the same design office. In 2013, Audi handed off responsibility for the corporation's V8 engines to Porsche. For production of the large powerplants,

Within the VW organization, Porsche was given responsibility for developing V8 engines, and developed a new 4.0-liter powerplant. Among other applications, it propelled the Porsche Panamera and Audi RS 6.

Audi's sister marque built a dedicated plant in Stuttgart-Zuffenhausen.

The new engine was intended to meet all worldwide emissions standards over a long term, tolerate fuels of varying quality, and had to be convertible to hybrid operation. In addition, its power output and power development had to be appropriate for models with sporting appeal. Within 34 months, Porsche developed a completely new V8 engine. Like Audi's own predecessor, it employed a 90-degree bank angle, but with a larger cylinder spacing of 93 instead of 90 millimeters.

Porsche designed a "square" engine, with bore and stroke identical at 86 millimeters. This yielded a displacement of 3,996 cc (244 cu. in.) A thin layer of iron on the cylinder walls, applied by means of a plasma spray, improved heat transfer and load-bearing capacity. Gray iron main bearing caps reinforced the aluminum block. These caps contained bearing inserts with a polymer coating to contend with the appreciably higher loading due to frequent engine starts in hybrid operation.

The engineers developed new, two-piece cylinder heads (lower level containing valve train, upper level with oil supply and camshaft bearings). These retained the cylinder deactivation system of the predecessor, in which cylinders 2, 3, 5, and 8 could be deactivated at part load.

Also carried over was the concept of centrally located turbochargers. In the new V8, however, they were mounted at the front of the engine. There was space behind them for the catalytic converters. Positioning these between the cylinder banks shortened their warm-up phase. Thanks to a special fuel-injection strategy, they reached operating temperature even more quickly.

Porsche first installed the new V8 in the Panamera Turbo. Audi converted the engine into a mild hybrid for service in the RS 6. A belt alternator starter took the place of the conventional alternator. This was fed by an auxiliary 48-volt electrical system and its own battery. While coasting or braking, it produced more energy than a conventional alternator. Conversely, under all other conditions, it put less load on the engine. At low engine speeds, the belt alternator starter added up to 60 Newton-meters (44 ft-lbs) of torque to the combustion-engine output, in other words relieving the gasoline engine of that much output. In addition, the system was able to start the engine imperceptibly. With this functionality, the RS 6 learned to sail. At speeds up to 160 km/h (100 mph), the combustion engine could be shut down and roll along without consuming any fuel, or creating any engine drag. That might not be typical RS behavior, but it helped ensure the continued existence of such large engines.

European Union CO_2 emissions limits put added pressure on carmakers. Fuel consumption in all segments would have to be reduced, otherwise financial penalties would be imposed. Audi's approach yielded results. In comparison tests by *Auto Zeitung*, the RS 6 beat the slightly more powerful Mercedes-Benz AMG E 63 S 4Matic+ in fuel economy by well over one liter per 100 km – a powerful argument toward its overall win in the test.

For the 40th birthday of the quattro, apprentices at Audi built the RS 6 GTO Concept. It quoted the 1989 Audi 90 IMSA GTO.

APPRENTICE PROJECT: THE AUDI RS 6 GTO CONCEPT (2020)

Right on time for the 40th birthday of Audi's all-wheel drive quattro, the manufacturer presented a special study. Apprentices at the company converted the RS 6 Avant into the GTO Concept. Visually, the car bore a strong resemblance to the legendary 1989 Audi 90 quattro IMSA GTO race car.

Audi chief designer Marc Lichte and his team drew an even wider body for the already wide RS 6. Components generated by a 3D printer added seven centimeters to the fenders. A huge rear spoiler, side exhausts, and warpaint faithful to the original cited the old racing touring car. In addition, the apprentices laminated wheel vents for the 22-inch rims in the style of the original.

Inside, the study eliminated almost everything that might be superfluous on the race track: rear bench seats and comfort seats were tossed out. Instead, racing bucket seats (Recaro Podium) with custom-fabricated consoles, racing safety belts and custom roll cage were fitted to the car. Window netting for the side windows and a safety harness were also included in the racing package.

The technology of the RS 6 GTO Concept remained largely stock. Its engine continued to develop 600 hp, a good 100 hp less than the race car. Despite the extensive effort involved in the conversion, series production of the car was not out of the question. At least, at its presentation in December 2020, Audi did not issue a firm denial of any production plans.

Audi quattro
Audi
quattro
GOODYEAR
BOSCH
GOODYEAR
BBS
Shell
Shell

PAINT CHOICES (EXCERPT)

Solid color: Nardo Gray
Metallic: Navarra Blue, Glacier White, Tango Red, Florett Silver, Mythos Black
Pearl effect: Daytona Gray
Crystal effect: Sebring Black

STANDARD EQUIPMENT (EXCERPT)

Exterior:

- 21-inch aluminum wheels with 275/35 tires
- LED headlamps (carried over from Audi A7), LED taillamps
- Rear spoiler, rocker panel skirts, RS-specific front and rear valance
- Black trim strips, outside mirrors, roof rails and radiator grille

The C8 generation of the RS 6 differed even more strongly from the A6 than ever. Its headlamps were taken from its sister model, the A7.

Individualization continued to be one of the competencies of Audi's performance-oriented subsidiary. For example, the RS 6 offered tasteful color combinations.

Inside, the RS 6 differed little from the A6. Audi programmed unique displays for its multitude of screens.

INTERIOR

- Leather and Alcantara "plus" front sport seats, electrically adjustable and heatable
- Three-spoke multifunction sport steering wheel, flattened at bottom, with shift paddles and RS button
- Décor inserts in Aluminum Race anthracite

FUNCTION

- Four-zone automatic climate control
- MMI Navigation plus with MMI touch response and virtual cockpit plus
- 20-inch brake system
- Parking assistant plus
- RS adaptive air suspension
- RS exhaust system

Audi RS 7 Sportback (C8)
Wide at last

2019

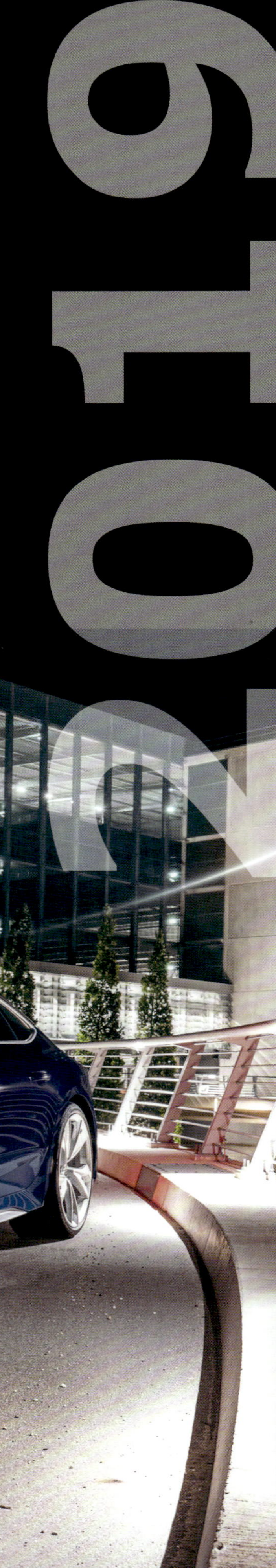

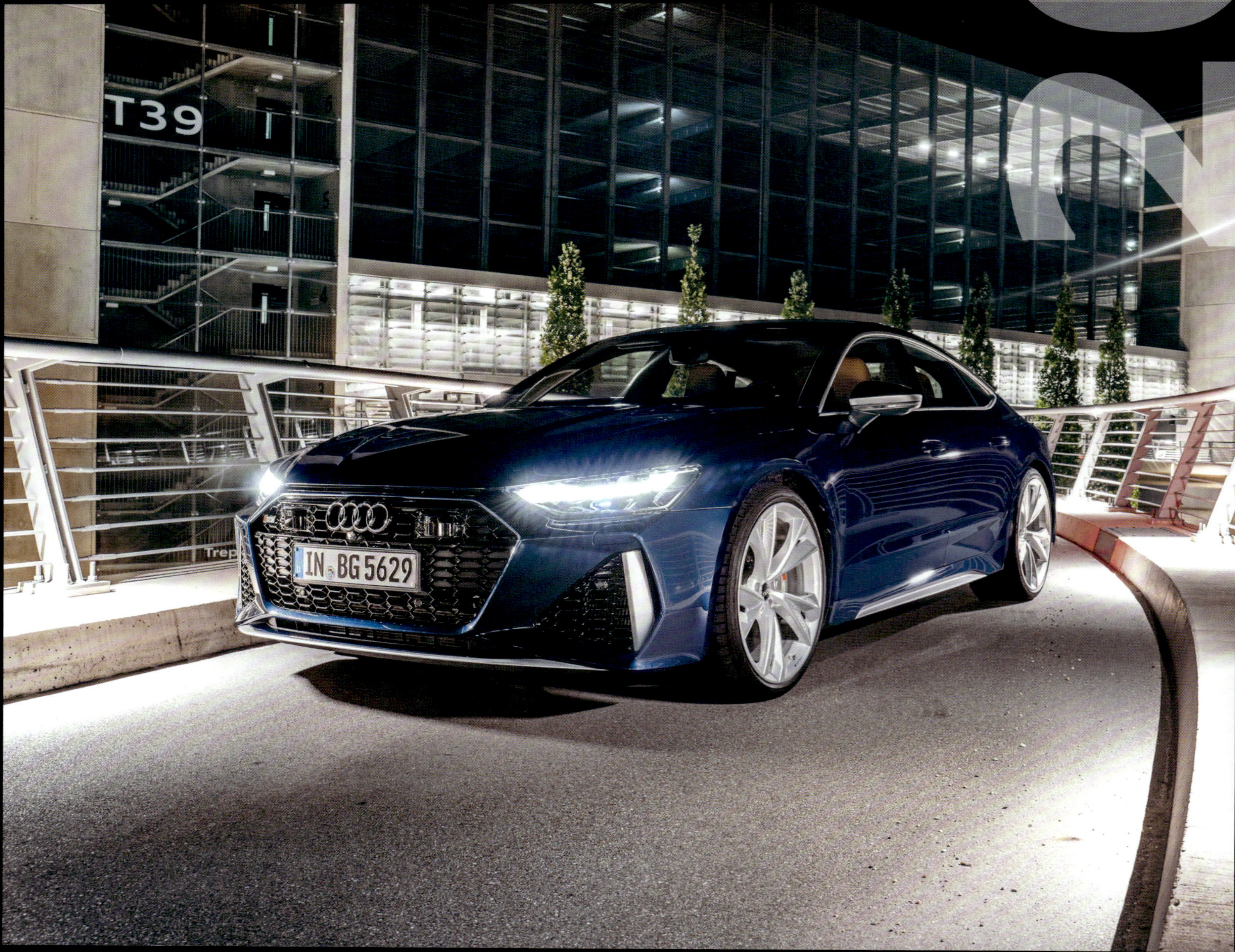

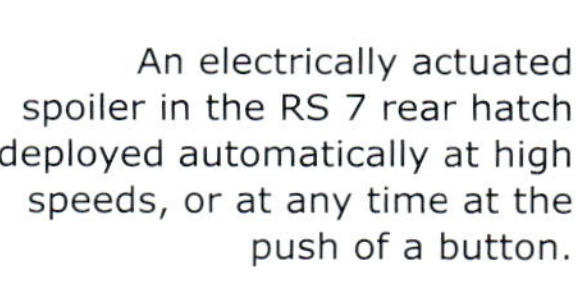

An electrically actuated spoiler in the RS 7 rear hatch deployed automatically at high speeds, or at any time at the push of a button.

A classic sedan body has never been able to firmly establish itself in Audi's larger sports models. Quattro GmbH tried an RS 6 sedan over the course of two different generations, but sales numbers were far below those of the Avant. In 2013, when the RS 7 Sportback replaced the notchback, customers welcomed the change. In the first full year of production (2013), 1,084 examples of the five-door coupe were built. The last RS 6 sedan managed the same numbers in the course of its three-year production run. Consequently, not only was a successor to the Sportback a possibility; it was obligatory.

In its second generation, the RS 7 construction edged even closer to that of the RS 6 Avant. Even in the predecessor, both models shared most of their drivetrain components. They still had detail differences due to different body widths. As of 2019, they were identical in terms of engineering, right down to track widths. Audi Sport developed the models simultaneously and tuned the axles, wheels, and wheel wells to the specific characteristics of both cars.

These efforts resulted in a significantly wider RS 6 (adding 8 cm – more than 3 in.) and a modestly wider RS 7 (with an extra 4 cm – 1.6 in.) – a costly innovation for the Sportback, which heretofore had only been available with the standard production A7 body. Now only five sheetmetal components were carried over from the base model to the top of the line (front doors, roof, engine hood, rear hatch), and the car finally had wide fenders – as it should be for an RS.

This was especially pleasing for Audi's creatives. Until then, they had been given a conservative assignment, to keep even the hottest cars visually close to the base models. In the course of the RS 7's first public appearance, the designers reported that they enjoyed far greater opportunities in the new car. The stylistic freedom allowed by the decision makers in terms of vehicle width and front "face" surprised even the designers.

TECHNICALLY AN AUDI RS 6

All of the things that made an RS 6 move, turn, and stop, were taken over without modification in the RS 7. The V8 biturbo with its mild hybrid system and 600 hp, eight-speed automatic with Torsen differential, air suspension and big steel brakes were installed as standard equipment in both cars. Rear sport differential, DRC suspension, dynamic all-wheel steering and ceramic brakes were available from Audi as options. Both cars were absolutely equal in terms of performance: acceleration to 100 km/h (62 mph) in 3.6 seconds, top speed 250 km/h (155 mph) or optionally 280 or 305 km/h (174 or 190 mph).

The higher positioned A7 brought innovative lighting technology. For that model, Audi offered optional laser high beams. A module provided by supplier Osram generated a blue laser beam, whose color was altered to white by a converter. This was capable of illuminating the road ahead twice as far as regular LED high beams. This system became active at speeds above 70 km/h (43 mph). Due to increased risk of dazzling oncoming traffic, the laser high beams shut off if another car was detected within visual range. The especially bright headlamps were available for both RS models.

The RS 7 exhibited less differentiation from its sister model, but all the more differences compared to its predecessor. This was above all attributable to the networking of its dynamic hardware. Drivetrain, suspension and sport differential now shared a single control module, making decisions for all components and combining their functions. Fine tuning of vehicle dynamics resulted in greater range and possibilities.

In the C8 generation, the oval exhaust tips were 33 percent larger than on the predecessor.

The second-generation RS 7 got what many had wished for at the model's debut: a unique, wide body to clearly differentiate it from the A7 and S7.

The RS 7 also built up a considerable lead over the base model. Its developers had to make fewer compromises than on the A7. With only two (instead of four) tire sizes listed in the development targets, they were able to tune the RS 7 more precisely. This they did successfully. *Motor1 Deutschland* enthused that the car had the "best steering since the sainted B7 RS 4."

Despite its significant mass, the RS 7 functioned well, according to *Auto Zeitung*. "In view of the test car's considerable weight of 2,165 kilograms (4,773 pounds), it does not feel anything like a go-kart, but it's astounding how light-footed and yet reliably solidly the RS 7 Sportback moves, even when grip is greatly reduced – in the wet, for example."

Still, a glance at the marketplace showed that the competitors were thinking differently from Audi. They chose stiff suspensions, while the RS 7 moved with more compliance. *sport auto* compared the Audi test car with the BMW M5 and Mercedes-Benz AMG GT 63 S 4Matic+. Having the greatest weight of the test candidates, and with softer chassis tuning, put the Audi into third place in the dynamics department. Its competitors, however, constantly showed off their sportiness, making them more annoying on anything but closed race courses. In everyday use, "the Audi, following along at the rear, was suddenly very popular."

It was a question of market positioning. Audi Sport regarded the RS 7 as a "Gran Turismo" – a successful compromise combining speed with comfort. *Auto Zeitung* summarized: "The Audi RS 7 Sportback manages to cover an astounding number of contradictions under a single, elegant hat, and wears it well."

IN BG 5629
RS 7

PAINT CHOICES (EXCERPT)

Solid color: Nardo Gray
Metallic: Navarra Blue, Glacier White, Tango Red, Florett Silver, Mythos Black
Pearl effect: Daytona Gray
Crystal effect: Sebring Black

STANDARD EQUIPMENT (EXCERPT)

Exterior:

- 21-inch aluminum wheels with 275/35 tires
- LED headlamps, LED taillamps
- Rocker panel skirts, RS-specific front and rear valance
- Black trim strips, outside mirrors, and radiator grille

Audi allowed the RS 7 designers a surprising degree of freedom. The reactions to so much daring were universally positive.

With a vehicle weight of more than 2.1 metric tonnes (2.3 tons) and 600 hp, the optional ceramic brakes were highly recommended for the RS 7.

Light played a major role in the Audi RS 7. Within the VW corporation, skillfully placed lamps serve as the "new chrome."

INTERIOR

- Leather and Alcantara "plus" front sport seats, electrically adjustable and heatable
- Three-spoke multifunction sport steering wheel, flattened at bottom, with shift paddles and RS button
- Décor inserts in Aluminum Race anthracite

FUNCTION

- Four-zone automatic climate control
- MMI Navigation plus with MMI touch response and virtual cockpit plus
- 20-inch brake system
- Parking assistant plus
- RS adaptive air suspension
- RS exhaust system

2021

Audi RS e-tron GT

The first electric RS

The first Audi model without an exhaust pipe, the RS e-tron GT operates strictly on electrical power.

History repeats itself. Audi's first electric sportster was born in a similar manner to the first sport wagon – in cooperation with Porsche. Other than the 1994 RS2, however, the project did not call for conversion of an existing Audi, but rather development of a new car and its integration within two marques. Both venture partners carried out their design work as a team, and their interpretations were sold independently. At Porsche, the result was called the Taycan. Audi called it the e-tron GT, in its most powerful variation it was the RS e-tron GT. It was the first all-electric RS model, and with 646 hp, the most powerful production car to carry the four Audi rings.

Why, of all things, an electric car, when tradition would dictate ingenious five, six, or eight-cylinder combustion engines? For one, because the European Union's strict CO_2 emissions limits could not be met without electric propulsion. Locally emissions-free cars are not yet mandated as replacements for those powered by traditional means, but must in any event supplement them. For another, the market has long demanded cars like the RS e-tron GT. In 2020, in the German market, Porsche sold nearly twice as many Taycans as Panameras. Even taken together, the Boxster and Cayman could not match the electric car's sales numbers.

There was yet another, conceptually bound advantage. An electric car delivers nearly its peak torque from the first revolution of its motor. In the RS e-tron GT, this measures about 830 Newton-meters (612 ft-lbs). It was capable of sprinting to 100 km/h (62 mph) in 3.3 seconds. *auto motor und sport* described the maximum-effort launch of the electro racer as follows:

"The light goes green. Off the brakes and we have liftoff. The seamless thrust is brutal, robs you of your senses, while you bravely keep it pointed at the finish line. Speed? Hmmm... 200 or 210 km/h (124 or 130 mph). Then feel the total darkness, open the window, fill up on oxygen, and back into the light. My goodness – what *was* that?"

TWO MOTORS IN THE ELECTRIC RS

The RS e-tron GT drew its power from two motors. At the front, Audi installed a permanently excited synchronous motor developing 175 kW (or, in old-school terms, 238 hp) and coupled this to the front wheels via a single-stage planetary transmission. Another motor of the same type was nestled below the trunk floor. This provided 335 kW (456 hp) to a two-speed transmission. The first, shorter gear was only active under full-load acceleration up to about 80 km/h (50 mph). The RS e-tron GT did everything else using second gear.

Added together, peak output of both motors resulted in 646 hp for the system. The car can maintain this power level for two and a half seconds. The so-called overboost reduced the time required to accelerate up to secondary-road speeds. Even before the car reached 100 km/h (62 mph), the total output of the motors was reduced to 440 kW (598 hp). This put the power at the same level as that of the Audi RS 7.

There were many parallels between the electro RS and the big Sportback. Both cars employed similar chassis components. Air suspension was standard on both, while rear-wheel steering, ceramic brakes (including ten-piston calipers in the e-tron RS!) and sport differential were added-cost options. Only the traditional DRC suspension was not available for the electric car.

Both cars measured about five meters (197 in.) and about 1.95 meters (77 in.) in width. Even the wheelbase of both cars was nearly identical (e-tron: 2.90 m, 114.2 in; RS 7: 2.93 m, 115.4 in.) However, the construction of the electric car, with a large battery in the floorpan, resulted in different spatial conditions. Its flat roof and bulky battery affected the interior arrangements. The developers incorporated recesses ("foot garages") in the energy packages, so that the occupants would not feel cramped.

The RS e-tron shared this unusual design feature with the Taycan. Similarly, both cars had an acoustic problem. For all their sporting claims, their motors sounded too emotionless. At Audi, sound engineers Rudi Halbmeir and Stefan Gsell used bass frequencies and a fan whose sound was directed through a composite tube to create a new, characteristic sound. A total of three speakers optionally transmitted the artificial sound to the interior as well as the outside world.

A NEW PORSCHE-AUDI

Technically, the Audi and Porsche electric four-seaters were nearly identical. Both were based on the "J1" electric car platform and shared motors, axles, suspension, two of the three different

Dimensionally, the RS e-tron GT and RS 7 were very similar. Both cars had almost the same overall length and width, but the electric car was a little bit lower.

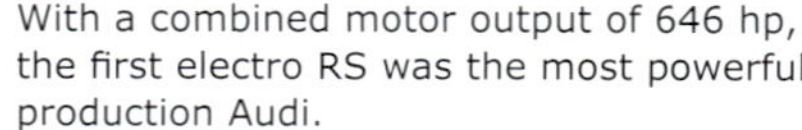

With a combined motor output of 646 hp, the first electro RS was the most powerful production Audi.

For the electric car, Audi deviated from its usual instrument panel layout only in minor details. It was significantly different from the Porsche Taycan.

brake systems, recuperation strategy (with as much as 265 kW) and battery package – in all, about 40 percent of the parts count. Differences could be found in the equipment and trim details, and tuning. Audi programmed in a different peak power (just under that of the Porsche Taycan Turbo), altered the suspension tuning, and equipped the car in keeping with its own ideas.

After its first drive in the e-tron, *Auto Bild* emphasized that Audi was not building a copy of the Porsche: "Anyone who thinks that the RS e-tron GT would drive like a Porsche Taycan with a different body, will be surprised. The Ingolstadters set their own benchmarks and put greater emphasis on comfort." Audi and Audi Sport positioned the e-tron as a "comfortable and dynamic touring sports car" – in other words, close to the current RS portfolio.

As befitting a touring sports car, the RS e-tron GT had long legs. On a single battery charge (net capacity: 85.2 kWh) the low-slung, aerodynamic car (drag coefficient Cd = 0.24) could cover about 470 kilometers (292 miles) in the standard test procedure. Its battery, employing 800 volt technology, made for quicker recharging stops. Underway, it could recharge at rates up to 270 kW at fast charging stations. At home, connected to a wall box, it could recharge at 11 kW. Audi promised a 22 kW option for a later date.

AUDI'S FIRST ELECTRIC SPORTSTER

With the e-tron GT, Audi achieved several firsts. It was based on a platform with no combustion-engine options, employed an operating voltage of 800 V, and had nothing in common with an SUV. Before the arrival of the e-tron GT, the only all-electric vehicles on the market were considerably taller, with limited sporting appeal. Now, an "electrodynamic" performance car boasted a lower center of gravity than even the Audi R8.

Above all, however, for the first time an RS model appeared on the market at the same time as its base-model stablemate. Audi built both the e-tron GT and RS e-tron GT at the Böllinger Höfen shops in its Neckarsulm facility, on a single assembly line shared with the Audi R8. Because an electric car must be environmentally friendly overall, production made use of biogas and ecologically sourced electrical power to achieve a CO_2 - neutral process.

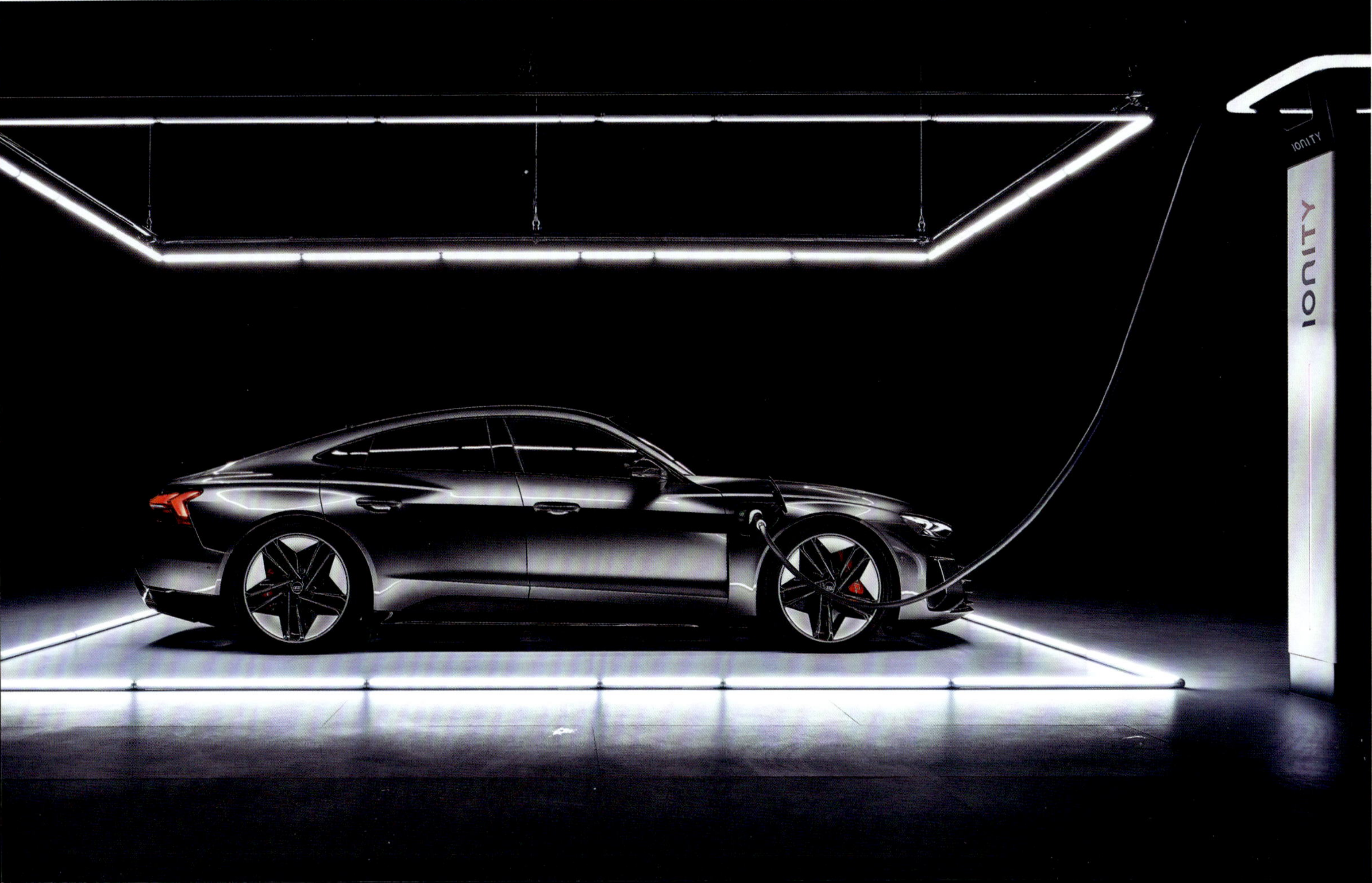

The 800-volt electrical system enabled high charging current; the RS e-tron GT could recharge at rates up to 270 kW.

TECHNICAL SPECIFICATIONS

<table>
<tr><th></th><th></th><th colspan="2">Audi S6 plus (C4)</th><th colspan="2">Audi RS 6 (C5)</th><th>RS 6 plus (C5)</th><th colspan="2">Audi RS 6 (C6)</th></tr>
<tr><td rowspan="2">MODEL</td><td>Body style</td><td>Avant</td><td>Sedan</td><td>Avant</td><td>Sedan</td><td>Avant</td><td>Avant</td><td>Sedan</td></tr>
<tr><td>Production timeframe</td><td colspan="2">1995-1997</td><td colspan="2">2002-2004</td><td>2004</td><td colspan="2">2008-2010</td></tr>
<tr><td rowspan="9">ENGINE</td><td>Engine configuration</td><td colspan="5">Longitudinal front-mounted V8 Otto cycle engine</td><td colspan="2">Longitudinal front-mounted V10 Otto cycle engine</td></tr>
<tr><td>Engine designation</td><td colspan="2">AHK</td><td colspan="2">BCY</td><td>BRV</td><td colspan="2">BUH</td></tr>
<tr><td>Displacement, cc</td><td colspan="2">4,172</td><td colspan="3">4,172</td><td colspan="2">4,991</td></tr>
<tr><td>Bore x stroke, mm</td><td colspan="2">84.5x93.0</td><td colspan="3">84.5x93.0</td><td colspan="2">84.5x89.0</td></tr>
<tr><td>Power output, hp (kw) @ rpm</td><td colspan="2">240 (326) at 6,500</td><td colspan="2">331 (450) at 5,700- 6,400</td><td>353 (480) at 6,000-6,400</td><td colspan="2">426 (580) at 6,250-6,700</td></tr>
<tr><td>Torque in Nm (ft-lbs) @ rpm</td><td colspan="2">400 (295) @ 3,500</td><td>560 (413) @ 1,950-5,600</td><td>560 (413) @ 1,950-5,500</td><td>560 (413) @ 1,950-6,000</td><td colspan="2">650 (479) @ 1,500-6,250</td></tr>
<tr><td>Valvetrain, valves per cylinder</td><td colspan="2">Timing belt, four overhead camshafts, four valves per cylinder</td><td colspan="3">Timing belt, four overhead camshafts, variable intake timing, five valves (three intake, two exhaust) per cylinder</td><td colspan="2">Timing chain, four overhead camshafts, variable intake and exhaust timing, four valves per cylinder</td></tr>
<tr><td>Fuel delivery</td><td colspan="2">Fully sequential multi-point fuel-injection, static high-voltage distribution, cylinder-selective lambda control with two knock sensors, hot film mass airflow metering, variable intake manifold, Bosch Motronic M 5.4.1</td><td colspan="3">Twin turbocharged, fully electronic sequential multi-point fuel-injection with mass airflow sensor, map ignition with static high-voltage distribution, cylinder bank selective exhaust gas temperature regulation, coordinated engine torque control, Bosch Motronic ME 7.11 engine management system</td><td colspan="2">Twin turbocharged, direct fuel-injection, individual pencil ignition coils, two control modules, E-Gas (electronic throttle), cylinder-selective adaptive knock control, adaptive lambda control (cylinder bank specific), map ignition with static high-voltage distribution, Bosch ME 9.1.2 engine management system</td></tr>
<tr><td>Compression ratio</td><td colspan="2">11.6:1</td><td colspan="3">9.8:1</td><td colspan="2">10.5:1</td></tr>
<tr><td rowspan="2">POWERTRAIN</td><td>Transmission</td><td colspan="2">Six-speed manual</td><td colspan="3">Five-speed torque converter automatic (tiptronic)</td><td colspan="2">Six-speed torque converter automatic (tiptronic)</td></tr>
<tr><td>Drivetrain</td><td colspan="2">All-wheel drive, Torsen Type B center differential</td><td colspan="3">All-wheel drive, automatically locking Torsen Type B center differential, EDS (electronic differential lock), ESP (Electronic stability program)</td><td colspan="2">All-wheel drive, self-locking Torsen Type C center differential, ESP, ASR (anti-slip regulation), EDS (electronic differential lock)</td></tr>
</table>

		Audi S6 plus (C4)		Audi RS 6 (C5)		RS 6 plus (C5)	Audi RS 6 (C6)	
CHASSIS AND SUSPENSION	**Front suspension**	McPherson struts with lower transverse arms, wheel-locating transverse anti-roll bar		Four-link independent suspension, transverse anti-roll bar			Four-link independent suspension, transverse anti-roll bar	
	Rear suspension	Trapezoidal four-link, suspension, struts, transverse link, anti-roll bar		Double wishbone suspension, anti-roll bar			Independent, trapezoidal link suspension, anti-roll bar	
	Steering	Rack and pinion, power assisted		Rack and pinion, power assisted			Rack and pinion with speed-sensitive power assist	
	Turning circle, m (ft)	11.4 (37.4)		11.68 (38.3)	11.4 (37.4)	11.68 (38.3)	12.2 (40.0)	
	Brake system	Dual-circuit brake system with ABS and EBV (electronic brake force distribution), brake booster, two-piston front calipers, ventilated discs front and rear		Dual-circuit brake system with ABS, ESP, EBV (electronic brake force distribution), brake booster, eight-piston front calipers, ventilated discs front and rear; Optional: cross-drilled discs		Dual-circuit brake system with ABS, ESP, EBV (electronic brake force distribution), brake booster, eight-piston front calipers, ventilated and cross-drilled discs front and rear	Dual-circuit brake system with ABS, ESP, EBV (electronic brake force distribution), six-piston front calipers, ventilated discs front and rear; Optional: ceramic brake system with eight-piston front calipers	
	Brake discs	Front: 323x30 mm Rear: 269x20 mm		Front: 365x34 mm Rear: 335x22mm			Front: 390x36 mm Rear: 356x28 mm Optional: ceramic, 420x40 Front: 356x28 rear	
	Wheel size, in.	8x17		8.5x18		9x19	9x19	
	Tire size	255/40 ZR 17		255/40 R18		255/35 R19	255/40 R19	
DIMENSIONS & WEIGHTS	**Length/width/ height, mm (in.)**	4,797/1,804/1,440 (188.9/71.0/56.7)	4,797/1,804/1,430 (188.9/71.0/56.3)	4,852/1,850/1,452 (191.0/72.8/57.2)	4,582/1,850/1,425 (180.4/72.8/56.1)	4,852/1,850/1,452 (180.4/1425/57.2)	4,928/1,889/1,460 (194.0/74.4/57.5)	4,928/1,889/1,456 (194.0/74.4/57.3)
	Wheelbase, mm (in.)	2,692 (106.0)		2,759 (108.6)			2,846 (112.0)	
	Track, front/rear, mm (in.)	1,563/1,528 (61.5/60.2)		1,578/1,587 (62.1/62.5)			1,614/1,637 (63.5/64.4)	
	Empty weight, kg (lbs)	1,745 (3,847)	1,695 (3,737)	1,880 (4,145)	1,840 (4,057)	1,880 (4,145)	2,025 (4,464)	1,985 (4,376)
	Trunk volume, liters (cu ft)	390-1,310 (13.8-46.3)	510 (18.0)	455-1,590 (16.1-56.2)	424 (15.0)	455-1,590 (16.1-56.2)	565-1,660 (20.0-58.6)	546 (19.3)
	Fuel capacity, liters (U.S. gal)	80 (21.1)		82 (21.7)			80 (21.1)	
PERFORMANCE	**Top speed, km/h (mph)**	250 (governed) (155)		250 (governed) (155)		280 (governed) (174)	250 (governed); Optional: 280 (governed); RS 6 plus: 303 (governed) (155; 174; 188)	
	Acceleration, 0-100 km/h, sec (62 mph)	5.7	5.6	4.7	4.9	4.6	4.6	4.5
	Fuel economy, liters/ 100 km (U.S. mpg)	14.9 (15.8)		14.6 (16.1)			14.0 (16.8)	13.9 (16.9)
MISC.	**Number built, by year**	1995: 3 1996: 561 1997: 291	1995: 5 1996: 82 1997: 10	2002: 1,781 2003: 2,597 2004: 437	2002: 271 2003: 2,244 2004: 232	2004: 564	2007: 30 2008: 3,326 2009: 541 2010: 564	2007: 5 2008: 545 2009: 313 2010: 221
	Total number built	855	97	4,815	2,747	564	4,461	1,084
	Price at market introduction	120,500 DM	116,300 DM	89,600 €	87,500 €	101,050 €	105,550 €	107,200 €

Source Audi AG

TECHNICAL SPECIFICATIONS

		Audi RS 6 (C7)		Audi RS 6 (C8)	Audi RS 7 (C7)		Audi RS 7 (C8)
MODEL	Body style	Avant	Avant Performance	Avant	Sportback	Sportback Performance	Sportback
	Production timeframe	2013-2018	2015-2018	2019 -	2013-2018	2015-2018	2019 -
ENGINE	Engine configuration	Longitudinal front-mounted V8 Otto cycle engine		Longitudinal front-mounted V8 Otto cycle engine	Longitudinal front-mounted V8 Otto cycle engine		Longitudinal front-mounted V8 Otto cycle engine
	Engine designation	CRDB	CWUC	DJPB	CRDB	CWUC	DJPB
	Displacement, cc	3,993		3,996	3,993		3,996
	Bore x stroke, mm	84.5x89		86x86	84.5x89		86x86
	Power output, hp (kw) @ rpm	412 (560) @ 5,700-6,600	445 (605) @ 6,100-6,800	441 (600) @ 6,000-6,250	412 (560) @ 5,700-6,600	445 (605) @ 6,100-6,800	441 (600) @ 6,000-6,250
	Torque in Nm (ft-lbs) @ rpm	700 (516) @ 1,750-5,500	700 (516) @ 1,750-6,000, 750 (553) @ 2,500-5,500 (Overboost)	800 (590) @ 2,050-4,500	700 (516) @ 1,750-5,500	700 (516) @ 1,750-6,000, 750 (553) @ 2,500-5,500 (Overboost)	800 (590) @ 2,050-4,500
	Valvetrain, valves per cylinder	Timing chain, four overhead camshafts, variable intake and exhaust timing, four valves per cylinder		Timing chain, four overhead camshafts, variable intake and exhaust timing, four valves per cylinder	Timing chain, four overhead camshafts, variable intake and exhaust timing, four valves per cylinder		Timing chain, four overhead camshafts, variable intake and exhaust timing, four valves per cylinder
	Fuel delivery	Twin turbocharged, indirect charge air cooling, direct fuel-injection, cylinder-selective lambda control, map ignition with static high-voltage distribution, cylinder-selective adaptive knock control, "cylinder on demand" cylinder deactivation, Bosch MED 17 1.1 engine management system		Twin turbocharged, direct fuel-injection, map ignition, cylinder-selective adaptive knock control, "cylinder on demand" cylinder deactivation	Twin turbocharged, indirect charge air cooling, direct fuel-injection, cylinder-selective lambda control, map ignition with static high-voltage distribution, cylinder-selective adaptive knock control, "cylinder on demand" cylinder deactivation, Bosch MED 17 1.1 engine management system		Twin turbocharged, direct fuel-injection, map ignition, cylinder-selective adaptive knock control, "cylinder on demand" cylinder deactivation
	Compression ratio	9.3:1		10:1	9.3:1		10:1
POWERTRAIN	Transmission	Eight-speed torque converter automatic (tiptronic)		Eight-speed torque converter automatic (tiptronic)	Eight-speed torque converter automatic (tiptronic)		Eight-speed torque converter automatic (tiptronic)
	Drivetrain	All-wheel drive, automatically locking Torsen Type CSM center differential, quattro all-wheel drive		All-wheel drive, automatically locking Torsen Type CSM center differential	All-wheel drive, automatically locking Torsen Type CSM center differential		All-wheel drive, automatically locking Torsen Type CSM center differential, quattro all-wheel drive

		Audi RS 6 (C7)		Audi RS 6 (C8)	Audi RS 7 (C7)		Audi RS 7 (C8)
CHASSIS AND SUSPENSION	**Front suspension**	Five-link suspension, dual upper and lower transverse arms, anti-roll bar, air suspension		Five-link suspension, tubular anti-roll bar	Five-link suspension, dual upper and lower transverse arms, anti-roll bar, air suspension		Five-link suspension, tubular anti-roll bar
	Rear suspension	Trapezoidal link rear suspension with transverse link, anti-roll bar, air suspension		Five-link suspension, tubular anti-roll bar, air suspension	Trapezoidal link rear suspension with transverse link, anti-roll bar, air suspension		Five-link suspension, tubular anti-roll bar, air suspension
	Steering	Electromechanical steering with speed-sensitive power assist		Electromechanical steering with speed-sensitive power assist	Electromechanical steering with speed-sensitive power assist		Electromechanical steering with speed-sensitive power assist
	Turning circle, m (ft)	11.9 (39.0)		12.1 (39.7)	11.9 (39.0)		12.2 (40.0)
	Brake system	Dual-circuit brake system with ESC, brake booster, hydraulic brake assistant, six-piston front calipers, ventilated front and rear discs (wave design); optional ceramic brake system		Dual-circuit brake system with front/rear split, ESC, ABS, EBV (electronic brake force distribution), brake booster, hydraulic brake assistant	Dual-circuit brake system with ESC, brake booster, hydraulic brake assistant, six-piston front calipers, ventilated front and rear discs (wave design); optional ceramic brake system		Dual-circuit brake system with front/rear split, ESC, ABS, EBV (electronic brake force distribution), brake booster, hydraulic brake assistant
	Brake discs	Front: 390x36 mm, Rear: 256x22 mm (wave design); Optional: ceramic; Front 420x40 mm, Rear: 370x30 mm		Front: 420x40 mm; Rear: 370x30 mm Optional: ceramic	Front: 390x36 mm, Rear: 256x22 mm (wave design); Optional: ceramic; Front: 420x40 mm, Rear: 370x30 mm		Front: 420x40 mm; Rear: 370x30 mm Optional: ceramic
	Wheel size, in.	9.5x20	9.5x21	10.5x21	9x20	9x21	10.5x21
	Tire size	275/35 R20	285/30 R21	275/35 R21	275/35 ZR20 102Y XL	275/30 ZR21 98Y XL	275/35 R 21
DIMENSIONS & WEIGHTS	**Length/width/height, mm (in.)**	4,979/1,936/1,461 (196/76.2/57.5)		4,995/1,951/1,487 (196.7/76.8/58.5)	5,012/1,911/1,419 (197.3/75.2/55.9)		5,009/1,950/1,424 (197.2/76.8/56.1)
	Wheelbase, mm (in.)	2,915 (114.8)		2,930 (115.4)	2,915 (114.8)		2,930 (115.4)
	Track, front/rear, mm (in.)	1,662/1,663 (65.4/65.5)		1,668/1,650 (65.7/65.0)	1,634/1,625 (64.3/64.0)		1,668/1,650 (65.7/65.0)
	Empty weight, kg (lbs)	1,950 (4,299)		2,075 (4,575)	1,920 (4,233)	1,930 (4,255)	2,065 (4,553)
	Trunk volume, liters (cu ft)	565-1,680 (20.0-59.3)		565-1,680 (20.0-59.3)	535-1,390 (18.9-49.1)		535-1,390 (18.9-49.1)
	Fuel capacity, liters (U.S. gal)	75 (19.8)		73 (19.3)	75 (19.8)		73 (19.3)
PERFORMANCE	**Top speed, km/h (mph)**	250 (governed); Optional: 280 (governed) or 305 (governed) (155; 174; 190)					
	Acceleration, 0-100 km/h, sec (62 mph)	3.9	3.7	3.6	3.9	3.7	3.6
	Fuel economy, liters/100 km (U.S. mpg)	9.8 (24.0)	9.6 (24.5)	11.6 - 11.5 (20.3 – 20.5)	9.8 (24.0)	9.5 (24.8)	11.6 - 11.5 (20.3 – 20.5)
MISC.	**Number built, by year**	2012: 39 2013: 2,191 2014: 2,508 2015: 3,451 2016: 777 2017: 484 2018: 159	2014: 11 2015: 229 2016: 2,952 2017: 3,161 2018: 1,233	2018: 3 2019: 894	2012: 24 2013: 1,084 2014: 2,392 2015: 1,920 2016: 771 2017: 304 2018: 22	2013: 10 2014: 15 2015: 110 2016: 1,188 2017: 766 2018: 79	2018: 32 2019: 557
	Total number built	9,609	7,586	Still in production	6,517	2,168	Still in production
	Price at market introduction	107,900 €	117,000 €	117,500 €	113,000 €	121,700 €	121,000 €

Source Audi AG

TECHNICAL SPECIFICATIONS

Audi RS e-tron GT

MODEL	Body style	Sportback
	Production timeframe	2021 -
ENGINE	Engine configuration	Permanently excited synchronous motors, transversely mounted, front and rear
	Power output hp (kW), front motor	238 (175)
	Power output hp (kW), rear motor	456 (335)
	Total system power output, hp (kW)	598 (440) overboost 646 (475)
	Torque in Nm (ft-lbs) @ rpm	830 (612)
	Traction battery	Lithium-ion, 396 pouch cells in thirty-three modules, 800 volts
	Battery capacity	93.4 kWh (gross), 85.2 kWh (net)
	Range	ca. 470 km (292 mi)
POWER-TRAIN	Transmission	Single-speed planetary transmission at front, two-speed planetary transmission at rear
	Drivetrain	Electric all-wheel drive
CHASSIS AND SUSPENSION	Front suspension	Aluminum upper and lower A-arms, air suspension, active tubular anti-roll bar
	Rear suspension	Aluminum multi-link air suspension, active tubular anti-roll bar
	Steering	Electromechanical power-assisted steering, four wheel steering
	Brake system	Regenerative braking system (maximum 265 kW braking power), electromechanical brake booster, ten-piston fixed front brake calipers, four-piston fixed rear brake calipers, ventilated discs with tungsten carbide coating
	Brake discs	Front: 410x40 mm; Rear: 365x28 mm; Optional: ceramic discs, Front: 440x40 mm, Rear: 410x32 mm
	Wheel size, in.	9x20 front, 11x20 rear
	Tire size	245/45 front, 285/40 rear
DIMENSIONS AND WEIGHTS	Length/width/ height, mm (in.)	4,989 (196.4); 1,964 (77.3); 1,396 (55.0)
	Wheelbase, mm (in.)	2,900 (114.2)
	Track, front/rear, mm (in.)	1,702/1,667 (67.0/65.6)
	Empty weight, kg (lbs)	2,347 (5,174)
	Trunk volume, liters (cu ft)	350 rear/85 front (12.4/3)
PERFORMANCE	Top speed, km/h (mph)	250 km/h, governed (155 mph)
	Acceleration, 0-100 km/h, sec (62 mph)	3.3
	Power consumption, kWh/100 km	ca. 19.3-20.2
MISC.	Price at market introduction	138,200 €

Source Audi AG

HN RS 3009
HN RS 8007
HN RS 3029

MODELS

It is well known that traditionalists do not handle change well. An RS SUV? One would think that is a bad idea; after all, the concept of a comfortable, high-riding vehicle is at odds with the basic values of the Audi sports department. The vehicles are taller and heavier than what would be considered appropriate for sports cars. But market demand guides supply. And Audi's marque sister, Porsche, showed the way. In Zuffenhausen, order books filled to overflowing were the best possible evidence for the Cayenne's success. Demonstrably, the power SUV concept works. So quattro GmbH had to follow suit.

The manufacturer first ventured into the new segment with the Q3, a compact SUV based on the A3. So the RS Q3 was created, with a respectable separation from the RS 3. It was not made any wider, but stouter; didn't have an abundance of power, but was powerful enough. The concept was so well received that its successor was sharpened up, and Audi even expanded the model with a second body. As a Sportback, the RS Q3 was less practical, but visually more attractive.

That was not the end of it. Audi developed an RS Q5 according to the same formula. In the end, the company decided against production; the reasons for this decision are not known. Still, the connection between RS and Q did not end with the numeral 3. The RS Q8 represented the pinnacle of Audi's SUV offerings. It proved that one of the heaviest cars in the manufacturer's lineup could move athletically. Despite the effort, however, it was apparent that classic sedans, wagons and coupes would remain the faster options.

2013–

Audi RS Q3 (8U)

The first RS-UV

For its first test, Audi presented the RS Q3 on a number of alpine passes, where it was to prove its dynamic abilities and membership in the RS family.

It was a year of intensive work for quattro GmbH. In its 30th anniversary year, 2013, the model palette grew to a total of six vehicles, in eight versions. Three models and one derivative were new to the market, including an all-new vehicle configuration. For the first time, quattro converted and SUV into an RS. The Audi Q3 was transformed into the RS Q3. It was the founding member of the sporty compact SUV segment.

At the time, cars with off-road attitude were the next big thing. They expanded (literally) into every market segment. It stood to reason that one should experiment with the concept. The RS transformation worked in the compact as well as the premium class. Porsche and Audi both built high-riding vehicles with sporting aspirations. Even as far back as 2008, quattro GmbH had been responsible for the immensely powerful Audi Q7 V12 TDI, decked out with a plethora of RS insignia. It was high time to create a proper RS SUV.

In short order, a decision was made to base the new car on the Q3 platform. Because, in quattro GmbH's opinion, center of gravity and weight were contradictory to the objectives of a sports car, the choice of Audi's smallest SUV for the RS program was obvious. Technically, the compact lump resembled the A3. It drew its DNA from the RS 3. The remainder was a mere formality. Ultimately, an internal demonstrator vehicle convinced the corporate decision makers.

quattro GmbH borrowed the familiar five-cylinder turbo of the RS 3, coupled it to a dual-clutch transmission and all-wheel drivetrain, and fitted this powertrain to the SUV. The car was given a specially tuned suspension and was reworked for higher speeds. Skirts and spoilers made it two and a half centimeters (one inch) longer than the "civilian" variant. There was no room under the car for a second exhaust tip; one would have to suffice. This was due to the architecture of the Q3. To make room in the engine compartment, the battery was moved to the back of the car. There, it took up the space that would have been available for a more appropriate exhaust system – the same situation as on the RS 3.

AN SUV IN THE RS FAMILY

In the first test drives with the motoring press, Audi emphasized that the SUV was a genuine RS, and would be a solid member of the RS portfolio. To that end, there was not just a conventional driving event, but rather a driving festival, packaged as a road trip. Along with the RS Q3, this expedition included several other vehicles bearing the RS badge – RS 5 Cabriolet, RS 6, and RS 7 Sportback were included, all recently introduced to the market. In addition, the ancestral five-cylinder Ur-quattro and Sport quattro tagged along. Audi happily talked about how the manufacturer was well-aware of its tradition.

As it turned out, the new car almost became a side issue. The large RS family, with its senior members and youngsters in attendance, turned into a huge show. Audi led the retinue of powerful cars and countless journalists over wonderful alpine passes. The "Land of quattro Tour" took twelve days, with stops in Germany, Austria, Switzerland, France, Italy, as well as Monaco. Every participant spent two days with the group, was given an Audi hiking rucksack as a gift, and after conquering every mountain pass at the wheel of an RS, received a specially created pin to affix to the backpack.

As early as 2012, Audi presented the RS Q3 concept at the Shanghai auto show. Many elements later appeared in the production car, but its wider, flared fenders and dual exhaust were not included.

Quattro GmbH left the wheel wells of the RS Q3 unchanged; they could easily handle large wheels and tires without problems.

SISTER TRIP

The alpine tour underscored the membership of the new vehicle class to the RS program. Still, the powerful fleet could not belie the fact that an SUV simply drives differently from a typical RS. Of necessity, it brings with it design-specific disadvantages that do not appear in the classical body styles. First and foremost is a higher center of gravity, which was only partially offset by the subtle lowering of the RS Q3. In every turn, the suspension perceptibly fought against body roll, but could not quite prevail against inertia and the laws of physics. Compared to the RS 3, the RS Q3 was less agile, less snappy.

The same was true on the straights. Although Audi had installed the five-cylinder engine of the RS 3 and TT RS, initially it throttled its output to 310 hp. The manufacturer emphasized that it was not just about maximum power, but rather about a performance level that fitted a segment that effectively did not yet exist. Given that, the RS Q3 made an impressive first appearance, but lagged behind its technological siblings. In a drag race, even an Audi S3 could leave it behind, though in testing by *auto motor und sport* the RS Q3 beat the factory claims for 0-100 km/h (62 mph) time by 3/10ths of a second, reaching that speed after 5.2 seconds.

An SUV brings new challenges. The center of gravity and weight are in opposition to quattro GmbH's ideals.

Still, Audi was testing the waters in the segment. New skirts, door sills, brakes and suspension were de rigeur, but not much more than that. The RS Q3, for example, dispensed with the widened fenders that characterized most of Audi's top models. The standard production body offered plenty of room for bigger wheels and tires. Composite fender extensions like those that had appeared on the styling study were not required.

In all, the RS Q3 brought several compromises to the spirit of the RS label. Its cargo space shrank, the body was hardly changed from regular production, and inside, it lacked the familiar sporty feeling of the seats. But one could forgive the RS Q3 – it was, after all, still new.

It would in any case be wrong to criticize the RS Q3 for its deficits. In the end, the first RS SUV fitted the basic RS concept – to transfer sports car qualities to comfortable body configurations. With it, Audi established a segment that the competition explored at a later date.

In the following year, Mercedes-Benz launched its GLA 45 AMG. In North America, BMW offered the X1 xDrive35I, with 306 hp, but gave it a less edgy feel. The first compact SUV out of Munich with an M in the name (and also with 306 hp) was not launched until 2019. Meanwhile, the second-generation RS Q3 was already in preparation.

The five-cylinder turbo engine of the RS Q3 initially developed 310 hp. For the facelift, quattro GmbH increased this to 340 hp, and to 367 in the RS Q3 Performance.

ALONG WITH THE FACELIFT, MORE POWER

Audi revealed the reworked RS Q3 at the end of 2014. It received the same updates as the base model: new lamps, now standard with LED technology instead of xenon; additional assistant systems; and a few visual touches. More important, finally it had power to match its siblings. The five-cylinder now developed 340 hp, the same as it had in the recent RS 3. That model was in hiatus; its successor would not appear for some time.

Naturally, the manufacturer did not make any fundamental changes to the car. But the RS SUV got faster. With more power and torque, faster shift times as well as optimized tuning, its sprint performance was improved. Audi claimed a 0-100 km/h (62 mph) time of 4.8 seconds – 0.7 seconds faster than before. In testing, *Auto Zeitung* even measured a fantastic time of 4.3 seconds.

The revision served the car well. Audi included an adaptive suspension system in the RS Q3 options catalog. Before the facelift, conventional shock absorbers lived in the wheel wells. Now, the SUV offered a number of damping profiles. In principle, this was not really necessary, as the standard sport suspension provided adequate reserves of comfort for conquering long stretches with the car. Still, this additional equipment benefited the RS Q3 within the portfolio.

TOP OF THE LINE: RS Q3 PERFORMANCE

For 2016, Audi offered an even faster version. The RS Q3 Performance boasted 367 hp, thanks to the five-cylinder turbo gasoline engine that had recently been introduced in the RS 3. In the SUV, it provided better acceleration and higher top speed. The RS Q3 Performance topped out at 270 km/h (168 mph).

The category of compact power SUVs was growing. In 2014, Mercedes-Benz added the GLA 45 AMG, initially with 360 hp, then as of 2015 with 381 hp. It was the lighter and more agile car. It bought its advantages by means of compact exterior dimensions. In the *auto motor und sport* comparison test, it only beat the RS Q3 because the latter stayed true to its segment. It felt like a real SUV, with higher seating position and useful everyday space. In terms of space concept, the Audi easily outclassed the Benz.

The RS Q3 showed that Audi was taking a cool, dispassionate approach to its development. The RS Q3 was no awkward attempt to justify the S in SUV. It expanded the RS palette. As part of that range, it took "sport" seriously. Audi recognized the potential of the newborn vehicle class and made good use of synergies in its platform system. What came out was a vehicle that, in the beginning, could not yet look its brothers and sisters in the eye, but did translate a good idea in its own charming way. Audi took note of criticism and introduced comprehensive improvements – even during the model cycle. What could not be achieved under that restraint, would appear in its successor.

PAINT CHOICES (EXCERPT)

Solid color: Cortina White
Metallic: Mythos Black, Hainan Blue, Glacier White, Florett Silver
Pearl effect: Misano Red, Daytona Gray, Sepang Blue
Exclusively for RS Q3 Performance: Ascari Blue Metallic

STANDARD EQUIPMENT (EXCERPT)

Exterior:

- 19-inch aluminum wheels; Performance: 20-inch aluminum wheels
- Xenon plus headlamps with cleaning system, LED taillamps; as of facelift, LED headlamps
- RS bumpers, roof edge spoiler
- Radiator grille, outside mirrors and roof rail in matte aluminum-look
- Brake calipers painted black

RS valances stretched the sports version of the Q3 by several centimeters. A sport suspension noticeably lowered the body.

The five-cylinder engine of the RS Q3 was similar in power and had the same intense sound as its lower-slung siblings.

An unusual sight in 2013: an Audi RS model with a tall seating position.

INTERIOR

- Leather and Alcantara front sport seats
- Piano black décor
- Multifunction sport steering wheel, flattened at bottom; RS gear selector

DIFFERENCES FOR RS Q3 PERFORMANCE

- 20-inch aluminum wheels
- Carbon fiber décor
- Outside mirrors in black; radiator grille and roof rails in titanium-look
- Brake calipers painted red

FUNCTION

- Automatic climate control
- "Concert" audio system
- RS sport suspension
- RS brake system
- RS exhaust system with oval exhaust tip, on left side

Audi RS Q3 & Sportback (F3)

SUV twin pack

2019

The most important difference between the RS Q3 and the RS Q3 Sportback was the latter's taut back end.

The erstwhile market niche turned into a segment. Soon, sporty compact SUVs and crossovers were no longer an oddity. Where the RS Q3 vainly sought competition in 2013, six years later every manufacturer with an appropriate base model touted its own more or less sporty contenders. Mini brought out the Countryman JCW, BMW the X2 M35i, SEAT subsidiary Cupra's Ateca and Formentor, and VW the T-Roc as well as the R version of the Tiguan. Mercedes-AMG again tuned the GLA, this time in three different performance levels. Still, the segment pioneer defended its position. From 2019, Audi Sport converted the newest Q3 into the RS Q3. This time, there was more RS in the car than at its debut. It was more powerful, faster, and had a more striking visual presence. Subtle composite fender flares widened the car by one centimeter per side (nearly one inch overall). At the base of the rear diffuser, Audi incorporated two oval exhaust tips. Inside, a comfortable sport seat supported the driver. Optionally, the car stopped using ceramic disc brakes at the front. Every detail of the new RS Q3 served as validation of the concept. And much of it was an improvement on its predecessor.

Audi expanded its presence in the segment. In late 2018, a second compact SUV served the lower rungs of the performance ladder. A four-cylinder turbo gasoline engine of 300 hp powered the AUDI SQ2. The RS Q3 continued to be a contender at the head of the class, with 400 hp. And now it was available in a choice of two models. Along with the classic body shape, Audi offered a version with a flat back end, an SUV coupe called the Sportback. Functionally, the two bodies differed only in height and cargo volume. Both variants of the RS Q3 were equally powerful and fast, and differed only in appearance.

Again, a five-cylinder powerplant was fitted under the hood of the RS Q3, playing its enchanting melody. The car was given a new, lighter engine. Audi again adapted the powerplant of the TT RS and RS 3. Nothing was altered on the concept. The powertrain was mounted transversely and sent its output to all four wheels. A seven-speed dual-clutch transmission shifted automatically.

UNIQUE FEATURE: FIVE-CYLINDER ENGINE

Journalists' first drives in the RS Q3 did not come off exactly as planned. Audi invited the motoring press to Arvidsjaur, a town in northern Sweden not far from the Arctic Circle. There, the intent was to have the car demonstrate, on the local frozen lakes, how much better its new all-wheel drive system, based on the Haldex 5 principle, functioned. However, many of the flights to the event were canceled due to bad weather, and a large portion of the invited guests stayed home. Those who did manage to arrive had opportunity to execute spectacular drifts with the new SUV on iced roads. Most test reports were delayed. The press would catch up later, by testing the cars on their home turf.

The motoring press was of one mind that Audi did well to oppose the prevailing four-cylinder monotony. Two-liter engines with four pistons propelled all of the market competitors. Often these were mass-production engines that, for sporting aspirations, had been squeezed into track suits. They were fast, but commonplace. The RS Q3 behaved differently. Its fifth piston was a unique feature; pure reason said that it was really not necessary. But in the 400 hp class, driving enjoyment is the primary consideration, and along with it, auditory pleasure. That came with the RS Q3, as standard equipment. "Heartwarming," said *Motor1 Deutschland*. "A real hoot," said *auto motor und sport*.

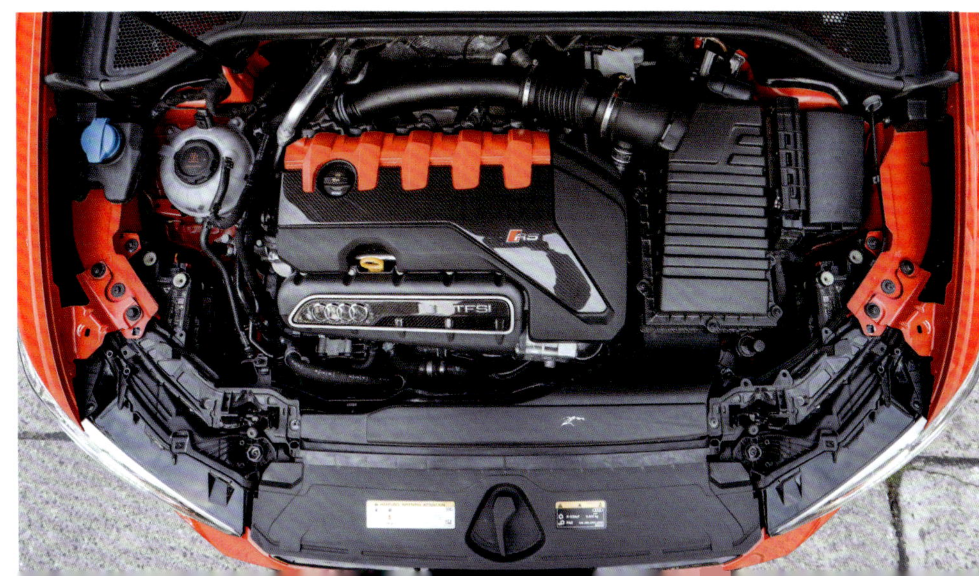

Audi did not throttle the output of the sporty SUV's five-cylinder engine – it produced 400 hp.

In its first public test drives in Arvidsjaur, Sweden, the RS Q3 showed how 400 hp and all-wheel drive behave on ice and snow – above all, when going sideways.

A second oval exhaust tip at the rear of the RS Q3 was a new feature in the second generation.

Auto Zeitung said that the car celebrated "the glory and honor of the sainted Urquattro." A manufacturer really could not wish for more laurels for an engine in a compact SUV.

The new powertrain made the car enormously fast. Up to 100 km/h (62 mph), not much changed; both body shapes returned acceleration numbers at the same level as the predecessor. It was at higher speeds that the RS Q3 set new standards. The new car knocked about two seconds off the 0-200 km/h (124 mph) time set by the first generation, even though particulate filters throttled the exhaust flow and pushed the torque curve backward. The stock top speed was still 250 km/h (155 mph), but now an option enabled a 280 km/h (174 mph) top end.

There were many improvements in the second-generation RS Q3. Still, it got its share of criticism. There was general doubt about the rationale behind the concept. The market segment was not yet as well established as that of the powerful sedans. A few criticized the execution, none more so than *Top Gear*, who felt that Audi had made the standard suspension far too stiff, describing the ride as "criminal." The British journalists reported that only "people who don't know about cars" would find such tuning "sporty."

When fitted with the optional adaptive shock absorbers, the press reports were uniformly better. *Auto Zeitung* recommended the medium driving mode, because in sport mode every bit of waviness on the asphalt was clearly conveyed to the interior. Opened shock valving calmed the body and provided ride comfort. There was also praise for the ceramic brakes, at least once they were warmed up. They reached their sweet spot after a couple of maximum-effort stops.

MORE SPACE AND A BETTER BASIS

Naturally, the new RS Q3 had its parallels to the preceding model. Still, it was a completely new car, which Audi Sport had pressed into a familiar shape. The car grew about 10 cm (4 in.) in overall length, because in the meantime the Q2 was putting on pressure from farther down in the model lineup. In its second generation, it was as big as a VW Tiguan. Eight centimeters (3.1 in.) longer wheelbase provided more rear-seat room, something lacking in the first generation.

Its new architecture, the VW corporate "modular transverse platform," reduced weight and improved space utilization. Although it was substantially bigger and offered more technology, the RS Q3 weighed less than the most powerful version of the preceding model. Above all, it brought with it some solid benefits that made the car more pleasant, in a classical way. Assistant systems, infotainment as well as networking were significantly optimized. All of this helped to underscore its sporting leadership.

Like the Q3, the modern RS Q3 did not employ analog instruments. Audi mounted a display behind the steering wheel, and simulated classical gauges. Special RS menus accessed an expanded on-board computer, capable of measuring lap times or acceleration values – a modern implementation of the classic tachograph analog trip recorder. Audi installed a large touchscreen display as standard equipment, and also expanded connectivity to smartphones and vital driving assistance devices. The RS Q3 grew along with the expectations of its customers, but continued to stand for sport, sound, and speed.

PAINT CHOICES (EXCERPT)

Solid color: Nardo Gray, Pulse Orange, Kyalami Green, Turbo Blue
Metallic: Glacier White, Mythos Black, Tango Red
Pearl effect: Daytona Gray
Exclusively for RS Q3 Performance: Ascari Blue Metallic

STANDARD EQUIPMENT (EXCERPT)

Exterior:

- 20-inch aluminum wheels
- LED headlamps, LED taillamps with dynamic turn signals
- RS bumpers, roof edge spoiler
- Gloss black front spoiler and outside mirrors, roof rail in matte black

The second RS Q3 grew considerably. Audi placed the base model at the level of the VW Tiguan, because the Q2 was applying pressure from below.

To stop the RS Q3, ceramic brakes were available as an option. These reached their best operating temperature after a couple of full stops.

The new, modern world of SUVs had display screens instead of round gauges, and touchscreens instead of rotary/push knobs.

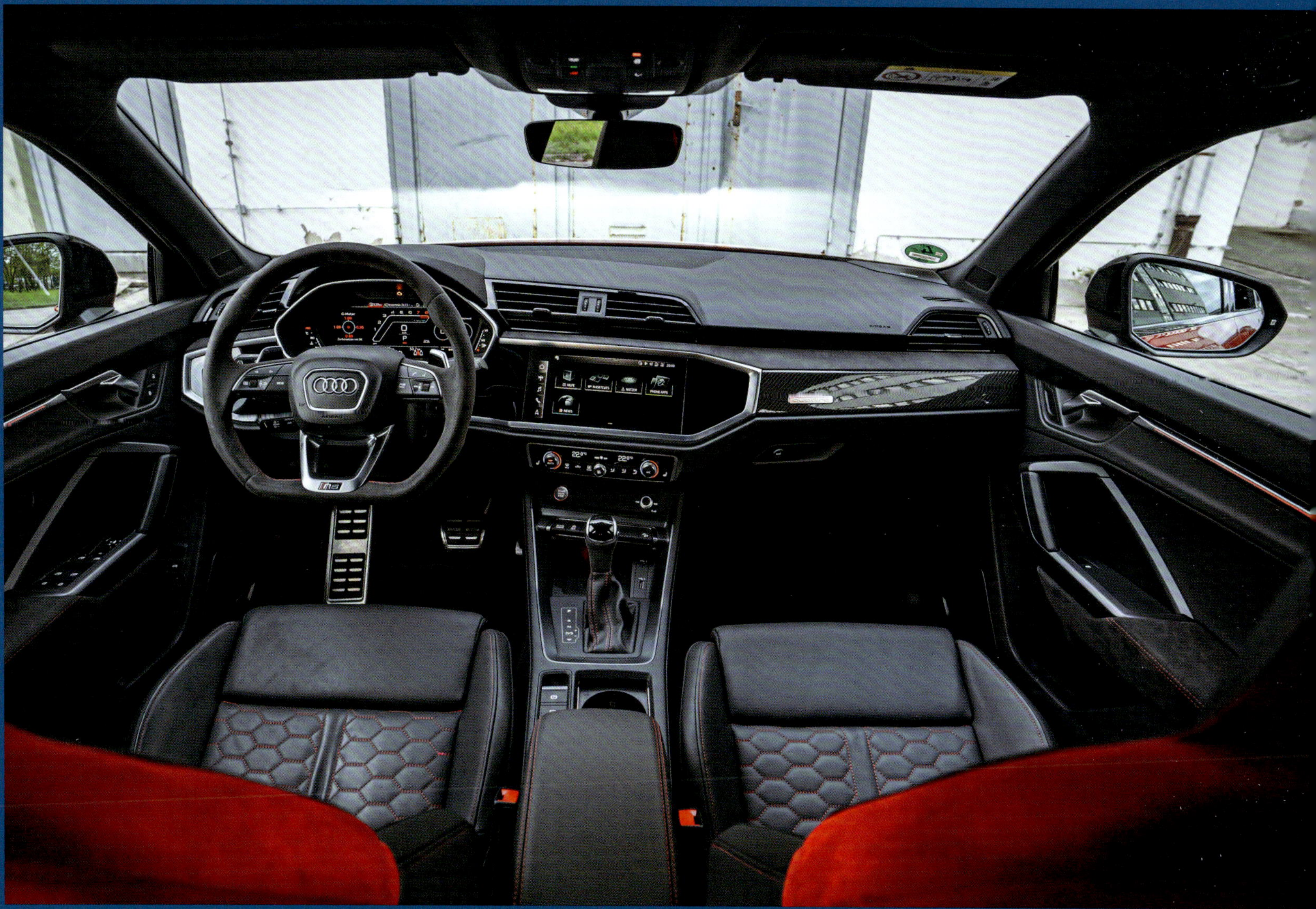

INTERIOR

- Leather/Alcantara combination front sport seats
- Aluminum Race décor
- Multifunction sport steering wheel, flattened at bottom; RS gear selector

FUNCTION

- Manual climate control
- MMI Radio plus, Audi virtual cockpit
- Lane departure warning
- Progressive steering
- RS sport suspension
- RS brake system
- RS exhaust system with left and right oval exhaust tips

2019

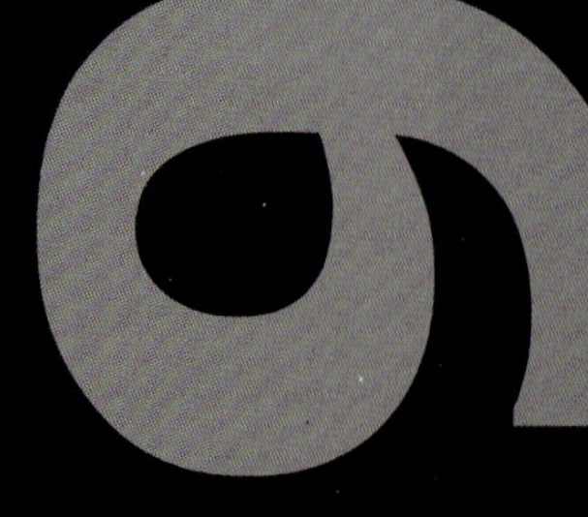

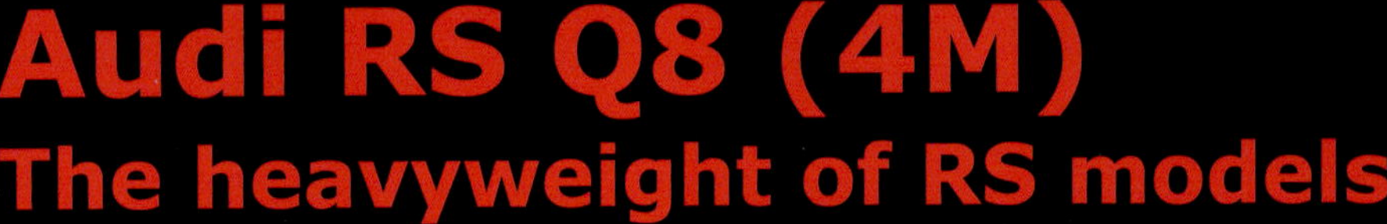

Audi RS Q8 (4M)

The heavyweight of RS models

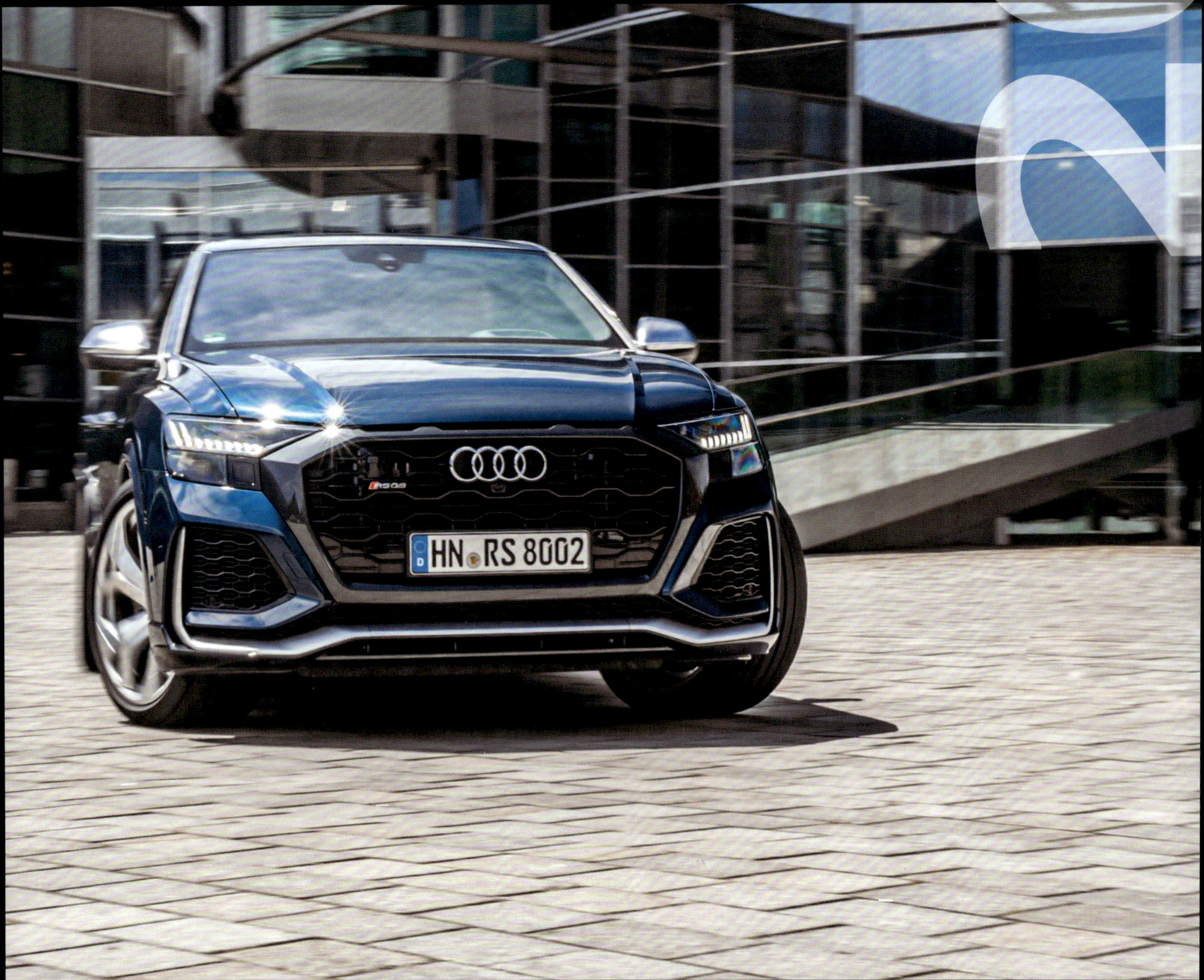

Big-league sports in a heavy car means gigantic brakes. In the RS Q8, the ceramic discs measured 44 centimeters (17.3 in.) in diameter.

SUV models enjoy a special place in the RS program. They are a direct answer to market demands. Customers desire powerful versions of the beefy vehicles, above all in North America and Asia. The heavyweights fight in their own class on the race track, the Autobahn, and the quarter-mile drag strip. Old rules about center of gravity and weight are seemingly forgotten. What counts is moving mass.

In 2019, the Audi RS Q8 brought the most mass of any vehicle in the RS portfolio. The specification sheet listed nearly 2.4 metric tonnes (2.65 U.S. tons), including driver and optional equipment. Its body stretched for a good five meters (more than 16 feet) and was 1.71 meters (5 feet, 7 in.) tall. It would be difficult to somehow associate this with any motorsports legacy – except for its high-speed potential. Audi equipped the RS Q8 with a 600 hp gasoline V8 engine that was capable of delivering the goods.

'RING RECORD IN THE HEAVIEST RS MODEL

To prove that even a heavy vehicle could move briskly, Audi sent the RS Q8 to the Nürburgring. Even before its official premiere, race driver Frank Stippler booted the SUV through the "green hell." Externally, Audi applied modest camouflage to the car so that the final design would not be recognized. Inside, the car was fitted with a roll cage, racing seats and safety harness – in case something went wrong. On the famous race course in the Eifel Mountains, that is always a possibility. A large, red emergency kill switch on the center console revealed that this was still a pre-production model.

As Stippler set forth on his record lap, Audi already sensed the outcome. By that time, 123 prototypes of the Audi RS Q8 had already covered countless test kilometers, of these 18,000 on the Nürburgring north circuit. The realization from all of these tests was that it paid to try the various driving modes. Just before the section called the Fuchsröhre, Stippler switched the sport differential for the rear axle from "balanced" to "sporty." Driving with maximum effort, he was only able to make the switch on the slippery touchscreen on his third attempt.

At Pflanzgarten, the RS Q8 went airborne, and at the Döttinger Höhe, reached a top speed of more than 300 km/h (186 mph). The north circuit lap time came in at 7:42.253 minutes. With that, the heaviest RS model was as fast on the world's most challenging race course as a Porsche 911 GT3 RS of the 997 series, with Walter Röhrl at the wheel. It set an absolute record in the SUV segment, and beat the Mercedes-AMG GLC 63 S by seven seconds.

Looking back on the achievement, the Audi works driver was amused by this result. Normally, he piloted an R8 LMS Ultra over the north circuit – a race car for the endurance racing championship. Stippler was impressed by the capabilities of the RS Q8, whose center of gravity and weight disadvantages were concealed by ingenious suspension tweaks. Audi spared no expense.

SOFTWARE MAKES THE DIFFERENCE

The Audi SQ8 formed the engineering basis for the Audi RS Q8. From this, the RS Q8 took its three-chamber air suspension, all-wheel steering, locking rear differential and roll stabilization. The anti-roll bars contained small electric motors coupled to short-geared transmissions. These were capable of stressing the spring steel of the anti-roll bars to counteract cornering forces. As a result, the body remained largely upright, where it would normally roll far to the outside of the turn.

Suspension components from the volume-production model were basically adequate for the RS Q8. However, their programming was different. The development engineers wrote a good deal of added sportiness into the code. They gave the springs more stiffness, locked the rear differential a bit sooner, and allowed slightly less roll. As a result, in the sporty driving modes, the RS Q8 was markedly more responsive than the less powerful SQ8.

LAMBORGHINI PARTS IN THE AUDI SUV

In fast turns, the car did not feel sluggish or ponderous, but rather quick and agile. This did not degrade comfort a bit, even though Audi had installed harder suspension bushings and bearings. These were in part sourced from the closely related Lamborghini Urus. The brake system was adopted from the same donor. Optionally, the front and rear ceramic brakes measured 44 and 37 centimeters (17.3 and 14.6 in.) in diameter. At the front, ten-piston calipers gripped the rotors. Audi did not expend as much effort on any other RS

suspension as they did on the RS Q8. That was consolation that the body did not entirely rise up to the usual RS standards. Skirts and rocker panel extensions gave the RS Q8 a beefy appearance. Its blacked-out lamps gave it an angry countenance, and it stood on imposing 23-inch wheels that just barely fit over the gigantic brakes. The body panels, however, remained stock. The hottest Q8 model shared all of its sheetmetal with the less powerful variants.

Audi had a good explanation for that: the normal Q8 was already so wide that its body barely passed through the paint facility. Composite trim strips along the sides were a nod to RS tradition. At the front, these widened the car by one centimeter (0.4 inch), at the rear, by half a centimeter (0.2 inch). Not including outside mirrors, the car measured 1,998 mm in width, almost 5 cm (2 in.) more than an RS 6. Even wider bodywork would make everyday use unnecessarily difficult, and the 295-series tires would again be too narrow.

QUICKER THAN MANY SPORTS CARS

The technical specifications indicated a close relationship between the RS 6 and RS Q8. Both were powered by a 4.0-liter, twin-turbocharged, eight-cylinder developing 600 hp, coupled to a mild hybrid system. The high weight, however, demanded some engine modifications; it could not be carried over to the larger car unaltered. In the SUV, Audi installed different pistons and turbochargers to compensate for the greater loads. Nothing changed as far as the engine characteristics or sound were concerned, not even the sound volume. According to government regulations, the larger body would allow one more decibel of sound, but Audi did not take advantage of this added margin.

The vehicle's mass, however, did have an effect on its dynamics. In the standing-start sprint to 100 km/h (62 mph), this was hardly apparent – the SUV reached country-road speeds in 3.8 seconds, according to the company only two-tenths slower than the wagon. However, increasing speed of necessity also increases aerodynamic drag. At 200 km/h (124 mph), the RS Q8 lagged behind by more than 1.5 seconds. Seen in absolute terms, however, it was still an impressively fast car. Porsche Boxster Spyder, Bentley Flying Spur and Jaguar XFR-S all took longer to reach 200 km/h.

Because of its engineering proximity to the Lambo SUV, *Motor1 Deutschland* joked that the RS Q8 was a "Lamborghini Urus for the people" – after all, with a base price of a relatively affordable 127,000 Euros, it cost about 80,000 Euros less than the Italian job. In an intra-corporate comparison, however, it was at a 50 hp disadvantage. It made up for this with better exhaust emissions numbers. In the RS Q8, particulate filters collected microscopic dust before it could escape from the oval exhaust tips. Due to its lower production numbers, Lamborghini was, at least for the time being, able to dodge this requirement.

SUV coupes have little in common with traditional coupes. Still, the RS Q8 looked sexier than the closely related Audi Q7.

MAXIMUM TOWING CAPACITY IN THE SUV

The motor noters praised the ability of the RS Q8 to compensate for its massive excess weight and high center of gravity. It moved like a much lighter, lower vehicle. *Auto Zeitung* spoke of a "successful symbiosis of light-footed dynamics, impressively responsive twin-turbo V8, and relaxed suspension and acoustic comfort." Its high fuel consumption might be forgiven. *Motor1 Deutschland* agreed, praised its comfort, power, and driving dynamics. Still, its road manners, despite the comprehensive efforts to leverage the laws of physics, did not seem natural enough.

In many aspects, the SUV resembled the RS 6. Both offered similar space, the same power, and brutal acceleration values. The RS 6 was nevertheless just a notch more dynamic. In exchange, the RS Q8 could pull a 3.5 tonne (nearly 3.9 U.S. ton) trailer. The wagon, on the other hand, was only permitted to pull 2.1 tonnes (2.3 tons).

Audi classified the Q8 model line as an SUV coupe. However, despite its brutal elegance, the giant had little in common with an old-school coupe. The roofline fell off smoothly and the back end was taut and attractive. The Q8 platform was largely identical to that of the Q7. Audi's big SUVs shared architecture and powertrain. However, Audi only sanctioned RS levels of sport in the Q8. In the Q7, the S model (diesel: 435 hp, gasoline: 507 hp) marked the apex of that model line.

THE STUDY: AUDI Q8 SPORT CONCEPT (2017)

In 2017, it was already obvious that an elegant SUV called the Q8 would appear in the following year. A near-production Q8 show car based on the Q7 had already been seen at the Detroit Auto Show in January. Despite this, for the Geneva show Audi brought along a new concept car. It carried yellow paintwork and fierce spoilers and skirts, along with 23-inch rims and oval exhaust tips. The cognoscenti could see that the RS Q8 was in the offing. For those who still did not "get" it, Audi provided some more or less subtle suggestions leading them in the right direction. The press release repeatedly mentioned Audi Sport GmbH, and digital press photographs contained the product designation "RS Q8" in their file names.

From an engineering standpoint, the study did not have anything to do with the final car. The concept contained a V6 hybrid developing 467 hp. Visually, however, the teaser and later production model were very similar. Wheel size and design, front valance and radiator grille, roof spoiler and rear valance with diffuser hardly differed from the later production standard. Air suspension and ceramic brakes were also solid evidence of what would be found on the coming RS Q8.

Audi showed a Q8 study in the spring of 2017, revealing most of what was to come in the later top-of-the-line model.

PAINT CHOICES (EXCERPT)

Solid color: Deep Black
Metallic: Glacier White, Florett Silver, Dragon Orange, Orca Black, Galaxy Blue, Matador Red, Navarra Blue
Pearl effect: Daytona Gray

STANDARD EQUIPMENT (EXCERPT)

Exterior:

- 22-inch aluminum wheels
- LED headlamps
- RS bumpers in contrasting color, roof edge spoiler
- Outside mirrors, front spoiler, radiator grille and window trim strips in gloss black
- Brake calipers painted black

Optionally, Audi Sport mounted 23-inch rims to the RS Q8 – the biggest wheels in the entire Audi program.

The RS 8 offered ample rear-seat legroom. Tall occupants had to be aware the hinges for the rear hatch.

Virtual cockpit: three displays and few genuine buttons, just as in the RS 6 and RS 7.

INTERIOR

- Leather/Alcantara combination power front sport seats
- Aluminum Race décor
- Power adjustable multifunction sport steering wheel, flattened at bottom
- Ambient lighting plus package

FUNCTION

- Four-zone automatic climate control
- MMI Navigation plus with touch response, Audi virtual cockpit
- Backup camera
- All-wheel steering
- Adaptive Air Suspension Sport
- RS steel brake system
- Left and right oval exhaust tips

TECHNICAL

		Audi RS Q3 (8U)		Audi RS Q3 (8U) Performance
MODEL	Body style	SUV		
	Production timeframe	2013-2014	2015-2016	2016
ENGINE	Engine configuration	Transverse front-mounted inline five-cylinder Otto cycle engine		
	Engine designation	CTSA	CZGA	CZGB
	Displacement, cc	2,480		
	Bore x stroke, mm	82.5x98.2		
	Power output hp (kw) @ rpm	310/228 @ 5,200-6,700	340/250 @ 5,300-6,700	367/270 @ 5,550-6,800
	Torque in Nm (ft-lbs) @ rpm	420 (310) @ 1,500-5,200	450 (332) @ 1,600-5,300	343 @ 1,625-5,550
	Valvetrain, valves per cylinder	Timing chain, dual overhead camshafts, variable intake and exhaust timing, four valves per cylinder		
	Fuel delivery	Direct fuel-injection, map ignition, exhaust turbocharger, Bosch MED 9.1.2 engine management system		Direct fuel-injection, map ignition, exhaust turbocharger, Bosch MED 17.1.1 engine management system
	Compression ratio	10:1		
POWER-TRAIN	Transmission	Seven-speed dual-clutch S-tronic automatic		
	Drivetrain	All-wheel drive on Haldex principle, Generation 4		
CHASSIS AND SUSPENSION	Front suspension	McPherson struts with aluminum lower A-arms, steel steering knuckles, aluminum subframe, tubular anti-roll bar		
	Rear suspension	Four-link rear suspension with non-coaxial spring/damper arrangement, subframe, aluminum hubs, tubular anti-roll bar		
	Steering	Electromechanical rack and pinion		
	Turning circle, m (ft)	11.8 (38.7)		
	Brake system	Dual-circuit brake system with ABS, ESP, eight-piston front calipers, ventilated discs front and rear		
	Brake discs	Front: 370x32 mm (Wave Design); Rear: 310x22 mm		
	Wheel size, in.	8.0x18		8.5x20
	Tire size	235/50		255/35
DIMENSIONS AND WEIGHTS	Length/width/height, mm (in.)	4,411/1,841/1,580 (173.7/72.5/62.2)		
	Wheelbase, mm (in.)	2,603 (102.5)		
	Track, front/rear, mm (in.)	1,571/1,577 (61.9/62.1)		
	Empty weight, kg (lbs)	1,730 (3,814)		
	Trunk volume, liters (cu ft)	356-1,261		
	Fuel capacity, liters (U.S. gal)	64 (16.9)		
PERFOR-MANCE	Top speed, km/h (mph)	250 (155) (governed)		250 (155) (governed); Optional: 270 (168) (governed)
	Acceleration, 0-100 km/h, sec (62 mph)	5.2	4.8	4.4
	Fuel economy, liters/100 km (U.S. mpg)	8.8	8.4	8.6
MISCELLANEOUS	Number built, by year	2012: 16 2013: 1,252 2014: 2,544 2015: 35	2013: 1 2014: 30 2015: 1,916 2016: 883 2017: 68 2018: 31	2015: 5 2016: 1,336 2017: 171 2018: 53
	Total number built	3,847	2,929	1,565
	Price at market introduction	54,600 €	56,600 €	61,000 €

SPECIFICATIONS

		Audi RS Q3 (F3)		Audi RS Q8 (4M)
MODEL	**Body style**	SUV	Sportback	SUV
	Production timeframe	2019 -	2019 -	2019 -
ENGINE	**Engine configuration**	Transverse front-mounted inline five-cylinder Otto cycle engine		Longitudinally front-mounted V8 Otto cycle engine
	Engine designation	DNWA		DHUB
	Displacement, cc	2,480		3,996
	Bore x stroke, mm	82.5x98.2		86x86
	Power output hp (kw) @ rpm	400 (294) @ 5,850-7,000		600 (441) @ 6,000
	Torque in Nm (ft-lbs) @ rpm	480 (354) @ 1,950-5,850		800 (590) @ 2,200-4,500
	Valvetrain, valves per cylinder	Timing chain, dual overhead camshafts, variable intake and exhaust timing, four valves per cylinder		Timing chain, four overhead camshafts, variable intake and exhaust timing, four valves per cylinder
	Fuel delivery	Direct fuel-injection, manifold injection, map ignition, exhaust turbocharger, Bosch MED 17.1.62 engine management system		Twin turbocharged, direct fuel-injection, map ignition, cylinder-selective knock control, "cylinder on demand" cylinder deactivation
	Compression ratio	10:1		9.7:1
POWER-TRAIN	**Transmission**	Seven-speed dual-clutch S-tronic automatic		Eight-speed torque converter tiptronic automatic
	Drivetrain	All-wheel drive on Haldex principle, Generation 5, ESP with wheel-selective torque vectoring		All-wheel drive, automatically locking Torsen CSM center differential; Optional: rear sport differential
CHASSIS AND SUSPENSION	**Front suspension**	McPherson struts with lower A-arms		Five-link suspension, links and subframe largely of aluminum, air suspension with 90 mm travel; Optional: active tubular anti-roll bar
	Rear suspension	Four-link suspension		Five-link suspension, links and subframe largely of aluminum, air suspension with 90 mm travel; Optional: active tubular anti-roll bar
	Steering	Electromechanical progressive steering		Electromechanical power steering, rear-wheel steering (maximum 5° steering angle)
	Turning circle, m (ft)	11.8 (37.8)		12.3 (40.4)
	Brake system	Dual-circuit brake system with ABS, ESP, six-piston front calipers, ventilated and cross-drilled front brake discs, ventilated rear brake discs		Dual-circuit brake system with ABS, ESP, ten-piston front calipers, ventilated and cross-drilled composite brake discs front and rear
	Brake discs	Front: 375x36 mm; Rear: 310x22 mm (Wave Design); Optional: ceramic front discs (380x38 mm)		Front: 420x40 mm; Rear: 370x30 mm; Optional: ceramic brake discs
	Wheel size, in.	8.5x20		10x22
	Tire size	255/40		295/40
DIMENSIONS AND WEIGHTS	**Length/width/ height, mm (in.)**	4,506/1,851/1,602 (177.4/72.9/63.1) 4,507/1,851/1,557 (177.4/72.9/61.3)		5,012 /1,998/1,694 (197.3/78.7/66.7)
	Wheelbase, mm (in.)	2,681 (112.6)		2,998 (118.0)
	Track, front/rear, mm (in.)	1,590/1,583 (62.6/62.3)		1,692/1,696 (66.6/66.8)
	Empty weight, kg (lbs)	1,790 (3,946)	1,775 (3,913)	2,390 (5,269)
	Trunk volume, liters (cu ft)	530-1,525 (18.7-53.9)	530-1,400 (18.7-49.4)	605-1,755 (21.4-62.0)
	Fuel capacity, liters (U.S. gal)	63 (16.6)		85 (22.5)
PERFOR-MANCE	**Top speed, km/h (mph)**	250 (155) (governed); Optional: 280 (174) (governed)		250 (155) (governed), Optional: 280 (174) or 305 (190) (governed)
	Acceleration, 0-100 km/h, sec (62 mph)	4.5		3.8
	Fuel economy, liters/ 100 km (U.S. mpg)	8.8-8.9 (26.7-26.4)		12.1 (19.4)
MISCELLA-NEOUS	**Number built, by year**	2018: 19 2019: 714	2018: 1 2019: 992	2018: 72 2019: 676
	Total number built	In production		
	Price at market introduction	63,500 €	65,000 €	127,000 €

Source Audi AG

SPOR
R

TS CARS & OADSTERS

It sounds paradoxical: for the time being, Audi's sportiest division was not building any sports cars. The time simply was not right. Even during its beginnings as a carmaker, quattro GmbH cast envious eyes on the low-slung sportsters out of Ingolstadt. But the TT was not as suitable for conversion to an RS model as the mid-range cars. The appropriate base engine was lacking.

The first forays in the segment did not bear an RS in their names. The Audi TT quattro Sport was not powered by the most powerful engine in the model line. But it became the fastest derivative. For the first TT generation, an RS model existed only as a study.

Only later did quattro GmbH convert the second-generation TT into an RS. It was an immediate hit. It also showcased the debut of Audi's first five-cylinder engine of the new era. It remained a hallmark of the top model, and in addition powered vehicles that shared the TT platform. So equipped, the little sportster even crowded the rear-view mirrors of more exclusive porsches.

Yet before the first TT RS appeared on the market, another sports car stood in the limelight. In 2006, quattro GmbH – a company that until then had only converted already existing cars – developed its first unique car. The Audi R8 super sports car shared its technology with the small Lamborghini models and roamed freely in the Porsche 911 turbo class.

Audi TT RS Coupe & Roadster (8J)

The return of the five-cylinder

2009–

2011

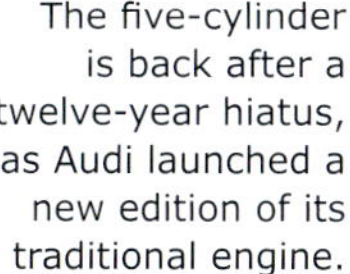

The five-cylinder is back after a twelve-year hiatus, as Audi launched a new edition of its traditional engine.

The inline five-cylinder engine is part of the Audi brand like an oil film on a cylinder wall. No wonder, then, that many Audi employees wished for a return of the iconic engine after production ceased in 1997. This dream drove two men in particular: Stephan Reil, head of development, and Michael Ganz, in charge of engines, were well-known proponents of the traditional engine. They would be especially happy to see a new edition in an RS Audi – even better if it appeared in a class that still lacked an RS model.

Audi's compact cars still did not include any powerplants with an RS qualification. The TT and A3 model lines used transversely-mounted engines. Available space and weight distribution considerations eliminated any large, heavy designs. For these cars, a five-cylinder engine would be a smart solution, just as it had been in the 1980 Audi quattro. As chance would have it, a corporate sibling had already been building an appropriate engine since 2004.

It was, of all things, a humble sedan that brought the five-cylinder back into the conversation. A 2.5-liter inline engine propelled the U.S. version of the VW Jetta. Thanks in part to a timing chain instead of a belt, it measured a compact 49 centimeters (19.3 in.) in length, and just barely shoehorned between the longitudinal frame members at the front of the car. VW and Audi shared the platform, therefore the Jetta engine also fit into the compact cars from Ingolstadt.

TURBO CONVERSION

Reil and Ganz based their efforts on this engine. The normally-aspirated, fuel injected engine had the correct shape, but not the required power. A mere 170 hp were adequate for mass-production vehicles but not for the top models in a line, intended to have sporting appeal. The engineers were well-aware that they had a great deal of work ahead of them. The engine was not yet capable of withstanding higher loads.

The men obtained the engine block's original tooling from VW and had a prototype cast using the material found in the Audi diesel engines. The alloy was capable of taking higher pressures than the standard gray iron, and provided a good basis for an appreciable increase in power output.

The man responsible for the engine knew how powerful a five-cylinder could be. In developing the new Audi five-cylinder, Michael Ganz was able to draw on his experiences with a proven racing engine. In the 1980s, he created the powerplant for a record-setting car. His five-cylinder turbo engine developed 650 hp and in 1986 propelled an Audi 200 to a top speed of 350 km/h (217 mph), and a closed-course speed record for all-wheel drive vehicles of 332.853 km/h (206.826 mph) at Talladega Speedway, driven by Bobby Unser.

The new prototype did not have that kind of power. Still, the project quickly gained friends at Audi, as secretly operated test engines functioned well, and fascinated all involved. The "what-if" musings turned into an assignment. Soon, a new five-cylinder would power a TT RS, later an RS 3. An RS Q3 was not yet under consideration.

REDISCOVERED DNA

An old idea finally became reality. As early as 2001, quattro GmbH had secretly built a fast TT. It was powered by the engine of the RS 4, but because

Based on a Jetta engine, quattro GmbH designed a 340 hp turbo engine.

An unusual feature of the first Audi TT RS: both manual and automatic transmissions were available.

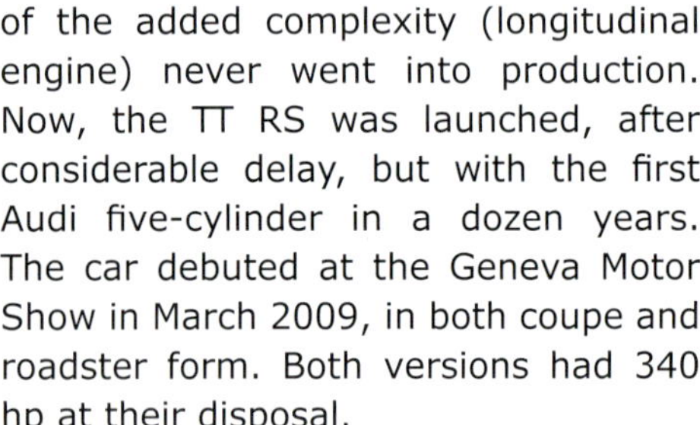

of the added complexity (longitudinal engine) never went into production. Now, the TT RS was launched, after considerable delay, but with the first Audi five-cylinder in a dozen years. The car debuted at the Geneva Motor Show in March 2009, in both coupe and roadster form. Both versions had 340 hp at their disposal.

The new engine pulled off the same trick as its predecessors. It repackaged the rough droning resonances from second-order inertia forces as "character" rather than poor tuning. As in "It's not running rough; it's supposed to be that way!" Anyone who remembered Audis from their years in rallying, carried fond memories of the quattro and Sport quattro, of Röhrl and Mouton, of roaring engines, twittering wastegates, drifting, and winning. It was a gift to the marketing effort; history helped at the introduction. "Five-cylinder engines are part of Audi's DNA," said the manufacturer in 2009, in the first line of the press kit.

Quattro GmbH invested less effort than usual in the body of the TT RS. It was already a sports car, so it did not need to be reshaped after the fact. Sufficiently wide wheels fit into the standard wheelhouses. All standard production aluminum and steel sheetmetal panels were retained, unaltered. The top model did, however, get wider door sill skirts, a front valance with large air inlet grilles and a diffuser at the rear. As standard equipment, Audi installed a fixed rear spoiler on the trunk lid, but offered the electrically deployed wing as a no-cost option.

THE ONLY RS AUDI WITH TWO TRANSMISSION OPTIONS

In its engineering, the little sportster carried over very little from the base car. Suspension geometry and steering knuckles were taken from the regular Audi TT, otherwise nearly everything else was changed. Until then, the most powerful Audi TT model had 272 hp. Quattro GmbH adapted all drivetrain components to the power of the new five-cylinder engine, beginning with the transmission.

Initially, the TT RS appeared with a manual transmission. It was the first to get Volkswagen's brand-new, manual six-speed corporate transmission. Audi called the gearbox the 0A6. It could handle up to 500 Newton-meters (369 foot-pounds) of torque, and employed a right-angle drive for the all-wheel driveline. Which of course was indispensable in RS models; quattro drive was part of the RS cachet. Later, the transmission would find application in other corporate products. VW installed it in the more powerful variants of the Tiguan and T5.

The fastest Audi TT was not limited to a single manual-shift gearbox. After many different manuals and several torque converter automatics, quattro GmbH installed a dual-clutch transmission for the first time ever in an RS model. From the second half of 2010, the TT RS was optionally available with the seven-speed S-tronic (internal designation: DQ500). For an added cost of 2,150 Euros, the unit reduced fuel consumption and acceleration times.

On cars like the Audi TT, added restraint at the gas pump was unlikely to make much difference. Launch Control, however, was a different matter; Audi combined this feature with the S-tronic. Thanks to this sprint-start assistant, any driver who could read the owner's manual could achieve a perfect drag strip launch. The car independently found the ideal engine speed (3,200 rpm), the optimum clutch slip, and rushed to the 100 km/h (62 mph) mark in 4.3 seconds. In the manual-transmission car, in the hands of a skilled driver, the same feat took 4.6 seconds. All versions were capable of

The TT RS was brilliant on secondary roads, and on the race track it could get dangerously close to the Audi R8.

The Audi TT RS came with a fixed rear wing as standard equipment. A more discreet variant was available at no added cost.

a top speed of 250 km/h (155 mph) in factory stock trim. Optionally, Audi could set the governor for 280 km/h (174 mph).

FIRST USE OF HALDEX ALL-WHEEL DRIVE

Another premiere for quattro GmbH was the Audi TT's all-wheel drive system. All other RS models distributed their power to the wheels by means of a Torsen center differential. However, this system was not used for transverse-engined vehicles within the Volkswagen concern. Such vehicles were equipped with a compact, attractively priced Haldex all-wheel drive system.

It functioned as follows. Alongside the front-axle shafts, a right-angle drive within the transmission provided power for the rear wheels. There, a multi-plate clutch determined just how much of the available torque was actually sent to the rear differential. With the clutches fully disengaged, the system was effectively that of a front-drive car. Audi nevertheless called it full-time all-wheel drive, because engine drag torque still caused a few Newton-meters of torque to be diverted to the rear wheels.

For service in the sports model, quattro GmbH designed the clutch package and differential to be more robust. The fixed right-angle drive within the transmission physically determined that at most, half of the available torque went to the rear wheels. This posed a limitation for the TT RS; it could not distribute its power as freely as other RS models. Within its limitations, however, the drive could be varied in response to conditions.

Quattro GmbH programmed the system with a progressive response. Better to have a rearward bias to the power distribution, than to have it feel like a front-drive car. In the "supertest" conducted by *sport auto*, this led to oversteer on wet pavement. The magazine's recommendation was that at least under slippery conditions, the car felt more secure with the electronic stability control activated.

Generally, however, the powerful TT tended to understeer. The testers found that this served to "emphasize safety" and described the handling as absolutely foolproof. Only in extreme cornering did the car resist tracking through turns, and then it exhibited a distinct push on the front wheels. On the world's most difficult race track, this was not a problem. The magazine measured a lap time of 8:09 minutes on the Nürburgring north circuit – eight seconds faster than a Porsche Cayman S with 295 hp. The Audi R8 4.2 with its 420 hp was within striking distance; on sport tires, that car lapped the course just five seconds faster.

With big brakes (*sport auto*: "... delivers good, but not outstanding results"), variable exhaust sound at the push of a button, and adaptive shock absorbers, the TT RS bridged the gap between sport and everyday utility. It was in everyday service that the magazine found the little sportster most surprising: "It behaves in an absolutely civilized manner, floats along relatively unobtrusively – and does not annoy." In a sports car developing 340 hp, that is not necessarily a given.

For the top-of-the-line TT RS plus, power output of the five-cylinder engine was increased to 360 hp.

360 HP IN THE AUDI TT RS PLUS

The ultimate version of the TT RS appeared three years after the model's introduction. With the suffix "plus," power output of the five-cylinder turbocharged engine was increased by 20 hp, due to software changes. Torque increased by 15 Newton-meters (11 ft-lbs). With the added power, the Audi took 0.3 seconds less to cover the standing-start sprint to 100 km/h (62 mph). Top speed in factory-standard trim was 280 km/h (174 mph).

The TT RS plus differed from the base model in several details. Audi installed 19-inch rims, outside mirror housings in carbon fiber, black exhaust tips, and special badging. The markup for performance, appearance, and speed: 3,900 Euros. At that time, just the higher top speed was a 1,600-Euro option on the regular TT RS. The manufacturer did not place a production limit on the special edition.

PARALLEL MANUFACTURING

Like all other RS models before it, the TT RS had to switch locations while being built. However, unlike other RS models, this was not due to any complicated assembly operations that could only be carried out by means of hand craftsmanship. In general, Audi split TT manufacturing between two different plants.

Ingolstadt built and painted the bodies. From there, they traveled by rail for completion in the plant in Győr, Hungary. There, TT, TTS and TT RS were all assembled on the same line. For quattro GmbH, this was something new. Until then, all other RS models had been assembled in Neckarsulm.

THE ENGINE OF THE AUDI TT RS: A NEW FIVE-CYLINDER

The new edition of Audi's legacy motor struck a balance between passion and economy. Its development goals were lofty: 100 kilowatts per liter (2.2 horsepower per cubic inch) and the typical five-cylinder engine sound, but also vital synergies with other Audi engine families and the basic powerplant of the U.S. model VW Jetta. Otherwise, the effort would not pay off.

Even with these requirements, many details had to be changed. The team around Reil and Ganz scored a direct hit on their first attempt. Their idea to use the diesel engine alloy made it into production. The block of a high-revving, supercharged gasoline engine was made of compacted graphite iron (also known as vermicular graphite iron, GJV). Audi had previously used this material for the V6 and V8 diesels. For the turbo variant, none of the block dimensions were changed.

Supplier Mahle provided special cast-aluminum pistons with asymmetrical skirts and angled wrist pin struts. With piston rings and wrist pins, each piston weighed 492 grams (17.35 ounces). In the turbo engine, these raised the compression ratio from the 9.3:1

The new five-cylinder engine shared construction details with diesel engines, the big V10 and its own roots in the VW Jetta.

This study heralded the TT RS. Audi presented the TT Clubsport quattro at the international Wörthersee GTI Treffen in Reifnitz, Austria.

(in the Jetta) to 10:1 (TT RS). Reinforced connecting rods with larger small-end bores and without deep-drilled holes were better able to withstand higher loads. A torsional vibration damper on the crankshaft improved engine smoothness.

The cylinder head, with its roller cam follower valve train, although based on the Jetta "donor" engine, had little in common with that more mundane unit. In converting the engine to direct injection, the engineers drew on their experience with the ten-cylinder powerplant of the Audi R8. Due to design differences between the two engines (cylinder spacing on five-cylinder: 88 mm; V10: 90 mm), the V10 head would not fit on the inline-five. There were however parallels in the layout of both engines.

For the cylinder head of the TT RS, Audi used a different aluminum alloy than VW used in the Jetta, added variable valve timing for the exhaust side, and optimized the cooling system. In addition, they added larger intake valves (33.85 instead of 32.35 mm), sodium-filled exhaust valves, and hardened valve seats. In its internal training materials, Audi described the cylinder head as a "modified carryover part." And with that, the design targets were met.

With a turbocharger (BorgWarner K16) and charge air intercooler, the engine developed its peak output of 340 hp with 1.2 bar (17.4 psi) – twice the power of the base motor. Beginning in 2012, the engine control system of the TT RS plus raised boost pressure to 1.25 bar (18.1 psi), yielding an additional 20 horsepower. The new engine design became Audi's most powerful production five-cylinder.

Along with its power, sound, and character, Audi also placed value on efficiency. With three catalytic converters, the engine of the TT RS met the requirements of the Euro 5 exhaust emissions standards. Thanks to direct injection and lightweight design, in the standard test cycle the car consumed just 8.5 to 9.1 liters per 100 km (25.9 to 27.7 miles per U.S. gallon). From 2010 on, the five-cylinder engine, with the internal designation EA855, repeatedly won the "International Engine of the Year" award in the 2.0- to 2.5-liter class.

THE TT CLUBSPORT QUATTRO STUDY

In May 2008, Audi announced the hottest derivative of the TT. The manufacturer presented the TT Clubsport quattro Concept at the GTI Treffen at Austria's Wörthersee. The TT Roadster was transformed into a Speedster. It arrived with a shortened windshield an entirely without a roof. Audi, however, was not inclined to build a radical cabriolet of the type shown at Reifnitz.

In fact, the point of the exercise was the styling study's details. Oval exhaust tips, wide wheel arches, slotted door handles and "more than 300 hp" hinted that a TT built by quattro GmbH was in the offing – a car that would give up nothing to the RS 4 and RS 6. The production car would not be as striking as the study shown at the VW GTI tuner meet. It would, however, get a bigger engine; the study had a mere four-cylinder under the hood.

PAINT CHOICES (EXCERPT)

Solid color: Ibis White
Metallic: Monza Silver, Suzuka Gray
Pearl effect: Misano Red, Daytona Gray, Sepang Blue, Phantom Black
Crystal effect: Panther Black
Top colors for TT RS Roadster: Black, Dark Gray

STANDARD EQUIPMENT (EXCERPT)

Exterior:

- 18-inch aluminum wheels with 245/40 tires
- TT RS plus: 19-inch aluminum wheels with 255/35 tires
- Bi-Xenon headlamps
- TT RS rear wing (no added-cost option: regular spoiler)
- RS bumpers, RS skirts, RS rear diffuser
- Outside mirrors in matte aluminum-look; TT RS plus: carbon fiber

Quattro GmbH converted TT coupes and roadsters into RS models.

The entire body of the TT RS was unchanged from the regular production model. Still, unique valances, skirts and the large rear spoiler clearly differentiated it.

Not spacious, but sportier for all that: the cockpit of the Audi TT RS.

For the TT RS, Audi added a Sport button to the interior.

INTERIOR

- Leather/Alcantara combination front sport seats
- Matte brushed aluminum décor
- Multifunction sport steering wheel

FUNCTION

- Automatic climate control
- "Chorus" sound system
- RS steel brake system
- RS exhaust system with two oval exhaust tips; TT RS plus: black exhaust tips
- Sport suspension

Same name, different concept: the Audi TT RS appeared in the VLN racing series in the SP 4T class, with front-wheel drive.

THE AUDI TT IN MOTORSPORTS

In 2010, Audi's motorsports department posed an existential question: how important is all-wheel drive? The answer: it depends. In roadgoing RS models, there was no alternative. On the race track, however, the manufacturer made an exception to this rule, insofar it might result in advantages.

The TT RS was to take part in the VLN endurance racing championship, a series of long-distance races conducted on the Nürburgring. Audi's participation was made possible by the special SP 4T class, for cars with turbocharged engines up to 2.6 liters, part of the organizers' policy of "if it has four wheels, we have a class for it." The rules for the Nürburgring north circuit prescribed a minimum weight of 1,100 kg (2,425 lbs). All-wheel drive cars would have to weigh an extra 100 kg (220 lbs). Audi weighed its options and chose the lighter, and therefore ultimately faster car.

For the VLN specifications, Audi raised power output of the TT five-cylinder to 380 hp, and used clever aerodynamics to compensate for the lack of thrust at the rear wheels – because the TT RS for the VLN was a front driver. Audi's calculation paid off. In the 2010 and 2011 seasons, the racing TT brought home multiple class wins. Its biggest success: in August 2011, it brought home an overall win in the ADAC Ruhr Cup six-hour race on the Nürburgring. Sales to racing customers commenced in September 2011, with a base price of 214,200 Euros in race-ready trim.

GRAN TURISMO
THE REAL DRIVING SIMULATOR
TT RS
H&R
Audi
Consulting

Audi TT RS Coupe & Roadster (8S)

Success through aluminum

2016

The first second-generation Audi TT RS ever built, in Audi's Győr works.

It would have been a mistake to make any fundamental changes to the Audi TT RS. With its modern interpretation of a traditional drivetrain, in its price class hardly any other manufacturer could serve its niche nearly as well. Still, when time came for a model change, there was room for improvement. Audi recognized the weaknesses of the first TT RS, and sought not to repeat these in its successor. For the second generation, the car was made lighter, more powerful, and faster.

HYBRID BODYWORK

From an engineering standpoint, the TT was one of Audi's showcase projects. Aluminum body components gave it light weight, the modular concept made it affordable. Nearly all of the oily parts were carried over from the A3. Still, it did not feel like a compact car wearing track shoes. On the contrary, Audi put a great deal of effort into the sports car qualities of the third TT.

In its bodywork, Audi combined the MQB (modular transverse) architecture of the A3 with additional lightweight elements. Cast aluminum (A-pillars), aluminum extrusions (door sills, roof frame, front crossmember) and aluminum pressings (rear inner wheel houses, and the complete exterior shell) were combined with various steel components. Compared to the predecessor, the new body was 23 percent stiffer in torsion. With all ancillary parts, the coupe body weighed only 276 kg (608 lbs). In the roadster, reinforcements around the passenger cell, and diagonal bracing at the axles, increased weight by 60 kg (132 lbs).

The materials mix did however make assembly of the car more complicated. Aluminum and steel are not easily welded together. To join the various elements, Audi utilized various cold and hot joining processes. With 3,020 spot welds, a total of 6.8 meters (22.3 feet) of MIG, MAG, and laser welded seams, 78 meters (256 feet) of bonded joints and 199 clinched joints, all of these parts were melded into a single body. Every third-generation Audi TT also contained 1,157 rivets and 128 self-tapping screws. To prevent anodic corrosion between steel and aluminum components, Audi primed the surfaces and applied a PVC or wax sealant. Audi welded, riveted, bolted, clinched and glued the car in its plant in Győr, Hungary.

The light, rigid shell was supported by proven suspension designs. At the front, Audi adapted the McPherson struts of the preceding model. At the rear, a four-link suspension was again chosen, with springs and shock absorbers mounted separately. As an added-cost option, Audi could install shock absorbers with adjustable characteristics. The front subframe and A-arms, as well as the rear hubs, were made of aluminum. At market introduction, the new 230 hp TT, with all-wheel drive and dual-clutch transmission, weighed just 1,335 kg (2,943 lbs).

MORE POWER, LESS WEIGHT

The new TT formed the perfect base for a serious sports car. Audi's speed subsidiary placed high value on keeping the TT's slim lines while building up muscle. Together with the parent company, quattro GmbH developed a

Compared to its predecessors, the new TT RS was above all lighter and faster.

new five-cylinder engine that addressed its predecessor's weight problem. With a lightweight crankcase and well-placed drillings, the engineers were able to cut significant mass out of the powerplant. All while raising power output to 400 hp, and torque to 480 Nm (354 ft-lbs).

Audi no longer offered a lightweight manual transmission in the new TT RS, because only a few buyers of the previous model had chosen to shift for themselves. Now, a seven-speed dual-clutch transmission was standard with the new engine. With a revised cranktrain and fifth-generation Haldex all-wheel drivetrain, the TT RS saved a few more hard-earned kilos. Despite this diet program, the RS conversion added about 100 kg (220 lbs) to the base weight. Without a driver, the top-of-the-line model, in coupe form, weighed 1,440 kg (3,175 lbs) – which was still 35 kg (77 lbs) less than the 8J generation with the same body configuration.

As before, the TT RS carried over the regular production bodywork and eschewed any add-on fender extensions. Big wheels already fit under the car, so additional fender flares were not needed. Valances, skirts and a fixed rear wing visually differentiated the top model from the base version, and improved its aerodynamics.

After quality and durability problems in the first generation, Audi developed a new brake system for the TT RS. At the front, eight-piston calipers clamped the brake pads to discs measuring 37 cm in diameter. Beginning in March 2017, Audi offered carbon ceramic brakes. These reduced unsprung weight by 13 kg (29 lbs), at an added cost of 4,650 Euros.

MEDIOCRE BRAKING PERFORMANCE ON THE RACE TRACK

The first road test reports published by *Auto Bild* and *auto motor und sport* praised the new TT RS for the things it did better than the old model: it showed hardly any noseheaviness, was stable under braking, and did not generate any irritating noises. Still, it fell down in precisely the department where sports cars are supposed to excel. *sport auto* put the model through its "supertest" on the Nürburgring north circuit. Even on the first hot lap, the new ceramic brakes failed. At racing speeds, it could not even manage a half marathon distance.

The test took place before the market introduction of the ceramic brakes. Audi was still experimenting with the brake pads, and their balance between performance and comfort. In a subsequent retest, the test car braked securely and lapped the "green hell" in a respectable 7:48 minutes, but in the course of ten laps, went through three sets of brake pads. Audi attributed the results to the car's layout: its transverse front engine led to high brake temperatures and severe stress on the brake materials. *sport auto* sensed that there was more potential in the car if Audi optimized the brake cooling. Apparently, Audi felt the same way, and as of 2018 offered new cooling ductwork in a retrofit kit. In online forums, many owners reported enormously improved brake durability after the kit installation.

Aside from its braking performance under racing conditions, the TT RS returned exemplary test results. From a standing start, it could sprint to 100 km/h (62 mph) in 3.9 seconds and could decelerate at 11.5 m/s² (37.7 ft/s², 1.17 g), exhibited hardly any aerodynamic lift, and tracked precisely, especially when fitted with the optional sport tires (Pirelli P Zero Corsa). New tuning of the all-wheel drive system, carried over to the TT RS from the RS 3, improved its handling in fast turns. Added to this was "...a highly emotional powertrain; one would instantly fall in love with its characteristic bass sound." (*sport auto*). In many respects, the TT RS did everything right.

Once again, the top of the TT model line appeared in roadster and coupe form.

That remained true even as new exhaust emissions standards curtailed automotive free expression. In 2018, the model went into a brief hibernation, to reappear half a year later with additional particulate filters and modestly reworked appearance. The clean-exhaust solution added about ten kg (22 lbs) of weight and cost the TT RS a few decibels of sound, as well as some spontaneity – but not enough to be obvious. *Auto Zeitung*, in its test report, said "When it comes to performance or sound, the TT RS is a full-fledged sports car that happily latches onto the exhaust pipes of cars costing two or three times as much." The trade magazine found no fault with the braking performance, either – hot or cold brakes, the car came to a stop from 100 km/h (62 mph) in 33 meters (108 feet). However, with the advent of the facelift, the ceramic brake system was no longer offered as an added-cost option, due to lack of interest. The test car stopped using conventional steel discs.

LIMITED EDITION: 40 YEARS OF QUATTRO

In 2020, Audi celebrated the 40th anniversary of its all-wheel drive. The company used the occasion to build a limited special edition of the TT RS. Visually (very much so) and technically (not quite so much), forty examples of the "Audi TT RS 40 years of quattro" recalled the history of the trailblazing drivetrain. The Haldex system of the TT RS had little in common with the Ur-quattro, but Audi paid much more attention to colors and aerodynamics.

The tiny production run was given an aero kit, consisting of side-mounted flics, a splitter, hood airscoop, sill trim, a larger rear wing, and a diffuser. Audi painted the cars Alpine White and applied decals with the marque's classic motorsports colors. Sport seats, Alcantara upholstery, white contrasts and a serial numbered plaque enhanced the interior. Optionally, Audi could replace the rear-seat bench with a carbon fiber strut cross brace. Audi left the drivetrain unchanged; the special edition extracted 400 hp from five cylinders. The package included an increase in top speed from 250 km/h (155 mph) to 280 km/h (174 mph). Also standard equipment: the potential to become a classic. This combination of exclusivity, aerodynamics and colors cost an additional 45,790 Euros.

THE ENGINE OF THE TT RS: AN ALUMINUM DIET FOR THE EA 855 EVO

Audi's five-cylinder engine had an enemy: (alleged) progress. Smaller engines had long been as powerful as the five-cylinder, sometimes more powerful. Nobody at Audi would openly admit that a four-cylinder could offer a valid, lightweight, economical alternative to the firm's traditional engine in a sports model. But the five-cylinder would have to be measured strictly against the advantages of the smaller engine.

For quattro's 40th anniversary, Audi Sport laid on a special edition of the TT RS.

Audi stayed true to the five-cylinder. The manufacturer developed a new, more powerful drive generation for the second TT RS.

For the new TT RS – and, in the long term, for the RS 3 and RS Q3 models – Audi and quattro GmbH designed a five-cylinder that could hold its own against the midget motors, at least in terms of weight. Little was changed in its configuration. It retained a displacement of 2,480 cc (151 cu. in.), 88 mm cylinder spacing, and an overall length of less than 50 cm. On the other hand, the engineers kept little of the old engine.

The most powerful lever in achieving the diet aims was the engine block. Audi shifted from the usual gray iron of its diesel engine family to an aluminum alloy. This measure alone saved 18.8 kg (41.4 lbs). Audi poured the block using tilt casting and an atmospheric plasma spray (APS) process to apply the cylinder wall wear surfaces. Additional coolant passages between the cylinders improved thermal management. The engine was to have more power, so it would have to reject more waste heat.

Audi found more unnecessary weight on the crankshaft. Thanks to holes in the crankshaft webs and a longitudinal bore, as well as reduced main bearing diameter, the forged, heat-treated steel component lost 1.5 kg (3.3 lbs) of weight. The engineers countered higher ignition pressures by means of improved bearing shells.

The development engineers found more weight savings potential in the two-piece oil pan. The new upper portion consisted of a magnesium alloy, the lower part of aluminum. This saved another 2.9 kg (6.4 lbs). In all, the new engine came in about 26 kg (57 lbs) lighter than its predecessor. With a total weight of 160 kg (353 lbs) it now weighed about as much as a comparable four-cylinder – mission accomplished.

The manufacturers also invested in power output and clean-exhaust emissions. In the new engine, manifold injection supplemented the predecessor's direct injection in order to reduce exhaust particulate formation at part throttle. New camshaft bearings reduced friction losses in the cylinder head. On the exhaust side, a new manifold optimized flow to the turbocharger.

Boost pressure of the new five-cylinder was increased to 1.35 bar (19.6 psi), compared the predecessor's 1.3 bar (18.9 psi). So equipped, the engine developed 400 hp and 480 Newton-meters (354 ft-lbs) of torque. This exceeded the output of the preceding engine's most powerful version by 33 hp and 15 Nm (11 ft-lbs). For 2019, Audi added a particulate filter to meet stricter exhaust emissions standards. With another increase in boost pressure (to 1.4 bar, 20.3 psi) the engine maintained its power output despite its now more restrictive exhaust tract.

RS
TFSI

With 400 hp out of a 2.5-liter five-cylinder, the TT RS returned acceleration times that until recently had been the exclusive domain of the most powerful RS models.

Audi Sport
DIESEL

PAINT CHOICES (EXCERPT)

Solid color: Nardo Gray, Vegas Yellow, Pulse Orange, Turbo Blue, Kyalami Green
Metallic: Glacier White, Mythos Black, Tango Red
Pearl effect: Daytona Gray
Crystal effect: Panther Black
Top color for TT RS Roadster: Black

STANDARD EQUIPMENT (EXCERPT)

Exterior:

- 19-inch aluminum wheels with 245/35 tires
- LED headlamps
- TT RS rear wing (no added-cost option: regular spoiler)
- RS bumpers, RS skirts
- Outside mirrors in black

The new TT RS did many things better than its predecessor, even though the brakes were still a topic of discussion.

Beefy without widening, big valances and an angry stare marked the top model of the TT line.

The digital speedometer was standard equipment on the Audi TT RS.

In the TT 8S, Audi generally renounced a central monitor. The driver would have to deal with entertainment and navigation functions on his own.

INTERIOR

- Leather/Alcantara combination heated front "plus" sport seats
- Race anthracite aluminum décor
- RS multifunction sport steering wheel, flattened at bottom, covered in Alcantara/leather
- Audi Virtual Cockpit

FUNCTION

- Automatic comfort climate control
- MMI radio with CD player and Bluetooth interface
- Parking assistant
- Audi drive select
- RS steel brake system
- RS exhaust system with two oval exhaust tips and RS sound button for manual control of exhaust flaps
- RS sport suspension

Sounding the all-clear: a second sporty TT study indicated that the five-cylinder engine would long remain part of Audi's engine lineup.

The source of many a rumor: this study prompted several journalists to assume that Audi's five-cylinder would soon cease production.

THE STUDY: AUDI TT QUATTRO SPORT CONCEPT

In March 2014, at the Geneva International Motor Show, Audi sought to display "the dynamic potential of the new Audi TT" by means of a design study. The rough outline of the showpiece: 420 hp, all-wheel drive, 3.7 seconds to 100 km/h (62 mph) and a clear focus on the race track – obviously, with a view to the TT RS. There was, however, one major problem: the "TT quattro sport concept" had a four-cylinder engine under the hood. An affront to the fans; ultimately, for them, five cylinders rule.

Reacting to the premiere of the study, several automotive media outlets announced that Audi's legendary five-cylinder was nearing the end. Simply from a pragmatic position, that made sense; with a "global" corporate engine, whose base version could power everything from the Audi S1 to the Škoda Octavia RS and several cars in between, the manufacturer could significantly lower its production costs. In addition, a lightweight four-cylinder would improve weight distribution (split 54/46 on the study). In the past, that had been the greatest handicap for Audi's heavy traditional engine. Better weight distribution, dual injection, pistons with a circumferential cooling passages and a fixed spoiler eventually made it to series production. The smaller engine, however, did not.

THE SECOND STUDY: AUDI TT CLUBSPORT TURBO

For the 2015 GTI meet at the Wörthersee, Audi had an especially powerful presence. The display stand, in auto show format, featured many fast production cars bearing the R and RS logos. And one that many a customer would have liked to see in production; the Audi TT Clubsport turbo allayed the fears of five-cylinder fans that a four-cylinder revolution was in the offing.

Audi called the 14 cm (just under 6 in.) wider TT a "technology study." In it, the manufacturer supplemented the turbocharged five-cylinder with an electrically powered compressor. With this twin turbocharging system, the 2.5-liter engine produced 600 hp and 650 Nm (479 ft-lbs) of torque. According to the factory claims, the manually shifted all-wheel drive car could sprint to 100 km/h (62 mph) in 3.4 seconds and reach a top speed of 310 km/h (193 mph). Yet all this *sturm und drang* remained no more than a conceptual exercise for Audi.

420

TECHNICAL SPECIFICATIONS

<table>
<tr><th></th><th></th><th colspan="2">Audi TT RS (8J)</th><th colspan="2">Audi TT RS plus (8J)</th><th colspan="2">Audi TT RS (8S)</th></tr>
<tr><td rowspan="2">MODEL</td><td>Body style</td><td>Coupe</td><td>Roadster</td><td>Coupe</td><td>Roadster</td><td>Coupe</td><td>Roadster</td></tr>
<tr><td>Production timeframe</td><td colspan="2">2008-2014</td><td>2010-2014</td><td>2011-2014</td><td colspan="2">2015 -</td></tr>
<tr><td rowspan="9">ENGINE</td><td>Engine configuration</td><td colspan="6">Transverse front-mounted inline five-cylinder Otto cycle engine</td></tr>
<tr><td>Engine designation</td><td colspan="2">CEPA</td><td>CEPB</td><td colspan="3">DAZA; as of 2019: DNWA</td></tr>
<tr><td>Displacement, cc</td><td colspan="6">2,480</td></tr>
<tr><td>Bore x stroke, mm</td><td colspan="6">82.5x92.8</td></tr>
<tr><td>Power output, hp (kw) @ rpm</td><td colspan="2">250 (340) @ 5,400-6,500</td><td colspan="2">265 (360) @ 5,500-6,700</td><td colspan="2">294 (400) @ 5,850-7,000</td></tr>
<tr><td>Torque in Nm (ft-lbs) @ rpm</td><td colspan="2">450 (332) @ 1,600-5,300</td><td colspan="2">465 (343) @ 1,650-5,400</td><td colspan="2">480 (354) @ 1,700-5,850
as of 2019:
480 (354) @ 1,950-5,850</td></tr>
<tr><td>Valvetrain, valves per cylinder</td><td colspan="6">Timing chain, dual overhead camshafts, variable intake and exhaust timing, four valves per cylinder</td></tr>
<tr><td>Fuel delivery</td><td colspan="4">Direct fuel-injection, map ignition, turbocharger, Bosch MED 9.1.2 engine management system</td><td colspan="2">Direct fuel-injection, manifold injection, map ignition, turbocharger, Bosch MED 17.1.62 engine management system</td></tr>
<tr><td>Compression ratio</td><td colspan="6">10:1</td></tr>
<tr><td rowspan="2">POWER-TRAIN</td><td>Transmission</td><td colspan="4">Six-speed manual (seven-speed dual-clutch S-tronic)</td><td colspan="2">Seven-speed dual-clutch S-tronic</td></tr>
<tr><td>Drivetrain</td><td colspan="4">All-wheel drive, Haldex Generation 4 principle</td><td colspan="2">All-wheel drive, Haldex Generation 5 principle, ESP with wheel-selective torque vectoring</td></tr>
<tr><td rowspan="8">CHASSIS AND SUSPENSION</td><td>Front suspension</td><td colspan="6">McPherson struts, aluminum lower A-arms, aluminum steering knuckles, aluminum subframe, anti-roll bar</td></tr>
<tr><td>Rear suspension</td><td colspan="6">Four-link rear axle with separate springs and shock absorbers, subframe, aluminum hubs, anti-roll bar</td></tr>
<tr><td>Steering</td><td colspan="4">Electromechanical steering with speed-sensitive power assist</td><td colspan="2">Progressive electromechanical steering with speed-sensitive power assist</td></tr>
<tr><td>Turning circle, m (ft)</td><td colspan="3">10.96 (35.96)</td><td colspan="3">11.0 (36.0)</td></tr>
<tr><td>Brake system</td><td colspan="4">Diagonally split dual-circuit brake system, ESP, hydraulic brake assistant, four-piston front calipers, ventilated discs front and rear</td><td colspan="2">Dual-circuit brake system, ABS, ESP, eight-piston front brake calipers, ventilated discs front and rear; Optional: front ceramic brake discs</td></tr>
<tr><td>Brake discs</td><td colspan="2">Front: 370x32mm
Rear: 310x22mm</td><td colspan="2">Front: 370x32mm
Rear: 310x22mm</td><td colspan="2">Front: 370x34mm
Rear: 310x22mm</td></tr>
<tr><td>Wheel size, in.</td><td colspan="4">9x18</td><td colspan="2">9x19</td></tr>
<tr><td>Tire size</td><td colspan="2">245/40 R18 93Y</td><td>245/40 R18 93Y
(255/35 R19 96Y)</td><td>245/40 R18 93Y</td><td colspan="2">245/35 R 19 93 Y XL</td></tr>
</table>

		Audi TT RS (8J)		Audi TT RS plus (8J)		Audi TT RS (8S)	
DIMENSIONS AND WEIGHTS	Length/width/height, mm (in.)	4,198/1,842/1,342 (165.3/72.5/52.8)	4,198/1,842/1,348 (165.3/72.5/53.1)	4,198/1,842/1,342 (165.3/72.5/52.8)	4,198/1,842/1,348 (165.3/72.5/53.1)	4,201/1,832/1,344 (165.4/72.1/52.9)	4,201/1,832/1,344 (165.4/72.1/53.0)
	Wheelbase, mm (in.)	2,468 (97.2)				2,505 (98.6)	
	Track, front/rear, mm (in.)	1,555/1,546 (61.2/60.9)				1,564/1,543 (61.6/60.7)	
	Empty weight, kg (lbs)	1,450 (automatic: 1,475) (3,197; auto 3,252)	1,510 (automatic: 1,535) (3,329; auto 3,384)	1,450 (automatic: 1,475) (3,197; auto 3,252)	1,510 (automatic: 1,535) (3,329; auto 3,384)	1,425 as of 2019: 1,450 (3,142 as of 2019: 3,197)	1,515 as of 2019: 1,540 (3,340 as of 2019: 3,395)
	Trunk volume, liters (cu ft)	292-700 (10.3-24.7)	250 (8.8)	292-700 (10.3-24.7)	250 (8.8)	305-712 (10.8-25.1)	280-803 (9.9-28.4)
	Fuel capacity, liters (U.S. gal)	60 (15.9)				55 (14.5)	
PERFORMANCE	Top speed, km/h (mph)	250 (governed) Optional: 280 (governed) (155/174)		280 (governed) (174)		250 (governed) Optional: 280 (governed) (155/174)	
	Acceleration, 0-100 km/h (62 mph)	4.5 (4.3)*	4.6 (4.4)*	4.3 (4.1)*	4.4 (4.2)*	3.7	3.9
	Fuel economy, liters/100 km (U.S. mpg)	9.0 (8.5)* (26.1 (27.7*))	9.1 (8.6)* (25.9 (27.4*))	9.0 (8.5)* (26.1 (27.7*))	9.1 (8.6)* (25.9 (27.4*))	8.0-7.9 (29.4-29.8)	8.1-8.0 (29.0-29.4)
MISCELLANEOUS	Number built, by year	2008: 11 2009: 1,095 2010: 1,009 2011: 1,140 2012: 434 2013: 138 2014: 32	2008: 9 2009: 275 2010: 200 2011: 315 2012: 124 2013: 40 2014: 21	2010: 5 2011: 368 2012: 973 2013: 622 2014: 148	2011: 1 2012: 188 2013: 133 2014: 43	2015:12 2016: 873 2017: 2,410 2018: 1,186 2019: 1,663	2015: 6 2016: 218 2017: 214 2018: 324 2019: 437
	Total number built	3,859	984	2,116	295	In production	
	Price at market introduction	55,800 €	58,650 €	63,000 €	63,700 €	66,400 €	69,200 €

* Values for dual-clutch transmission

Source: Audi AG

STUDIES

Dreams. What would the world be without dreams? Volume-production cars are bounded by the constraints of technology, taste, and purchasing power. Anything that pleases the customer, functions well, and is affordable, has a chance in the marketplace. This does not mean that engineers and developers only think rationally. Sometimes, they are allowed to daydream, to work their magic. The results are often just finger exercises that do not even escape the walls of corporate internal secrecy. Sometimes, however, these turn into studies for the public, and even genuine, drivable cars.

Carmakers' most daring visions are therefore destined for auto shows. Usually, these are empty shells, standing around without drivetrains and whose main task is to look cool. They show what elements of the past are to be preserved, how the future might look, and what might be possible if only the dear customers would shake loose enough money to pay for it all. Fictitious technical specifications animate the wishful thinking. These do not have to represent the actual level of development, but rather just make promises. Depending on project status and its separation from reality, there might even be a spark of truth in the spec sheets.

Mostly, it is about design – of the entire car or some details. Often, some minor features manage to secretly slip into production. For example, the digital outside mirrors of Audi's e-tron concepts were later to be found, unaltered, on production cars. The Avantissimo anticipated the cockpit of the C6 platform A6. Sometimes, concepts herald certain drivetrain configurations, but rarely do they reach the marketplace unaltered. There is no guarantee for their success.

Not all studies of sporty Audi models carry the letters RS. This is for a variety of reasons – because an official name announcement might be premature, or for reasons of secrecy, or because a final name has not yet been chosen. Other studies borrow the significant RS insignia to showcase sporty innovations. A survey of beautiful, fast, and interesting Audi dream cars illustrates concepts that did not make the leap into series production.

2001

Audi TT 2.7 T RS

The only distinguishing feature of the hot TT was an expansive rear wing that was obviously not sourced from any production car.

Audi's sports department was facing a problem. Together with Cosworth, they had developed a superlative engine with plenty of power and fine character – and then had only one car that could handle the power of this development stage. The tuned 2.7-liter turbocharged gasoline engine remained a distinctive feature of the first RS4. It might have been fine for the fast wagon, but a waste of an outstanding engine – or so thought a number of Audi engineers who had the urge to experiment a bit.

After the RS4, quattro GmbH would have preferred to build a sports car. This came to pass in 2001, based on the Audi TT. A few more years would pass before the R8 appeared. The TT, however, carried its engine crosswise at the front, between the wheels. For this layout, there was not an available drivetrain with sufficient urge. And what about the RS4 engine? It was mounted lengthwise in the chassis, with the transmission behind it. The engine was simply not compatible. Yet precisely this engine found its way into the TT.

This departure represented added effort and expense. The development engineers did not fit the engine to the car, but rather the car to the engine. They shortened the RS4 floorpan by 17 cm (nearly 7 in.) and dropped the TT body onto the technology package.

Such a radical conversion had no chance to attain production status. It was all the more astounding, then, that during its development period, the prototype rolled on public roads, openly and without camouflage. The hot Audi TT 2.7 T RS was so well executed that nobody even noticed. Visually, it hardly differed from the original. Only experts might recognize the larger rear wing, the wide 18-inch wheels, and the six-cylinder sound that, at that time, did not yet exist in the production TT. Nobody caught on to the RS4 engine.

Chief developer Stephan Reil said that his prototype could outrun a Porsche 911. No wonder; the Carrera models of that time had only 300 to 345 hp. The 2.7-liter V6 in that very special TT could draw on 381 hp, just as in the RS4.

So equipped, the car weighed less than 1.6 tonnes (1.8 tons). In a drag race, it could just beat its own donor car; in top speed, it could exceed it handily. It could sprint to 100 km/h (62 mph) in 4.8 seconds, and, without an electronic speed limiter, topped out at 295 km/h (183 mph).

The TT prototype covered 20,000 kilometers (12,400 miles) on the Nürburgring and on public roads. Reil said that it was a completely developed car, with outstanding driving qualities. However, the project was stillborn because of the cost and complexity; the TT 2.7 T RS remained a study. The first generation of the production sports car never featured an RS version, but there was an optimized variant with more power and less weight – the Audi TT quattro Sport.

It was not until the second generation that the TT earned its RS spurs. With a five-cylinder engine developing up to 360 hp and all-wheel drive, it was called the TT RS. Its successor even surpassed the study in terms of power and acceleration – but not in top speed. The prototype remained the fastest-ever TT.

A longitudinal engine in a transverse-engined car: for conversion to the RS 4 powerplant, quattro GmbH swapped floorpans.

Audi (Sport) quattro Concept

quattro

The quattro Concept could have been the successor to the Sport quattro.

No, there's little likelihood that Audi will ever again build a car like the 1984 Sport quattro. It is not for lack of motivation. Time and again, that legend of a bygone age has served as inspiration for something new. Usually, the only elements of the original that survive to appear in a modern interpretation are wide fender flares or a front face broken up by multiple air inlets. But sometimes a little more gets through. For example, in 2010, when Audi tried something daring. For the 30th anniversary of the marque's all-wheel drive debut, a study that might be more than just another homage was rolled out for the Paris auto show.

The pretty thing was the quattro Concept, as Audi wistfully recalled the good old days. Historically correct, once again a coupe served as the base. The RS 5 donated its chassis. As in the 1980s, the engineers chopped material out of the floorpan and shortened the wheelbase. Fifteen centimeters – six inches – fell by the wayside, and another 20 cm (8 in.) behind the rear wheels. Compared to the donor car, four centimeters were taken off the top. With that, the quattro Concept was purely a two-seater; it did not even bother to include an unusable rear bench like the original.

What was not discarded was the concept of lightweight construction. Aluminum bodywork and a carbon fiber roof reduced weight to about 1.3 tonnes (1.4 tons, 2,860 lbs) – putting it on an equal footing with the original, at least in theory. In fact, the study weighed more than claimed in the factory specifications. Still, Audi promised, at its presentation, that a production car would be more than 400 kg (880 lbs) lighter than the RS 5. That in itself is something.

For the drivetrain, Audi again stayed true to history. The company had recently rediscovered the five-cylinder and installed it in the TT RS. Now, mounted longitudinally, it was hung under the hood of the study, backed by a six-speed manual-transmission, all-wheel drive of course, and a sport differential. Audi claimed 408 hp, 3.9 seconds to 100 km/h (62 mph) and a top speed of 300 km/h (186 mph). This, too, was all theoretical – because although the car was drivable, but could never survive a full-throttle orgy in the form displayed at auto shows.

Still, dreaming is vital. The concept awakens recollections of the past, and of Walter Röhrl in full drift at the wheel of the "shorty." The nav system offered an appropriate "pace note" mode. Notes were communicated with the voice of Röhrl's navigator, Christian Geistdörfer. Center-lock wheels imparted a hint of sport in everyday driving – exactly as Porsche had done in its hotter 911 models.

Prototypes wearing RS 5 disguises indicated how far the project had advanced. Audi even created tooling for the production car. The official go-ahead seemed a mere formality. But it was not to be. Internal strife about hierarchies within the company, and the design of the new Audi quattro, ended its career before it even began. The cancellation was made official in 2012. This hit development boss, Stephan Reil, especially hard. Later, he would call the quattro Concept a car that he always wanted to build, but was never allowed to.

A SECOND ATTEMPT, WITH EIGHT CYLINDERS

The wounded hearts of fans healed as the manufacturer again held out hope for a new Sport quattro. Another study appeared in 2013, this time at

A tidy cockpit with a special feature: the navigation system spoke with the voice of Walter Röhrl's co-driver, Christian Geistdörfer.

the Frankfurt International Auto Show, the IAA. The new study was bigger and more powerful, measuring 4.6 meters (just over 15 feet) in length and almost two meters (6 feet, 6 in.) in width. Any thoughts of the smaller, lighter car had been forgotten, as was the five-cylinder engine. The quattro Concept was followed by the Sport quattro Concept. With new hybrid power, Audi predicted astonishing fuel economy figures.

While the new car bore visual reminders of the legendary predecessor, its technology had nothing in common. The traditional drivetrain was replaced by the gasoline V8 of the RS 6 and RS 7, supplemented by an electric motor. Taken together, both power sources generated a total of 700 hp and 800 Nm (590 ft-lbs) of torque. Despite weighing 1.85 tonnes (2.04 tons or 4,080 lbs), this was enough power to accelerate to 100 km/h (62 mph) in 3.7 seconds. Top speed was electronically limited to 305 km/h (190 mph). If and when the study reached production, it would be able to drive for 50 km (30 miles) on electric power alone.

In 2013, however, the technology to actually implement the hybrid scheme had not yet been developed. The new concept had to be rolled onto the stage using human muscle. Still, it caused quite a stir. During the show, even Chancellor Angela Merkel took a look at Audi's sporty concept. Her main interest, however, was not top speed, but rather the claimed fuel consumption in the standard test cycle – two and a half liters to cover 100 km (94 miles per U.S. gallon).

The show car still contained a great deal of show. The concept was built for looks, not for testing. By the second day, the driver's seat had come loose, and the interior reeked of adhesive. Audi had a demo video play on the speedometer display. The idea was that at some point, one could configure personalized displays, including a lap timer and maps of favorite race circuits. The steering wheel, with its starter button and driving mode switches, already foreshadowed a production car, as did the minimized cockpit with fewer buttons and switches.

A firm statement regarding start of production could not be coaxed out of Audi. The press spokespersons evaded, said they were still evaluating reactions. There were rumors of a limited production run of 250 to 500 examples, and an entry price of at least 250,000 Euros. The car remained a topic of discussion within Audi, but was ultimately canceled. The new edition of the Audi Sport quattro would not appear in the marketplace.

NO SERIES PRODUCTION OF THE NEW EDITIONS

Neither of the two Audi Sport quattros would have been a vehicle for the masses, but rather a car for enthusiasts. Power in excess is not something to be proud of when the entire world is expecting efficient, long-distance endurance runners. Nevertheless, here and there, an odd feature of the studies would eventually find its way into the production cars.

These included, for example, interior details. In the RS 3, TT RS, and RS Q3, the five-cylinder continued to gain power, and ultimately nearly equaled the output of the quattro study. The drivetrain of the second concept made it into a production car, virtually unchanged. The 2017 Porsche Panamera Turbo S E-Hybrid was driven by a very similar combination of twin-turbo engine and electric motor. Performance, range in battery operation, and battery capacity virtually matched what Audi had claimed for its show car in 2013. Still, this was little consolation for quattro fans.

A drivable version of the second study was a painful reminder of how attractive tradition can be. Unfortunately, it is seldom affordable.

With hybrid power in the study, 700 hp would have moved the attractive coupe, if it only had gone into production.

Audi A1
Clubsport quattro

2011

RS 3 technology in the Audi A1 was appropriate for a tuner meet, but not an option for possible series production.

Austria's Wörthersee, Lake Wörth, is properly the province of the Volkswagen Golf GTI. Since 1982, every year around Ascension Day (end of May), enthusiasts have gathered in the town of Reifnitz to celebrate the quick VW. The company values its connection with the fans, and regularly attends to showcase some of its most interesting developments. It is not unusual for various marques to set up display stands to show off their fastest cars. They bring along highly tuned models created especially for the meet. The bandwidth ranges from the tiny Škoda Citigo to the massive Volkswagen Amarok.

In 2011, Audi brought along seventeen production cars – and one car that stood out from this collection like steel rims on a sports car. The Audi A1 Clubsport was a brutal little one-off, an exercise for its designers and the attendant enthusiasts. It was in effect the RS 1 that many a fan of subcompact cars longed for – a reworked Audi A1 with wider bodywork, five cylinders and 503 hp.

At Audi, a small team had transplanted the TT RS drivetrain into the tiny A1 engine compartment. Modifications to the turbocharger, intercooler, intake tracts and exhaust system raised power output by an additional 160 hp. Maximum torque of 660 Nm (487 ft-lbs) was available over a rev range from 2,500 to 5,300 rpm. The manual six-speed transmission directed power to all four wheels.

Audi's smallest car was available only with front-wheel drive. Therefore, the factory tuners mated the A1 chassis to the driveshaft, rear differential, and suspension of the TT RS donor vehicle. Audi cited firm performance numbers: the A1 Clubsport could accelerate to 100 km/h (62 mph) in 3.7 seconds and reach a top speed of 250 km/h (155 mph). Any more would have been reckless, given the short wheelbase.

The body of the show A1 gained 6 cm (2.4 in.) in width. Wheels measuring 19 inches in diameter were mounted over ceramic brake discs. Inside, anything that could slow down a car was removed: comfort items, needless electronics, and the rear bench seat were thrown out. Instead, there was a roll bar and bucket seats from the R8. Thanks to this lightweight philosophy, the study tipped the scales at less than 1.4 tonnes (1.5 tons or 3,086 lbs).

AUDI A1 QUATTRO: LIMITED SPECIAL EDITION

Of course, this A1 did not go into production. It was too powerful, too difficult to build, and too expensive. Audi consoled its fans at the Wörthersee that sporty decals would be available for the production A1. They could drive the A1 Clubsport virtually; for the duration of the Wörthersee meet, the car was available in the online racing simulation *Need for Speed World*.

A bit of the Clubsport eventually did make it to the street. In 2012, Audi laid on a small production run of 333 examples of the Audi A1 quattro. It was powered by only four cylinders, but these produced 256 hp, coupled to all-wheel drive and rims that were strongly reminiscent of the study. Later, Audi brought out an S1 with 231 hp. That was the limit for the A1 model line.

The bucket seats of the A1 study were borrowed from the Audi A8. The rear bench seat was completely eliminated.

Audi RS 8
Innovation vehicle (D4)

Audi never seriously planned to build an RS 8. Still, the study showed how such a car might look.

Quattro GmbH is always probing its own limits. The RS portfolio is expansive, but consistently avoids the very top and bottom ends of the Audi product range. Subcompacts and the luxury class are allowed to carry the "S" suffix, but no more. In RS trim these would be too expensive (at the low end) or too sporty (at the high end). According to the manufacturer, it would be difficult to reconcile the customers' demand for luxury with the RS badge. Off the record, Audi explained that an RS 8 would simply have to be too powerful to maintain the customary distance to the S model.

For prototypes, such arguments become irrelevant. For that reason, in 2013 Audi built a car that at least looked like an RS 8. The sedan featured widened fenders, aggressive-looking front and rear valances, a diffuser and two oval exhaust tips at the rear. Air suspension lowered the body so far that its 285-series tires disappeared under the edges of the wheel cutouts. Two-tone 21-inch wheels were fitted over ceramic brakes. All of this looked like the stuff of serious sporting pretensions.

And there it remained. The pipe dream embodied in the sheetmetal stretched its muscles visually, just as a real RS 8 might. Its powertrain, however, was that of the conventional S8. The twin-turbo V8 produced 520 hp. It was fast, but not fast enough. It could sprint from a standing start to 100 km/h (62 mph) in 4.1 seconds and was governed to a top speed of 250 km/h (155 mph) – just like the production model. Because an RS 8 was really not under consideration, the back of the car did not even sport an R badge, just an S8 emblem. Officially, however, Audi called it the RS 8.

ON THE TOPIC OF SAFETY

Indeed, the propulsion system of the prototype was at best a secondary consideration, and its visual appearance more an exercise than a serious effort. The project was an "innovation vehicle," a technology demonstrator. Development departments create such cars as a foretaste of what technologies, if they prove themselves, might appear on the road in five or ten years. In general, they remain secret projects. Audi only showed the RS 8 seven years after it was built, when it was part of the 25th RS anniversary festivities held in the Audi Forum, the company museum, in Neckarsulm.

There, it demonstrated what might have been. For example, part of its equipment was a so-called "3G brake." Under maximum-effort braking, skids in the side longitudinals would deploy to brace against the asphalt road surface to provide additional deceleration. The idea remained unrealized; Audi never put it into production.

The car also contained airbags of a new type. These were mounted in the seats and when deployed, would extend so far forward that the regular passenger bag became superfluous. This freed up space in the dashboard. Audi did not provide any other details. Many an innovation might still be in the planning stages.

The interior of the RS 8 harbored a few other interesting details. The seat belts were made of silk and contained additional airbags. These were intended to better protect passengers who might be in a reclined position. The motto of the technology demonstrator was "Vision Safety." The car remained a solitary example.

Nevertheless, sovereignty over the fast Audi S8 plus resides in Neckarsulm. That car was given the power of the RS 8 and RS 7 in its S8 Performance edition, with 605 hp.

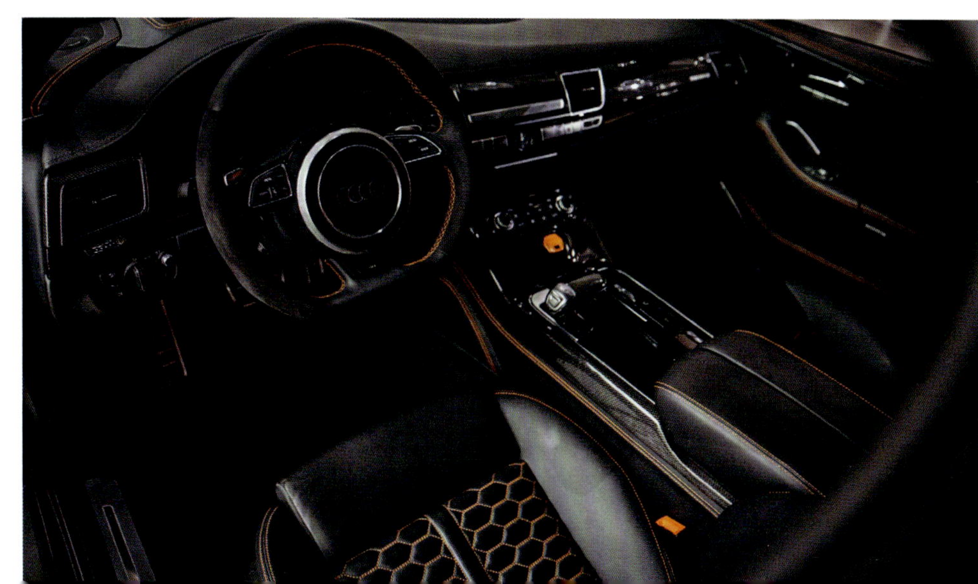

The modified cockpit included innovative airbags and safety belts made of silk.

The RS Lexicon

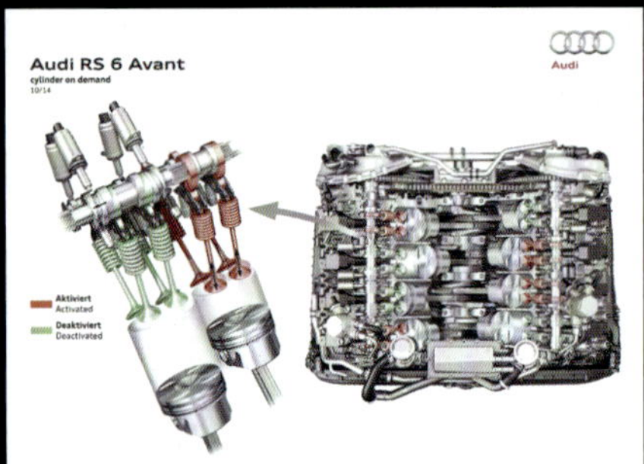

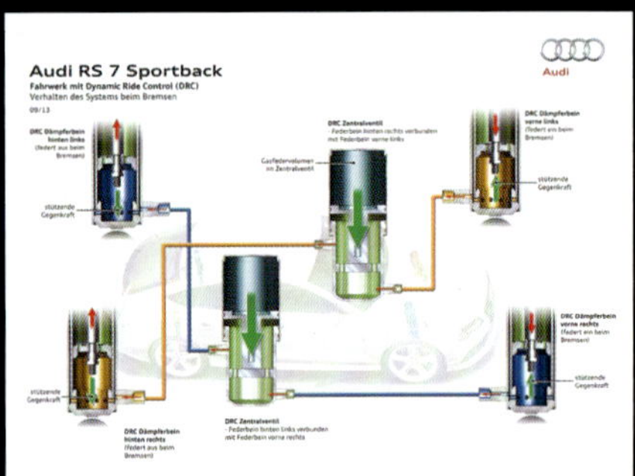

Active engine mount – Engine mounts connect the engine to the chassis. They prevent drivetrain vibrations from being transmitted to the body. Active engine mounts help to enhance ride comfort by generating compensating counter-oscillations.

Audi valvelift system (AVS) – A system that employs electromechanical actuators to select between two different levels of valve lift according to engine load and speed

Avant – Body style; Audi's name for its station wagon/estate body style vehicles.

B-Cycle process – A special combustion process based on the Miller cycle. The intake valves close well before the pistons reach bottom dead center. This reduces throttle losses. Compared to the short compression phase, the expansion phase is lengthened, which significantly boosts efficiency.

Bedplate construction – The layout employed by many RS engine blocks. The two-piece design encompasses all crankshaft main bearing seats in a single bridge. This further enhances the block's rigidity.

Belt alternator starter – A component of Audi's mild hybrid system. An electric motor is connected to the crankshaft of the combustion engine by means of a belt. Like an alternator, it can generate electrical energy, or like a starter, turn the crankshaft.

Ceramic brakes – More precisely, carbon fiber ceramic brakes. Brake discs made of carbon fiber reinforced silicon carbide are more heat resistant and resist fading (loss of braking performance due to overheating), but cost considerably more and often have associated comfort disadvantages.

Crown gear all-wheel drive – All-wheel drive using a special center differential, used in RS models with longitudinal engines. In the event of a rotational speed difference between front and rear axles, the design, using crown-like gears and multi-plate clutch packs, independently and without electronic control diverts more power to the axle with greater traction.

Cylinder on demand – At low to medium load and engine speed, the system deactivates half of the cylinders. The COD system shuts off fuel-injection and ignition, and also closes the valves. The engine runs on fewer cylinders; the COD system can reduce fuel consumption by several tenths of a liter per 100 kilometers.

DRC suspension – Dynamic Ride Control. Diagonally opposed pairs of shock absorbers are linked by hydraulic lines and a central valve. When cornering at speed, the valves regulate the oil flow in the shock absorber of the spring-deflected front wheel at the outside of the curve. This increases the support provided and reduces pitch and roll movements.

Drive select – Audi's selectable dynamic handling system. Depending on vehicle options, drive select controls the characteristics of engine, transmission, suspension, steering, exhaust system, differential and assistance systems.

Dynamic steering – Superposition gearing in the steering system, driven by an electric motor, modifies the steering ratio independently of road speed.

Dynamic package – An option package in association with increased maximum speed.

Electric powered compressor (EPC) – An electrically-driven turbine which supplements the work of the turbocharger(s) during start-up and acceleration at a very low engine speed. It therefore enables instant responsiveness and dynamic start-off performance from standstill.

Fixed brake caliper – A brake caliper design in which pistons on either side press the brake pads against the brake disc. In contrast to floating brake calipers, the fixed caliper is rigidly bolted to the hub or steering knuckle.

Five-valve technology – A valve layout used in several Audi engines. Three (instead of the conventional two) intake valves provide better cylinder filling. Audi first used this principle in the 1986 Talladega world record car.

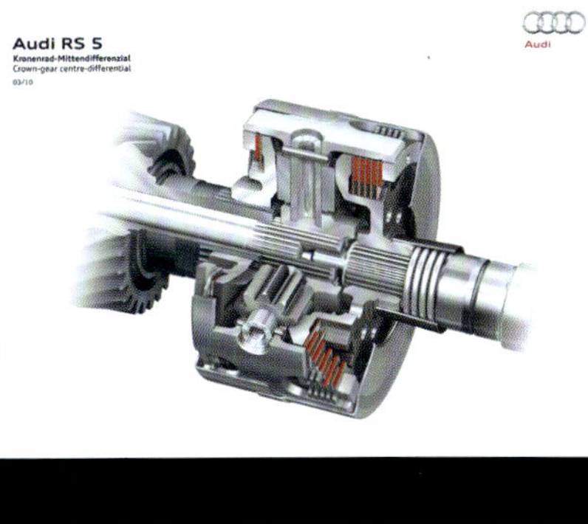

Floating caliper – One or more brake pistons press the brake pad against the brake disc. Because the caliper is free to move from side to side, it also presses the pad on the opposite side against the disc.

Haldex all-wheel drive – All-wheel drive for RS models with transverse engines. A rigid right-angle drive diverts half of the engine's propulsive power toward the rear axle. There, a laminar clutch determines whether, and how much, torque is transmitted to the differential and the individual wheels.

Mild hybrid – A form of hybrid drive that does not permit purely electrical operation. In certain situations, small electric motors, in the case of Audi connected to the crankshaft by belts, provide a certain amount of torque for forward propulsion, thereby reducing fuel consumption. This also significantly increases the comfort with an automatic start-stop system.

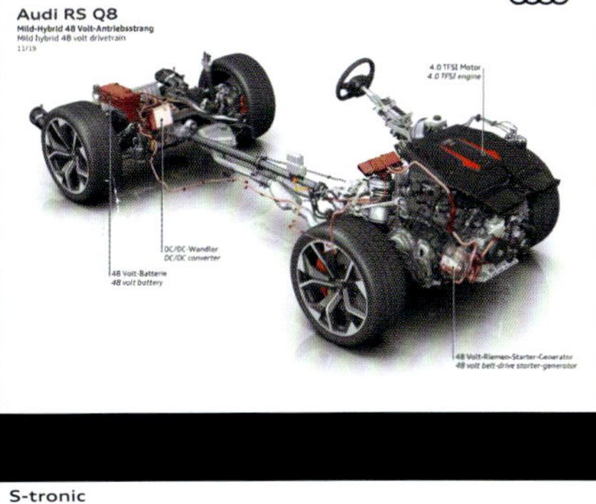

Permanently excited synchronous motor – A form of alternating current electric motor with magnets in the rotor to generate a permanent magnetic field.

Progressive steering – A special geared steering rack increases the steering ratio with increasing steering angle, for improved driving dynamics.

quattro – Audi's name for its all-wheel drive systems. Depending on model and generation, this has been applied to a variety of technologies.

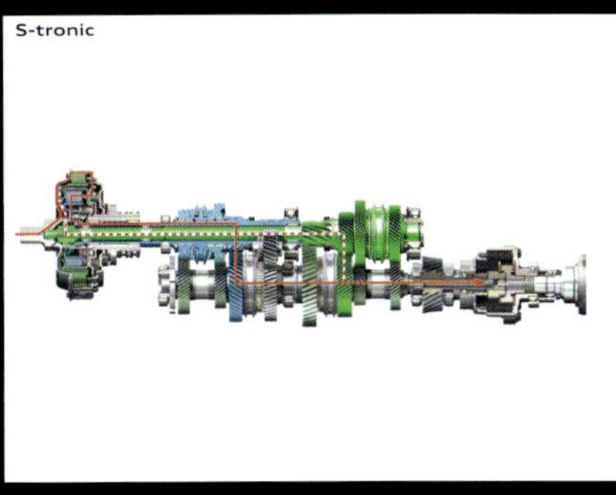

Recuperation – Increased work performed by the alternator under braking or coasting. In normal driving, the engine uses less power to generate electricity, resulting in improved fuel economy.

S-tronic – Audi's name for its dual-clutch transmission. Two transmission halves each use a single clutch. While one gear is selected, software preselects the next gear in the other transmission half. When a gear shift takes place, the clutches exchange duties. Gear shifts are quicker than with manual transmissions, and take place without interrupting power flow.

Sportback – Sales designation for several body configurations at Audi, for example the five-door Audi RS 3, or the five-door RS 7 sedan.

Sport differential – Special rear axle differential, offered as an option on several RS models. Multi-plate clutches, controlled by software, actively distribute drive torque between the rear wheels, adding a self-locking center differential to the quattro drive.

Tiptronic – designation for torque converter automatic transmissions used in Audi models.

Torsen all-wheel drive – All-wheel drive with self-locking center differential for Audi models with longitudinally mounted engines. Torsen gets its name from TORque and SENsing. If the rotational speeds of the axles differ (implying wheel slip), the differential locks. The configuration of the system varied greatly over the course of several vehicle generations.

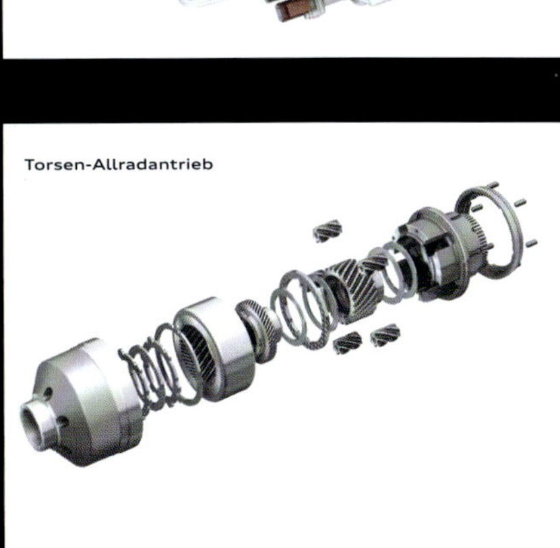

Twin scroll turbocharger – A turbocharger configuration with improved response. A divided turbine housing receives two different exhaust stream from various cylinders. This eliminates mutual interference between exhaust streams from different cylinders.

Wave brake disc – Brake disc with a wavy circumference. This configuration reduces weight and promotes improved heat rejection.

Wheel-selective torque control – Software uses directed brake application to control power flow. In cornering, the system gently brakes the inside wheels to divert torque to the outside wheels. The difference in drive forces turns the car into the bend.

The center differential

Milestones of a development

The center differential is the key element in many Audi quattro models with a longitudinally installed front engine. It distributes the drive torques optimally between the driven wheels and is the subject of continuous development.

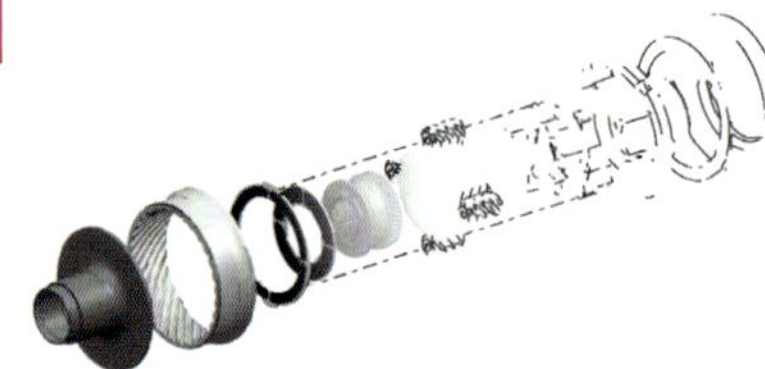

2022

Outlook
Weight: <3,000g
Basic distribution front/rear axle: 40:60
Optimized vehicle dynamics close to handling limits and further weight reduction.

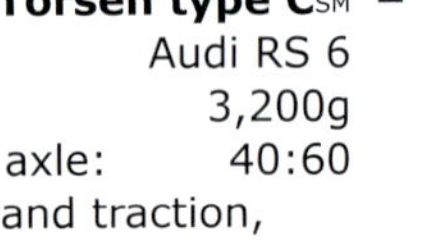

2013

Torsen type C_{SM}
Model example: Audi RS 6
Weight: 3,200g
Basic distribution front/rear axle: 40:60
Enhanced vehicle dynamics and traction, clear weight reduction.

2010

Crown gear differential
Model example: Audi RS 5
Weight: 4,800g
Basic distribution front/rear axle: 40:60
Improved traction for top engine/transmission versions, combined with wheel-selective torque control.

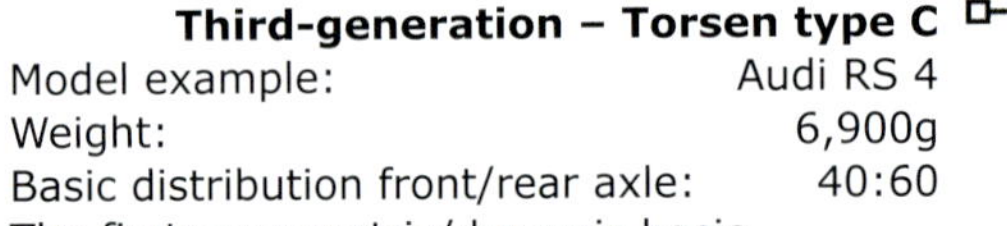

2005

Third-generation – Torsen type C
Model example: Audi RS 4
Weight: 6,900g
Basic distribution front/rear axle: 40:60
The first asymmetric/dynamic basic distribution of 40:60 brought a clear improvement in vehicle dynamics.

1994

Second-generation – Torsen type B
Model example: Audi A4/A8
Weight: 4,800g
Basic distribution front/rear axle: 50:50
Lower locking values for easier maneuvering.

1986

Second-generation – Torsen type A
Model example: Audi 80/100
Weight: 4,800g
Basic distribution front/rear axle: 50:50
The first self-locking center differential can be combined with brake control system.

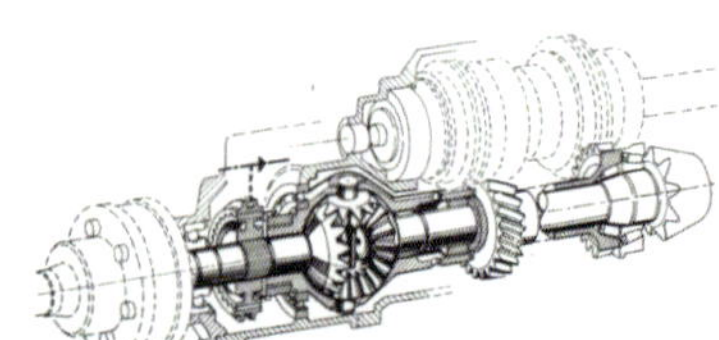

1980

Open bevel-gear differential
Model example: Ur-quattro
Basic distribution front/rear axle: 50:50
Open differential with manually selectable 100 percent interlock.

IN GT 118E